First Certificate GOLD

coursebook

Richard Acklam with Sally Burgess

LONGMAN

Contents

Reading	Listening	Speaking	Writing
Why do we risk it? (matching pictures to paragraphs)	*Disaster at sea* (note taking, True/False)	Interviewing a famous person Describing memorable journeys	An informal letter and checking accuracy
Would you set yourself on fire for £75 a day? (gapped text)	*Hated jobs* (multiple matching) Song: *9 to 5* (Dolly Parton)	Discussing: 1) value of different jobs 2) qualities/abilities that different jobs require Explaining how to play a sport	A transactional letter (1) Using sequencers
Twins (True/False) *Open house* (multiple matching)	*Grimble* (ordering pictures)	Discussing being an only child, a twin, etc. Describing family trees	Drafting and redrafting
Hype or hyper-reality? (multiple matching)	*Lies* (multiple matching) *Extracts* (multiple choice)	Discussing: 1) technology and the future 2) computer games and virtual reality 3) lies 4) UFOs	A narrative
Extract from *The Go-between* (reading between the lines)	Song: *Your song* (Elton John) *Wedding upset* (multiple matching)	Discussing 1) 'love triangles' 2) good books Problem solving: present giving Describing marriage customs	Background reading texts
The mind machine (multiple matching) *101 ways to avoid studying* (multiple choice)	*Exam crazy* (note taking)	Discussing: 1) purpose of schools and the qualities of good students/teachers 2) exams	Discursive (1) and punctuation
Superbrats (multiple choice)	*Stagefright* (multiple matching)	Roleplay: giving advice Roleplay: landlord/unhappy tenant Problem solving: museum exhibits	A report (1)
Supermodel sensation (jigsaw reading) *Why laughter is the best medicine* (gapped text)	Song: *Blue suede shoes* (Elvis Presley) *Designer row!* (comprehension questions)	Discussing fashion Describing an accident, an illness, etc. Roleplay: parent and son/daughter discuss party rules	A description of a person
Irish Stew (multiple choice) *Are you hooked?* (multiple matching)	*Tunisian brik à l'oeuf* (blank filling) *An addict* (True/False) *Shop complaint* (ordering pictures)	Discussing eating and cooking Explaining how to cook something Discussing shopping Roleplay: making a complaint	A formal letter (complaint)
The man who broke the pound (gapped text)	*Inventors* (note taking)	Discussing money Problem solving: 1) awarding a scholarship 2) ranking inventions Describing an invention	An application
Weird weather facts (question formation) *Easter Island* (gapped text)	*Biosphere 2* (significance of key words)	Discussing environmental issues Problem solving: selecting personal items	A transactional letter (2) and informal/formal style
The Eiffel Tower conman (True/False) *TV ration box* (question formation)	*Radio advertisements* (assessing effectiveness)	Roleplay: door-to-door salesman Product survey Creating a new TV channel	Discursive (2) and linkers
Mad as a hatter /or geniuses at work? (multiple matching)	*Vampire woman* (comprehension questions)	Discussing eccentricity Describing animals Discussing different types of accommodation	A description of a place
Batman (comprehension questions)	*Extracts* (multiple choice) *Guardian Angels* (True/False)	Roleplay: deciding what to do with a young criminal Ordering a picture story Discussing the role of vigilantes	Making your writing more interesting
Chatting with chimps (selecting correct sentences) *Graffiti* (multiple choice)	*Extracts* (multiple choice) Song: *I wish it would rain down* *Handwriting* (True/False)	Discussing differences between people and animals Discussing graffiti Analysing handwriting	Discursive (3)

Communication activities p.184   Language index p.191

Exam information

Overview

The Cambridge First Certificate Examination in English consists of five papers. Each paper tests a different area of your ability in English and is worth twenty per cent of your total result. After you take the exam you will receive a grade: A, B and C are pass grades; D, E and U are fail grades.

Paper 1 Reading

This paper contains four parts. Each part has at least one text with a task. There is a total of 35 questions. A variety of types of texts may be used, including letters, advertisements, extracts from works of fiction, newspaper articles and information from brochures. You will have 1 hour and 15 minutes to answer all the questions.

There are three main types of task:

1   Multiple matching: this may involve, for example, matching headings to their appropriate paragraphs in a text or deciding which of a number of places or people specific sentences are referring to. (See examples on pp.10–11 Exam focus, Exercise 2 and pp.130–131 Reading, Exercise 3.)

2   Multiple choice questions: in this case you will have to choose answers or finish sentences. (See example on pp.68–69 Reading, Exercise 3.)

3   Gapped text: in this case you are given a number of sentences or paragraphs which have been removed from a text. You must decide where they should go in the text. (See example on p.85 Reading, Exercise 4.)

Paper 2 Writing

In this paper you have two tasks. You will have 1 hour and 30 minutes to complete the two tasks and you will be required to write between 120 and 180 words for each task.

Part 1 is compulsory and requires you to write a 'transactional' letter based on information and prompts. (See example on p.20 Exam focus, Exercise 1.)

In **Part 2** you have a choice from four tasks. These will be a selection of the following:

● a letter, which could include a 'letter of application' (See example on p.12 Writing, Exercise 1.)
● an article (See example on p.126 Exam focus, Exercise 2.)
● a report (See example on p.73 Exam focus, Exercise 2.)
● a discursive composition (See example on p.156 Writing, Exercise 3).
● a descriptive composition (See example on p.81 Writing, Exercise 1.)
● a narrative composition (See example on p.44 Writing, Exercise 3.)
● a composition, article, report or letter on one of the background reading texts (See example on p.51 Writing, Exercise 2.)

Paper 3 Use of English

This paper contains five parts with a total of 65 questions. You will have 1 hour and 15 minutes to answer all the questions. The five different parts are as follows:

Part 1: this consists of a multiple choice cloze text. This is a text with 15 gaps, followed by 15 four-option multiple choice questions. The focus is on vocabulary. (See example on p.143 Use of English.)

Part 2: this consists of an open cloze text. This is a text with 15 gaps which you must fill with an appropriate word. The focus is on grammar and vocabulary. (See example on p.135 Exam focus.)

Part 3: this consists of 10 'key' word transformations. You are required to complete a sentence using a given word, so that it means the same as a previous sentence. The focus is on grammar and vocabulary. (See example on p.83 Exam focus, Exercise 2.)

Part 4: this consists of an error correction text. This is a text where some lines are correct and some contain an extra and unnecessary word which must be identified. The focus is on grammar. (See example on p.28 Exam focus, Exercise 2.)

Part 5: this consists of a word formation exercise. You will read a text in which there are 10 gaps. You are given the stem of the word which you must use to complete each gap. The focus is on vocabulary. *(See example on p.45 Review, Exercise 1.)*

Paper 4 Listening

This paper contains four parts with a total of 30 questions. In each part you will hear the text(s) twice. The texts will be a variety of types, possibly including phone messages, lectures, news, stories, interviews, advertisements, conversations, quizzes and extracts from plays. There will be a mixture of native and non-native speaker accents. This paper will last approximately 40 minutes.

Part 1: you will hear 8 short, unrelated extracts and have to answer a multiple choice question about each one. You may be asked to decide on, for example, the general subject of the text, the relationship of the speakers or the purpose of the conversation. *(See example on p.146 Exam focus, Exercise 1.)*

Part 2: you will hear a monologue or conversation lasting about 3 minutes. You will have to take notes or fill in blanks to complete missing information. *(See example on p.91 Exam focus.)*

Part 3: you will hear a series of short, related extracts of about 30 seconds from monologues or conversations. You will then have to complete a multiple matching task in which you match the speakers to given prompts. *(See example on p.17 Listening, Exercise 2.)*

Part 4: you will hear a monologue or conversation lasting about 3 minutes. You will have to answer questions which involve selecting between 2 or 3 possible answers, for example True/False, Yes/No, which speaker said what, multiple choice, etc. *(See example on p.148 Listening, Exercise 2.)*

Paper 5 Speaking

This paper contains four parts. The standard format involves an interview between two candidates and two examiners. One of the examiners is an interlocutor who speaks to the candidates; the other examiner only assesses the candidates and does not speak. In Parts 1 and 2 of this paper candidates speak mainly to the interlocutor. In Parts 3 and 4 the candidates speak mainly to each other. The different parts are as follows:

Part 1: the interlocutor asks each candidate to say a little about themselves, for example where they come from, what they like doing in their free time, etc. This will last approximately 4 minutes.

Part 2: candidates describe two photographs they are given by the interlocutor and talk about them in relation to themselves and their own experience. This will last approximately 4 minutes. *(See example on p.104 Exam focus.)*

Part 3: candidates are given visual prompts (e.g. photographs, line drawings, diagrams, maps) and are asked to carry out a task together which may involve planning, problem solving, decision making, prioritising or speculating. This will last approximately 3 minutes. *(See example on p.53 Exam focus, Exercise 3.)*

Part 4: the interlocutor develops the topic covered in Part 3 and asks the candidates to discuss and give opinions on more general questions related to the same theme. This will last approximately 4 minutes.

In total this paper will last approximately 15 minutes. *(For an example of a complete Paper 5 interview see p.158 Exam focus.)*

A sense of adventure

Speaking

1 Look at the picture below and discuss the following questions.

1 Why do you think the woman is doing this?
2 Would you be prepared to try this? Why?/Why not?
3 What type of character would you need to have to do this?

2 Complete the questionnaire opposite. Then compare your answers with other students in the class and find someone whose answers are similar to your own.

Are you a THRILL-SEEKER?

Choose the alternative that best describes your likes or dislikes, or the way you feel.

1a) I sometimes like to do things that are a little frightening. ✓ ......
 b) Sensible people avoid dangerous activities. ......
 c) I love being terrified! ......

2a) I enter cold water gradually, giving myself time to get used to it. ......
 b) It's fun to dive or jump right into the ocean or a cold pool. ......
 c) I won't go in the water unless it's very warm. ......

3a) When I go on holiday, I want a decent room and a bed at least. ......
 b) I like going camping and doing without the conveniences of everyday life. ......
 c) I expect a bit of luxury on holiday. ......

4a) My friends are pretty crazy. ......
 b) I prefer calm, conventional people. ......
 c) I like having a mix of friends of all different types. ......

5a) I think it would be really exciting to do a parachute jump. ......
 b) Jumping out of a plane, with or without a parachute, is crazy. ......
 c) I'd consider doing a parachute jump if I had proper training. ......

6a) I think it would be fun to be hypnotised. ......
 b) I wouldn't mind being hypnotised by a professional. ......
 c) I would hate to be in the power of a hypnotist. ......

7a) People who ride motorbikes must have some kind of unconscious desire to hurt themselves. ......
 b) Riding a motorbike at high speed is one of the most exciting things you can do. ......
 c) Motorbikes are just another means of transport. ......

To see how you did on the test, turn to page 184.

Vocabulary: feelings

1   Look at the groups of words below and answer the following questions. Use your dictionary where necessary.

1   Which word is the odd one out in each group? Why?
2   On which syllable does the main stress fall in each word?

EXAMPLE: *ex'cited – second syllable stress*

a) frightened excited terrified scared
b) happy lucky thrilled glad
c) depressed miserable sad confused
d) astonished upset amazed surprised
e) angry cross furious nervous

> — **Watch Out!**   *nervous* ◀
>
> 1   Please stop whistling. It's making me *nervous./It's very irritating.*
> 2   I get very *nervous/irritated* just before an exam.
>
> Which is the most likely alternative in each sentence?

2   Decide which is the correct form of the adjective in each of the following sentences.

1   I had never done a parachute jump before. It was very *frightening/frightened.*
2   I had never done a parachute jump before. I was very *frightening/frightened.*

Which of the other adjectives in Exercise 1 have an *-ed* form and an *-ing* form?

Grammar reference p.162 (1.1/1.2)

3   Complete the following sentences with a suitable adjective from Exercise 1 in the correct form.

1   That film was very .... – all the main characters died!
2   I was .... to hear that he had passed his exams because he never seemed to do any work. It's so annoying!
3   It makes me so .... when people drop litter in the street!
4   Mike was .... when they asked him to be godfather of their first child. Nothing could have made him happier!
5   It was a very .... match. The score was 2–2 until just before the end.

4   Tell a partner how you would feel in the following situations and what you would do next.

1   You hear you have passed all your exams.
2   You are in a lift which suddenly stops and won't move.
3   Your brother/sister/flatmate has borrowed some of your clothes without asking permission.
4   You are walking home late at night and you think someone is following you.

5   Choose three more adjectives from Exercise 1. Tell your partner the last time you felt like that.

6   How are you going to record new vocabulary?

1   Are you going to have a special vocabulary notebook? If so, are you going to organise it:
   ● by day (like a diary)?
   EXAMPLE:

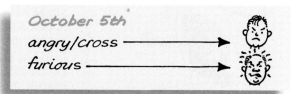

   ● by topic area?
   EXAMPLE:

   ● alphabetically (like a dictionary)?
   EXAMPLE:

   A
   amazed /ə'meɪzd/ adj.: to feel very surprised
   e.g. They were all <u>amazed</u> by her new hairstyle.

2   What information are you going to put in your vocabulary notebook? It is a good idea to include the following things:
   ● the part of speech e.g. noun, verb, adjective, etc.
   ● a definition
   ● an example sentence
   ● the translation
   ● the phonemics and word stress

Reading

1 Look at the pictures below and describe what you can see happening in each one.

A

B

C

D

E

2 Now read the text opposite and decide which paragraph each picture belongs to. Then tell a partner how each picture relates to the text.

3 In most texts you read there will be some words that you do not understand. It is important that you are able to make sensible guesses as to what these words might mean from the surrounding context.

1 The words opposite come from the text. Look at each word in context and choose the correct meaning a) or b).

Why do we risk it?

Ordinary people all over the world are willing to risk their lives for the ultimate experience – an 'adrenaline buzz'. What basic human need is driving them to do it?

1 RISK SPORTS are one of the fastest-growing leisure activities. Daredevils try anything from organised bungee jumps to illegally jumping off buildings. These people never feel so alive as when they are risking their lives. In their quest for the ultimate sensation, thrill-seekers are thinking up more and more elaborate sports. 'Zip wiring', for example, involves sliding down a rope from the top of a cliff suspended by a pulley attached to your ankle.

2 So why do some people's lives seem to be dominated by the 'thrill factor', while others are perfectly happy to sit at home by the fire? Some say that people who do risk sports are reacting against a society which they feel has become dull and constricting. David Lewis, a psychologist, believes that people today crave adventure. In an attempt to guarantee safety, our culture has eliminated risk. 'The world has become a bland and safe place,' says Lewis. 'People used to be able to seek adventure by hunting wild animals, or taking part in expeditions. Now they turn to risk sports as an escape.'

3 Risk sports have a positive side as well. They help people to overcome fears that affect them in their real lives. This makes risk sports particularly valuable for executives in office jobs who need to stay alert so that they can cope when things go wrong. They learn that being frightened doesn't mean they can't be in control.

4 Of all the risk or adrenaline sports, bungee jumping is proving the most popular. Worldwide, one-and-a-half million people have tried it. You hurtle towards the ground from 200 metres up and, at the last moment, when you are about to hit the water or land and death seems certain, a rubber band yanks you back to life. You can decide whether to jump from a crane, a bridge or a balloon. Attached to a length of elastic rope, jumpers experience a free fall of nearly 100 mph, before they're slowed by a quickly increasing pull on their ankles.

5 After five or six bounces jumpers are lowered on to a mattress and set free. Almost inarticulate, they walk around with idiotic grins on their faces. Their hands can't stop shaking, they can only use superlatives and say repeatedly how amazing it was. 'As you're falling, all you see are things flying around as you turn,' says one breathless bungee jumper. 'You don't think you're ever going to stop and when you rebound, it's like weightlessness. You feel as if you're floating on air. My legs are like jelly, but I feel so alive!'

from *Focus* magazine

1 quest *(noun)*	a) search	b) fear
2 crave *(verb)*	a) want very much	b) dislike strongly
3 bland *(adjective)*	a) frightening	b) without excitement
4 alert *(adjective)*	a) full of anxiety	b) quick to notice what is happening
5 hurtle *(verb)*	a) move very fast	b) be sick
6 yank *(verb)*	a) hit violently	b) pull suddenly
7 inarticulate *(adjective)*	a) unable to speak clearly	b) unable to move

2 Now choose two other words that you don't know in the text and try to work out their meaning from the context.

Grammar: questions

1 Here are some incorrectly formed questions. Try to correct them. Then read the information about QUESTIONS opposite and check your ideas.

1 Why people take such dangerous risks?
2 Can you tell me how did you feel afterwards?
3 Did he was waiting for you to jump?
4 Let's go home, do we?
5 When you went bungee-jumping?
6 Are you agree?
7 How many time have you been doing this sport?
8 Of what are you afraid?
9 Who did asked the instructor?
10 Do you know if is he coming?
11 He used to hate motorbikes, wasn't he?

2

1 Question tags are used to check information.

   EXAMPLE: *You've got two brothers, **haven't you?***

   - If you are fairly sure that your information is correct, your voice should <u>fall</u> on the question tag.
   - If you are not very sure whether your information is correct or not, your voice should <u>rise</u> on the question tag.

   Listen and decide if the person saying the above sentence is fairly sure or not very sure that their information is correct.

QUESTIONS

a) Questions are often formed in this way:

Question word(s) +	auxiliary verb +	subject +	main verb
How much	*does*	*this bag*	*cost?*
When	*did*	*he*	*go?*
What	*have*	*they*	*done?*

b) *Be, can* and *have (got)* just change the order of the subject and auxiliary verb.
e.g. *He is watching TV.* > ***Is he watching** TV? They can swim.* > ***Can they** swim? You have got time.* > ***Have you got** time?*

c) If *who/which/what* is the **subject** of the sentence, do not use *do/does/did.*
e.g. ***Who invented** the telephone?* (**not** ~~Who did invent the telephone?~~) ***What happened** to Mike last night?* (**not** ~~What did happen to Mike last night?~~)

d) With 'indirect' questions the word order of the subject (and auxiliary) and main verb is the same order as in statements.
e.g. *Do you think **he is doing** his homework? Are you going to ask me what **I bought**?*

e) Question tags are generally formed with the auxiliary of the verb in the first part of the sentence. Positive statements generally have negative question tags, negative statements generally have positive question tags.
e.g. *You don't like him, **do you**? They haven't taken it, **have they**?*

shall we is the question tag used after *Let's*
e.g. *Let's watch TV, **shall we**?*

did/didn't is used in the question tag after *used to*
e.g. *You used to like swimming, **didn't you**?*

f) Prepositions generally come at the end of questions (except in very formal situations).
e.g. *Who did you go to the cinema **with**?* (**not** ~~With whom did you go to the cinema?~~) *What were you talking **about**?* (**not** ~~About what were you talking?~~).

g) To ask about a period of time we can use *How long ... ?*
e.g. ***How long** have you known him? **How long** are they staying?*

Grammar reference p.171 (13)

2 Listen to five other people using question tags. Are they fairly sure or not very sure that their information is correct?

3 Work with other students and check what you know about them using question tags and the appropriate intonation.

   EXAMPLE: *You're eighteen, **aren't you**?*

3 In small groups consider the following two problems. Try to solve the problems by asking your teacher questions which she/he can answer 'Yes' or 'No' to. Your teacher will not answer your questions unless they are grammatically correct.

Cindy and Sebastian are lying dead on the floor. They are surrounded by broken glass and water. The window to the room is open and the curtains are flapping in the breeze.

Who are they? How did they die and why?

EXAMPLE: *Were they murdered?*

A man is lying dead on the floor. Next to him is a piece of wood, some sawdust and a gun. Another man comes to the door, opens it, looks in, sees the dead man and smiles. He walks away extremely happy.

How did the man die? Why is the second man so happy?

EXAMPLE: *Did the second man kill the first man?*

4

1 A young Australian actress was recently interviewed for a popular magazine. These were the answers she gave. Work with a partner and try to imagine the kinds of questions she might have been asked. See how many different questions your class can think of for each answer.

a) About two years now.
b) Chocolate cake with fresh cream.
c) Heights.
d) Madonna, I suppose.
e) Biting my nails.
f) Getting up before 8.00 in the morning.
g) About once every five years.
h) No, actually, I'm twenty.
i) Yes, but I gave up a few months ago.
j) He's a good friend. Nothing more.
k) My hair. I wish it was blonde.
l) The fact that I am very loyal.
m) My mother. I tell her everything … nearly.

2 Now choose some of your questions and interview a partner.

5

1 Work with a partner. Together, choose two famous people that you are both interested in. Write at least six questions that you would like to ask them.

2 Now take it in turns to be a journalist and the famous person. One of you should ask the questions, the other should answer as if you were that famous person. Be as imaginative as you can in your answers.

Exam focus
Paper 1 Reading (multiple matching)

1 In Paper 1 of the First Certificate exam you will have a section where you are required to match prompts to different elements of a text.

With all the texts you need to read in the exam, it is a good idea to look through them quickly first to get a general idea of what they are about, who they were written for and what context they might originally have come from e.g. a newspaper, a biography, etc.

To help you do this, quickly look through the text opposite and decide if you think it comes from:
a) a geography book
b) a general interest magazine
c) a novel

2 When you have got the general idea you will need to look at the text more closely. This is an example of the type of question you might have:

Which holiday(s) would you recommend for someone who likes:

1 beautiful scenery?
2 serious exercise?
3 historical sites?
4 swimming?
5 wildlife?

Read the information on each holiday and decide which of the above types of people it would be suitable for. (Each holiday may be suitable for more than one type of person.) Make a note of the part of the text which helps you decide.

ADVENTURE *HOLIDAYS*

ALGERIA

Trek through the Saharan wilderness on a camel accompanied by blue-robed Tuareg guides deep into the heart of nowhere. You will discover a world of silent beauty and infinite horizons. Holidays on the beach will never be the same again.
- Getting there: *Explore Worldwide* (01252 319448)

AUSTRALIA

On walkabout safaris in the Kakadu National Park you can learn how the Aborigines live off the land and see their 20,000-year-old rock paintings. Even more famously, Kakadu is the place to see crocodiles, some of which grow up to 9 metres long.
- Getting there: *Austravel* (0171 734 7755)

BORNEO

Travel through the jungles of Borneo by boat and visit the gigantic Mulu caves. Then put on your boots for a two-day climb up Mount Kinabalu, followed by a train ride through mountainous forests, then relax at the coast with some excellent snorkelling.
- Getting there: *Explore Worldwide* (01252 319448)

BRAZIL

The 150,000 square miles of the Pantanal swampland is the world's largest wetland sanctuary, home to 600 species of birds including enormous flocks of parrots. It is the best place in the Americas for a safari.
- Getting there: *Cox and Kings* (0171 834 7472)

GREENLAND

For a tough and exciting challenge, try hiking along the mountainous east coast of Greenland. Most people walk in one direction, following tracks across the tundra and staying overnight in huts, then flying back by helicopter.
- Getting there: *High Places* (01748 822333).

PERU

In Peru you can encounter almost every climate in the world. It has a desert coastline, fertile valleys and a vast area of tropical rainforest. As well as this, there are glaciers and snowy mountain peaks that rise to over 6,700 metres. Despite this wealth of natural beauty, the country is best known for a man-made sight: Machu Picchu, the 'Lost City of the Incas'. High up in the Andes, it is entirely hidden from the valley below and its existence was forgotten until 85 years ago.
- Getting there: *Explore Worldwide* (01252 319448)

THAILAND

'Backroads' is a 12-year-old US company specialising in cycling trips. Each day you cycle anything from 10 to 60 miles while your luggage is transported by van. The Thailand trip costs about £800 for nine days, including meals, good accommodation, elephant-riding and foot treks, but excluding airfares.
- Getting there: *Backroads* (0171 435 1403)

3 Look at the texts again. Tell a partner which two places you would be most interested in visiting and why.

Writing:
informal letters

1 Look at the example of an informal letter opposite written in answer to the following question:

> You have recently got back from a holiday. You decide to write back to an English friend who wrote to you some time ago. Apologise for the delay in replying and tell her/him about your holiday.

Unfortunately, the letter contains a number of spelling, grammar and vocabulary mistakes. Try to find and then correct them. The number of mistakes is indicated at the end of each sentence.

2 Before you practise writing an informal letter, answer the following questions about how you write informal letters in English.

1 Where do you write your address?
2 Do you write the address of the person you are writing to in the letter?
3 Where do you write your name?
4 Where do you write the date?
5 How do you usually begin an informal letter?
6 How can you finish an informal letter?

Apartado 134,
02640 Almansa,
(Albacete),
Spain
5/8/95

Dear Chris,

Thanks for your last letter. I am really sorry I didn't write back earlier, but I have only just got back from holiday. I went with three friends to a little place called Mojacar which is near of Almeria, but it wasn't exactly that we expected (2)!

We booked some rooms in hotel in the village, but when we arrived to the hotel, we were very disappointing (3). It was very old, rather dirty and we couldn't to see the sea (1). So, we decided change (1).

The next hotel was perfectly (1). It was very clean and it had the biggest swiming pool I ever seen (3). But it was one problem – it was so much expensive (2)! We stay one night, but then there was time to change again (2)!

On the end we found the beautiful apartment with a balcony and it was cheap (2). Unfortunatly, we only had four days of our holiday left (1)!

Anyway, I must go and unpack my suitcase! I will write again soon.

Love,

Natalia.

3 Now write an informal letter in answer to the question in Exercise 1 in 120–180 words. Your letter should follow this order:

- Apologise for not writing sooner and explain why.
- Say where you went on holiday and who with.
- Say why you enjoyed/didn't enjoy your holiday and describe any special things you did.
- Say when you hope to see or contact your friend.

When you have finished, show your work to a partner who should check your grammar and spelling.

4 When your teacher has corrected your letter, make a note of some of your more serious spelling, grammar and vocabulary mistakes.

EXAMPLE:

GRAMMAR	SPELLING	VOCABULARY
We couldn't find our luggage *not* ~~luggages~~	Unfortunately *not* ~~unfortunatly~~	I've sent for a brochure about skiing holidays. *not* ~~prospectus~~

- Build up a list of your common mistakes and try to avoid them in your future writing.

Vocabulary: transport

1   How many different ways can you think of to travel by sea, air or land?

EXAMPLE: *by sea > submarine, canoe, motor-boat, etc.*

2   Put the words in the box into categories according to whether they relate to *ships, trains, planes, cars* or *buses*. Which of the words can go in more than one category?

> a dual carriageway   to check in   the fast lane   a guard   Customs
> roadworks   a lifeboat   a lay-by   a platform   a compartment
> a fare   a ticket   a cabin   a seatbelt   a deck   a liner   a cruise
> a passenger   a port   a single   an inspector   a stop   to take off
> a parking meter   a ferry   a departure lounge   a life-belt   a flight
> first-class   a track   a driving test   a steward   a yacht   Duty Free

3   Complete the following table.

	car	bicycle	train	motorbike	plane	bus
get into/ out of	✔	✗				
get on/ off						
drive						
ride						
catch/ miss						

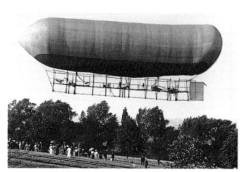

> **Watch Out!**   *journey/trip/travel*
>
> 1 I've got to go on a business *journey* to Rome next weekend.
> 2 The *travel* to New York was long and tiring.
> 3 *Trip* makes you more sensitive to other cultures.
>
> What is the mistake in each of these sentences?

4   Answer these questions to describe the last/longest/worst journey you have ever made by *ship, train, plane, car, bus* or *motorbike*.

1 When did you go?
2 Who did you go with?
3 Where were you going?
4 Who or what were you going to see?
5 What was the journey like?
6 What did you do during the journey?
7 Did you meet anyone interesting?

Listening: disaster at sea

1 Look at the picture above and discuss the following questions.

1 What can you see happening? What do you know about this ship? Why is it so famous?

2 How do you think these words will be important in the story of this ship?

> iceberg   look-out   bridge (of a ship)   sink   icy   lifeboat

2 Listen to the first part of the story and see if your ideas were correct.

3 Listen again and make a note of the significance of these numbers.

a) 2 hours and 40 minutes
b) 2,300
c) 11.40 p.m.
d) 1,513
e) 22 knots
f) 16
g) 1,250

4 What do you think happened next on board the *Titanic*? Discuss your ideas with a partner and then listen to the second part of the story to see if you were right.

5 Listen to the second part again and decide if the following statements are True or False.

1 The passengers of the *Titanic* weren't particularly worried at first.
2 Emily Richards had just left the USA.
3 She had her two children with her.
4 She regrets not being able to save more people.
5 The ship was completely under the water at 2.20 a.m.
6 Music was heard as the ship went under the water.
7 There were four similarities between what happened to the *Titanic* and the ship in the story written by Morgan Robertson.

6 Discuss the following questions.

1 Who do you think was responsible for the sinking of the *Titanic*?
2 Do you know of any other major transport disasters? What happened and why?

Vocabulary: word formation

● *And so began two hours and forty minutes of **dis**belief ...*

1 What do the following prefixes in **bold** mean?

EXAMPLE: *re-* means 'again'.

1 **re**play/**re**do
2 **dis**belief/**im**polite/**il**logical/ **un**usual/**ir**responsible/**in**visible
3 **over**crowded/**over**charge
4 **under**estimate/**under**weight
5 **post**graduate/**post**mortem
6 **ex**-husband/**ex**-President
7 **sub**marine/**sub**way

2 What parts of speech (nouns, adjectives, or adverbs) do the suffixes in **bold** indicate?

1 quick**ly**/back**wards**
2 employ**ment**/happi**ness**/ inflat**ion**/social**ism**
3 employ**ee**/teach**er**/conduct**or**
4 fam**ous**/sunn**y**/hope**ful**/ brown**ish**/use**less**

3 Make as many words as you can by combining different parts of the box.

dis	**excite**	ful	ment
un	**appoint**	less	ness
im	**honest**	able	ion
	patient	ly	
	success	y	
	direct	ship	
	kind		
	profit		
	help		
	friend		
	luck		
	like		

4 Choose six words you formed and write a sentence for each to illustrate the meaning.

1 Match the two halves of the following conversations. Imagine who is speaking and where they might be.

1 A return to Manchester, please.	a) Look, I'm really sorry, but I had it a minute ago.
2 I can't believe it. We've been stuck in this traffic jam for hours!	b) Oh, well ... why don't we go and have a look round the Duty Free shop?
3 Tickets, please.	c) And did you ever have dinner with the captain?
4 The 19.30 Los Angeles flight will be delayed by one hour due to poor weather conditions.	d) Will you be coming back today?
5 We generally got up early and went for a walk round the deck before breakfast.	e) Can you wait for a second because I think there's a petrol station just a bit further on?
6 Can you stop at the next lay-by? I think there's something wrong with my seatbelt.	f) There are probably roadworks ahead.

2 Complete the following sentences with the **opposite** of one of the words in the box.

> forwards   underweight   legal   lucky   polite   responsible   useful   honest   patient   kind

1 It's .... for people under seventeen to drive a car in Britain.
2 Don't be .... ! Let your sister play with your toys.
3 This knife is .... It can't cut anything.
4 You shouldn't drive when you are feeling sleepy. It's very ....
5 Why are you so .... ? Just relax. It will be your turn soon.
6 Don't step .... or you will fall in the swimming-pool.
7 Some people believe it is .... to walk under ladders.
8 You know that taking that money without asking was a .... thing to do.
9 I don't know why you are on a diet. You are certainly not ....
10 I thought it was rather .... of her not to say goodbye.

3 Look at the pictures and think of a word to describe how the people are feeling. What do you imagine has made them feel this way?

A   B   C   D   E

4 This informal letter contains various mistakes of organisation and punctuation. Rewrite the letter correcting the mistakes.

> Chris Parker
> 19/5/96
> 181 Dover House Rd.,
> Putney,
> london SW5 5AE
>
> Dear natalia,
> thanks very much for your letter, your holiday sounds like it was very interesting!! I have been very busy at work recently but Sam and I are going on holiday to Greece next week for ten days, we are really looking forward to it. I promise IU send you a postcard! Hope to see you soon, best wishes,
> Chris

5 Put the words in these questions in the correct order. Then answer the questions in complete sentences.

1 free do doing like you what time your in ?
2 place the been what most to is ever interesting have you ?
3 holidays best of what you kind like do ?
4 studying for English long been you how have ?
5 English learning thing the you about find do what difficult most?
6 pass exam you you the Certificate do think will First ?

Work and play

B

C

D

a dustman

E

F

Speaking

Look at the pictures of people with different
jobs and discuss who you think should
be paid the most/the least and why.

Vocabulary: jobs

G

1 Describe what these different people do in their jobs.

EXAMPLE: *A nurse takes care of people who are not well.*

a nurse   a debt collector   an undertaker   a referee   a tax inspector
a bouncer   a plumber   a traffic warden   a conductor   a bookmaker
a social worker   a surgeon   a dustman   an artist   a chef   a miner
a private investigator   a librarian   a caretaker   a stockbroker
an editor   a vet   a wrestler   a lifeguard

2 If you had the necessary skills/qualifications, which of these jobs:

1 might you be interested in? Why?
2 would you definitely not be interested in? Why?

H

3 Work with a partner.

1 Choose one of the jobs from Exercise 1, but don't tell your partner
which one you have chosen.

2 Your partner must ask you questions to find out what the job is.
EXAMPLE: A: *Do you wear a uniform?* B: *Yes.*

3 You can only answer 'Yes' or 'No' to the questions. When your partner
has discovered the job, change over.

4 See who can discover the other person's job in the least number of
questions.

Listening: hated jobs

1 You are going to hear four people talking about their jobs. Each job appears in the box in Vocabulary Exercise 1. Listen and decide what each person's job is.

2 Now listen again and decide which speaker each of the following sentences applies to. (One of the sentences does not apply to any of them.)

A This person says she/he was physically threatened.
B This person says her/his salary is the most important thing.
C This person has actually cried at work.
D This person most enjoys the contact with people.
E This person has had an embarrassing experience at work.

3 Look at the phrasal verbs with *on* in the sentences below and decide if the common meaning of them all is:

a) to move
b) to complete
c) to continue
d) to change

- One individual did say he would break my legs if I *kept on* asking him for money.
- Let's *hold on* for a little bit longer. I'm sure he will be here soon.
- I will *carry on* working here until I can find a better job.
- The book was so interesting that she wanted to *go on* reading it until she had finished.

4 Discuss the following questions.

1 Would you be interested in doing any of the four jobs that you have heard about?
2 What qualities/abilities do you need to do each of these jobs well?

Grammar: present tenses

1 Read the following rules for when the Present Continuous is used. Then match one of the sentences below to each rule.

The Present Continuous (or Progressive) is used for:

1 actions happening now or over a period of time around now.
2 changing/developing situations.
3 temporary situations.
4 future arrangements.
5 annoying habits.

a) Why are you always telling me what to do?
b) The level of unemployment is getting worse.
c) I'm sorry, but he is doing his homework right now.
d) We are having dinner with Julie on Friday night.
e) She is staying with friends in York for a few days.

Grammar reference p.175 (17.2)

2 Now do the following exercises with a partner to practise the Present Continuous.

1 Think of members of your family or close friends and say what you think they are probably doing at the moment.
 EXAMPLE: *I think my father **is probably having** a meeting in his office.*

2 Think of the same people again and tell your partner about any annoying habits they may have.
 EXAMPLE: *My younger brother **is always leaving** his shoes and socks around the house.*

3 Tell your partner what things you have arranged to do this weekend.
 EXAMPLE: ***I'm meeting** Maria on Saturday morning and **we're going** shopping together.*

4 Tell your partner if you think the people you know and the place where you live are changing. Think about things such as: fashion/unemployment/cost of entertainment/pop music/inflation/pollution/the weather.
 EXAMPLE: *The pollution where I live **is getting worse** all the time!*

3 Read the following rules for when the Present Simple is used. Then match one of the sentences below to each rule.

The Present Simple is used for:

1 routine or regular, repeated actions.
2 time clauses after *when, as soon as, if, until,* etc.
3 permanent situations.
4 the future as expressed in timetables.
5 scientific or natural laws.
6 with 'state' verbs (which we do not usually use in the continuous form) e.g. *be, believe, feel, hate, hear, know, like, look, love, prefer, realise, remember, see, seem, smell, suppose, taste, want.*

a) Water freezes at 0°C.
b) I work five evenings a week.
c) I'll ask him when I see him.
d) I live in Athens.
e) It's the people I like most about the job.
f) The train arrives in Edinburgh at 5.00 p.m.

Grammar reference p.175 (17.1)

4 Now do the following exercises to practise the Present Simple.

1 Complete the following sentences with the Present Simple or Future Simple (*will*) form of the verbs in brackets.
   a) I .....will......... (*paint*) the kitchen when I .... (*have*) some free time.
   b) We ....will....... (*start*) the meeting until everybody .... (*arrive*).
   c) If she .... (*find*) a better job, I think she .... will .... (*leave*).
   d) They ....will.... (*move*) house as soon as they .... (*find*) a buyer.
   e) When he .... (*come*) back, I ....will.... (*tell*) him what we have decided.

2 Write five sentences about yourself in the Present Simple. Each time you should use one of the words/expressions in the box below.

> quite frequently/about two or three times a year/
> very often/from time to time/hardly ever/
> as often as I can/never/once or twice a week/
> more often than I'd like to

EXAMPLE: **I visit** my grandmother **as often as I can**.

3 Work in a group with two other students. Describe your typical routine at the weekend. Are there any major differences between your routine, and the routines of the other students in your group?

EXAMPLE: *I usually **get up** at about 7.00 a.m. and **have** a shower. Then I ...*

5 Complete the following dialogue with the Present Continuous or Present Simple form of the verbs in brackets.

RUPERT: Hi, Nigel! How are you?
NIGEL: Fine, fine. It's been a long time.
RUPERT: Yes, nearly four years now.
NIGEL: So, tell me about yourself!
RUPERT: Well, I (1) ....work..... (*work*) in this language school in Cairo.
NIGEL: Oh, really? So what (2) .....are you doing.... (*do*) here in London?
RUPERT: I (3) ...am having... (*have*) a holiday.
NIGEL: Oh, I see. And what (4) ......do you think.... (*think*) of Cairo?
RUPERT: Oh, I (5) ....like...... (*like*) it very much. It's a very exciting place.
NIGEL: And what about your job?
RUPERT: Well, I generally (6) .....get up....... (*get up*) about 8.30 and (7) .... (*plan*) some lessons. Fortunately, with time, it (8) ....gets...... (*get*) easier and easier to plan lessons – in the beginning it took me ages! I usually (9) .... (*teach*) from 11 a.m. to 1 p.m. and later again from 6.30 to 9.30. We all (10) .... (*finish*) at 9.30 p.m. and we often (11) .... (*go*) into town in one big group, to a disco or something.
NIGEL: When (12) ...are you going back... (*go back*) to Cairo?
RUPERT: Next week, on Friday. The plane (13) .... (*leave*) early, about 7.00 a.m.
NIGEL: And how's your brother?
RUPERT: Chris ... oh, he's OK. I (14) .... (*see*) him as often as I can. He is married with two children and he never (15) ....stops..... (*stop*) telling me that I should get a regular job and settle down! He (16) .... (*play*) a lot of football at the moment. I (17) ....think..... (*think*) he (18) .... (*try*) to get fit!
NIGEL: That's new!
RUPERT: And what about you? What (19) .... (*do*)?

Vocabulary: employment

1   Read the following questions and check that you understand the meaning of the words in *italics*. Use a dictionary where necessary.

1   What do you think is a good *salary* or *wage* in your country? How much would you like to *earn*?
2   Would you like to work on *commission*? Why/Why not? Do you think people should get paid a *bonus* for especially good work?
3   What different information should you put in a *C.V.*?
4   What should you do to make a good impression at a job *interview*?
5   Think of the job you do at the moment or that you would like to do in the future. What *skills* and/or *qualifications* do you need to do it?
6   How many years' *training* do you need to do before you can become a doctor in your country?
7   Is it common or unusual for *employees* to *go on strike* in your country. Do you have *trade unions*?
8   For what reasons can people be *sacked*? For what reasons can people be *made redundant*? Why do people sometimes *resign* from their jobs?
9   What help do people get from the government if they are *unemployed* in your country?
10   At what age do men and women usually *retire* in your country? Do you think this is early, late or about right? Do they usually get a *pension*?

2   Now discuss the questions in small groups.

Watch Out!   *experience*

1   He did a scientific *experiment/experience* in the laboratory.
2   He has a lot of *experience/experiences* as a salesman.
3   He had some terrible *experience/experiences* while he was travelling in the USA.

Which alternative is correct in each sentence?

Use of English: word formation

In Paper 3 of the exam you will be required to read a text and put key words into the text in the correct part of speech. Here is a procedure for doing this type of task:

● Read the text quickly to get the general idea.
● Look at each gap. Decide what part of speech is required and whether it needs to be positive or negative.
● Fill in the gap with a word in the appropriate form.

Now follow this procedure for the text below. To help you this time we have given you a choice of two alternatives in each case. If you are still not sure, you should refer to your dictionary.

---

hon·est /ˈɒnəst ‖ ˈɑːn-/ *adj* **1** open and direct: *To be quite honest with you, I don't think you'll pass.* **2** not likely to lie, steal, or cheat: *An honest employee is a rare thing.* **3** truthful and sincere: *an honest face | an honest opinion* – opposite **dishonest**

Father fires son for 10 years of laziness

A businessman sacked his son because he was lazy, incompetent and (1) **dishonest/dishonesty**. Stuart Bidwell, 26, was handed dozens of (2) **undisciplined/disciplinary** letters about his work during his ten years with the firm. Manager and father Stephen Bidwell said: 'He got (3) **numerate/numerous** warnings and was just no good. He didn't really have the right (4) **qualifications/disqualified** for the job anyway. We only gave him the job because he was family and we didn't want him to be (5) **unemployed/unemployment**.'
The final straw came when Stuart was caught making long-distance phone calls to his girl-friend in Australia during office hours. Apparently Stuart was finally asked to hand in his (6) **resigned/resignation** but he refused, so he was sacked.
Stuart Bidwell told the court that he had been (7) **unfairly/unfairness** dismissed. Stuart said he had worked for his father's company since leaving school at 16 and that he had only ever had two warning letters.
Stuart's father has already put an (8) **advertisement/advertising** in the local paper for a replacement and says that they have already had over 100 (9) **applicants/applications** through the post. The case continues.

HONEST
DISCIPLINE
NUMBER
QUALIFY
EMPLOY
RESIGN
FAIR
ADVERTISE
APPLY

from *Today* newspaper

Listening: song

1 What does the expression 'the rat race' mean? Why would some people want to get out of it? What might they do instead?

2 You are going to listen to a song called *9 to 5*. What do you imagine the song will be about? Listen and see if you were right.

3 Here are the words to the song, but in each verse the lines are in the wrong order. Put them in the correct order. Then listen to the song again to check your answers. You have been given the first line of each verse.

And the blood starts pumping
And yawn and stretch
Out on the streets
Tumble out of bed *(1)*
Pour myself a cup of ambition
With folks like me
And try to come to life
Jump in the shower
On the job from 9 to 5
And I stumble to the kitchen
The traffic starts jumping

Chorus
And they never give you credit
What a way to make a living
It's all taking and no giving
It's enough to drive you crazy
Working 9 to 5 *(1)*
Barely getting by
If you let it
They just use your mind

You would think that I
But the boss won't seem to let me
9 to 5 for service and devotion *(1)*
I swear sometimes
Want to move ahead
Would deserve a better promotion
That man is out to get me

Exam focus

Paper 2 Writing Question 1 (transactional letter)

1 In Part 1 of Paper 2 you must write a letter based on certain information. There is no choice and you must write between 120 and 180 words.

Read the following example of a typical task.

You see the following job advertisement in a local newspaper. You are quite interested but would like some extra information. Read carefully the advertisement and the notes which you have made below. Then write your letter:

a) saying why you think you would be particularly suitable for this job.

b) asking for extra information as suggested by the handwritten notes below.

Write **a letter** of **between 120 and 180** words in an appropriate style. Do not write any addresses.

WORK WITH ENGLISH-SPEAKING TOURISTS

Have you been looking for a chance to improve your English and earn good money at the same time? Well, this is an ideal opportunity!

Our company specialises in providing package tours for British and American tourists all over the world, and we are looking for local people who are interested in acting as tour guides around major cities and places of national interest. You would also be responsible for looking after the general welfare of your group while they were in your care.

Letters of application should be sent to:

*BritAm Tours,
Empire House,
176 Piccadilly,
London W1 9FQ*

Short-listed applicants will be called for interview locally.

- *when job start?*
- *hours of work + pay?*
- *'be responsible for looking after the general welfare' – what does it mean?*
- *available for interview – evenings only!*

2 Here are two different attempts to answer the question in Exercise 1. Read Letter A and Letter B and then complete the table according to the characteristics which you think each letter has.

	Letter A	Letter B
• answers the question directly and completely	✔	✘
• communicates the message effectively		
• begins and ends the letter appropriately		
• organises it well with clear paragraphs		
• has a good range of grammatical structures and vocabulary		
• uses the grammatical structures and vocabulary accurately		
• has correct punctuation and spelling		
• includes a range of linking expressions e.g. *although, furthermore*		
• uses language of an appropriate style		

Letter A

Dear Sir/Madam,

I am writing with reference to your advertisement in todays paper concerning possible work with English-speaking tourists. I am very intrested in doing this kind of job and will be available from the begining of next month. I need to know exactly when the job would start, I should say that my level of english is good, I can communication well and fairly fluently. I have spent time on holiday in britain and really enjoy meeting people from other countrys. i have always been interested in the history and cultur of my local area. before I can consider the job I need to know what the hours of work and pay would be. I would like to know more about what 'be responsable for the general welfare of your group' means and what they could inwolve. I am afraid that I will only be available for interview in the evening (due to present work commitements). I look forward to hearing from you in the near future.
Yours faithfuly,

Ingrid Nelson

Letter B

Dear Sir/Madam,

I write about your advertisement in today's newspaper concerning possible work with English-speaking tourists. I am very interested by this job and can be start next month. However, I need knowing when job start.

First of all my English level is quite well. I went to England and very enjoy meeting people from others countries. Moreover, I had interested in the all history and culture of my town.

I looking forward hear from you.

Lots of love,

Luis Sanchez

3 Now write your own letter in answer to the question above, trying to incorporate the best features of Letter A and Letter B.

Would *YOU* set yourself on fire for £75 a day?

... OR LAUNCH yourself off the Great Wall of China without a parachute? It's all in a day's work when you're a nerves-of-steel stuntwoman. And as it's a profession where there is very little female participation – there are only sixteen stuntwomen in the whole of Britain – it's a job consideration worth taking seriously. Sue Dando finds out the facts.

A stuntperson is a man or woman who does all the really dangerous bits of acting work in films or on TV. **(1 ———)** Sarah Franzi, 24, is one of Britain's 16 professional stuntwomen (as against 160 men). Like many of her female colleagues, it was a career she'd never seriously considered. 'From when I was young I'd trained to be a dancer, and for seven years after school I was rarely out of work. A dancer's life is pretty short, though, and it was my father who suggested I should think about doing stunt work after I'd given up dancing. **(2 ———)** For six months, I worked really hard, every day, all day. I had to learn six different skills – sub-aqua, sky diving, horse riding, stuff like that – to a high standard of training.'

Sarah finished all the requirements in just five months – it can take as long as three years to qualify. Two weeks after Sarah's completed application was accepted by the Stunt Committee, she was launching herself off the Great Wall of China in *Superman IV*. 'I was very lucky to get work so quickly. I had a small part, playing a tourist who fell off the Wall after an earthquake, only to be rescued from death by Superman. In reality, I fell 15 metres onto a pile of cardboard boxes!

(3 ———) You just have to suffer the discomfort and fall properly. I was paid £210 a day for it, and because it was considered dangerous, another £200 "adjustment" fee was added for every extra take.' This may sound like a lot but, as Sarah explains, 'The film company is paying for the risk. If I'd broken a bone, that isn't very much money at all when you're out of work for the next few months, and there is a risk involved. Safety procedures are very strict, but it's still a danger. **(4 ———)**.'

As yet, Sarah has received injuries no more severe than bangs and bruises, though she does admit to having been scared on at least one occasion.

'I was set alight for *London's Burning* (a TV programme about the London Fire Brigade). It was a full fire job, which meant that my whole body – I was wearing protective clothing – was set alight. **(5 ———)** The difficulty with that kind of job is that you're never fully in control of the fire, so it's easier for something to go wrong.

'It's jobs like that which make people think we must be completely mad to do this kind of work.

(6 ———) There are so many safety precautions, with so much mental concentration involved, that what we're really doing is creating an illusion of danger. If people think, "How could you do that? You must be mad!" then we're just doing our jobs properly.'

How to qualify

To be accepted onto the Stunt Register – the official list of qualified stuntpeople, and the only means by which you're able to get work – you have to be between 18 and 30 years old, and a full member of Equity, the actors' union. Once you've got these qualifications, you then have to reach the required standard in at least six of the categories listed below. **(7 ———)** The groups are:

Group A – Fighting
Fencing
Judo/Aikido/Wrestling
Other martial arts
Boxing

Group B – Falling
Trampolining
Diving
Parachuting

Group C – Riding and driving
Horse riding
Car driving
Motorcycle riding

Group D – Agility and strength
Gymnastics

Group E – Water
Swimming
Sub-aqua

Group F – Miscellaneous
Evidence of a high standard of qualification in a skill not listed e.g. ballet, athletics, dance.

Further help

For more details write to:
Stuntperson Enquiries, Equity, 8 Harley Street, London W1N 2AB. (Don't forget to enclose a stamped addressed envelope.)

from *Just 17* magazine

Reading

1 Describe to a partner the most dangerous and/or exciting thing you have ever done.

2 Read the text opposite and then answer the following questions. (Certain sentences have been taken out of the text which will be inserted later.)

1 What is Sarah Franzi's job?
2 What made her decide to do it?
3 Has she been seriously injured?
4 Do you think she is well paid?

3 The sentences below have been removed from the text. Decide which sentence goes in each of the numbered gaps in the text. Here is a procedure for doing this type of task:

- Read the text once to make sure that you have a good general idea of what it is about.
- Look at the sentences that have been removed and try to get an idea of the subject of each one.
- Look at each gap in the text in turn, at the sentence before it and the sentence after it. In your mind, try putting in the most likely missing sentences. Look for clues to help you e.g. words like *that*, *it* or *he* which refer to something or someone in the sentence before.
- Decide on one sentence for each gap. If later you want to use a particular sentence again, go back and check where you used it before. There may be a different sentence that would fit in this gap.

A But that's not the case at all.
B You can't use anything softer than that, like mattresses for instance, because you'd bounce back up into view of the camera.
C I was on fire for 15 seconds and towards the end it was incredibly hot.
D They should fall within at least three of the groups, but not more than two categories should fall within any one group.
E This can be anything from a relatively simple fall into a swimming pool, to jumping off the top of a skyscraper.
F Fortunately, the risks are one part of the job I really enjoy.
G I did think about it for the next two years – then decided to take the plunge and have a real go.

4 Compare your answers with a partner and say what you think the underlined words in Exercise 3 refer to.

EXAMPLE: *In A I think that refers to the idea that stuntpeople must be completely mad.*

5 Discuss the following questions.

1 What would you feel about doing Sarah's job?
2 Have you ever done any of the sports in Groups A–F? Are/Were you good at them? Would you like to do any of them? Why?/Why not?

Vocabulary: sports

1 Match the words in the box to one of the listed sports below. Some of the items go with more than one sport.

| a glove a net a hole a set a ring a green |
| a goal a racket a round an umpire a court |
| a pitch a linesman a club a referee to serve |

1 tennis   4 volleyball
2 golf   5 boxing
3 football

2 Describe how the following pairs of sports are similar to and different from each other.

1 volleyball/basketball
2 tennis/table-tennis
3 boxing/wrestling
4 football/American football
5 surfing/windsurfing

3 Discuss the following questions.

1 What sport do you enjoy playing most? Are there any other sports that you would like to try?
2 What sport do you enjoy watching most? Do you prefer going to sports events or watching them on TV?

Writing: sequencers

_1_ Read the text and put the following pictures in the order in which they happen.

Mountain Men

The history of Sumo wrestling goes back over 2000 years. Its origins are connected to the Japanese belief in Shinto, the 'way of the gods', where winning gains favour with the gods. This is why the ritual of a sumo match is taken so seriously.

The clay fighting ring is itself a sacred shrine. On entering it, the enormous wrestler first claps, to attract the gods' attention and indicate his own purity of heart. Having done that, he shakes his apron to drive away evil spirits, and raises his arms to show he carries no weapons. Next comes his most dramatic gesture. With his left hand on his heart and his right arm extended to the east, the huge fighter raises his right leg as high as possible – to send it crashing down with all his force. Then he performs the same earth-shaking stamp with the other leg. After that, he purifies himself and the ring by throwing salt, wiping himself, and rinsing his mouth with water. Finally, the opponents spend three or four minutes trying to intimidate each other with grimaces and threatening postures.

The fight itself is brief and brutal and consists of a thunderous collision that rarely lasts more than ten seconds, which ends when one giant is pushed to the ground or outside the circle.

_2_

1 What seven different words or grammatical structures can you see in the second paragraph for describing a sequence?
   EXAMPLE: **On enter*ing*** it, the enormous wrestler **first** claps, ...

2 Think about a typical morning in the week. Describe what happens when you wake up. Use some of the 'sequencers' from the text.
   EXAMPLE: *The first thing is that my alarm goes off. Then I get up ...*

_3_ Work in a group with other students and describe a sport that you know.

- Refer to the following if appropriate:
- where you play
- what you play with
- what you wear
- who you play with
- the object of the game
- the basic rules
- what makes a good player
- Use some of the words and structures from the text to describe sequences.
- If the other students know how to play the sport, they should imagine they don't and make you explain very clearly!

_4_ Write a short introduction to your particular sport for people who have never played it before. Divide it into paragraphs referring to the different areas listed in Exercise 3 above.

1 Look at the following characteristics and think of two jobs for which each one is necessary. Use different jobs each time.

EXAMPLE: *strength: a wrestler, a bouncer*

1 strength 2 kindness 3 patience
4 reliability 5 creativity 6 attention to detail

2 Explain the difference in meaning between the following pairs of words/phrases.

1 an employer/an employee
2 to win/to earn
3 a salary/a wage
4 unemployed/on a pension
5 to be sacked/to be made redundant
6 a perk/a bonus
7 to retire/to resign

3

1 Write the verb form of the following nouns. Then mark the position of the stress in both forms.

Noun	Verb
qualifi'cation	to 'qualify
resignation	
employment	
advertisement	
application	
replacement	
information	
specialisation	
protection	
concentration	

2 Now write a sentence using either the noun or the verb form of each of the words in the table.

EXAMPLE: *It takes many years to **qualify** as a doctor.*

4 Choose the correct alternative in the following sentences.

1 The job situation *slowly gets/is slowly getting* better.
2 I *only occasionally go/am only occasionally going* to the theatre.
3 You *don't believe/aren't believing* him, do you?
4 I *stay/am staying* with Paul for a few days.
5 Ask him to give me a call, when you *see/are seeing* him.
6 I *probably play/am probably playing* football tonight.
7 The flowers *come out/are coming out* in early March.
8 I think he *realises/is realising* that you are serious.

5 Read the following text and choose the correct alternative below to fill in the gaps.

I never really enjoyed sports at school. I remember when I played football, I was always put in (1) ...., but I used to get bored and read a book. Then when the other side (2) ...., the rest of my (3) .... would shout at me. Later on I tried tennis which wasn't much better. I used to have this habit of dropping the (4) .... each time I went to hit the ball. The worst thing was once when I actually won a (5) .... – I was so pleased that I ran and jumped over the (6) ...., but caught my foot on it, fell and broke my arm.

   My latest attempt to get fit was when I tried boxing at a local gym. I remember my first (7) .... I climbed up inside the (8) .... and the bell went for the start of the first (9) .... I just shut my eyes and swung my fist. Unfortunately, I hit the (10) .... and not my opponent. Needless to say, that was the end of my boxing career.

(1) net/goal   (6) line/net
(2) scored/pointed   (7) fight/struggle
(3) club/team   (8) court/ring
(4) racket/bat   (9) round/game
(5) play/game   (10) umpire/referee

'Disadvantage Brown'

UNIT 3

Nearest and dearest

Speaking

1 Fill in the gaps in the following poem with the words in the box. Then listen and check your answers.

> twin (x 2)   same   trick   out   pain   win   sick
> again   blame   shout   sin

MY SISTER

My younger sister is a (1) _pain_ ,
She's so naughty again and (2) _again_ .
Every morning is the (3) _shout_ ,
And what is worse I get the (4) _blame_ .
It is so sad, I just can't (5) _win_ ,
'Cos after all she is my (6) _twin_ !!

My Dad says,'I'll sort her (7) _out_ ,'
But all he does is shout and (8) _shout_ .
But shouting doesn't do the (9) _trick_ ,
It isn't fair, it makes me (10) _sick_ .
It's such a crime, 'Oh! What a (11) _sin_ .'
Please, oh please DON'T HAVE A (12) _twin_ !!

2 Discuss what the advantages/disadvantages are of:

a) being an only child.
b) having brothers and sisters.
c) being a twin.

Reading

1 Read the following article and decide what you think is the most appropriate title.

a) Twins reunited after a lifetime apart.
b) Twin sisters trapped in a single mind.
c) Bringing up twins – the parents' story.

1 AT FIRST IT'S HARD TO BELIEVE. They speak in unison, walk in step, dress identically to the last button and match each other mouthful for mouthful at the dinner table. But this is no trick with mirrors. This is everyday East London, where everyone knows Greta and Freda Chaplin, the identical twins.

2 The twins do everything together. Whether they are out shopping or doing the housework they mirror each other's actions and mannerisms down to the finest detail. To vacuum the floor both twins grasp the handle of the hoover at the same time as they guide it slowly around the carpet together. If they make tea, both their hands are on the bottle as they pour the milk. Listening to them talk is like hearing one person with a slight echo a split second later. If someone gives them a bar of soap in different colours, they will cut theirs in two and swap a half. They have two black coats, but one came with green buttons and one black. They swapped the buttons around so that each twin had two green and two black buttons on each coat. The sisters themselves say that they feel like one person, not two. Sometimes it's almost as though they inhabit the same mind.

3 The sisters, now 48, live in a flat in Hackney, East London. They are a familiar sight in the area, where they are often seen out shopping together in their long clothes and waist-length hair. Some people are frightened of their strange telepathic bond, others laugh at them. The twins realise this and don't like it, so they avoid crowds. They rely a great deal on the protection and friendship of Jack Davenport who has been like a father to them. 'Sometimes it's as if you're seeing double,' he says. 'If we go out shopping, they automatically buy the same thing in the same colour at the same price, although it might be from a different counter. They do everything at the same time – clean their teeth, eat, drink. If they're having fish and chips, they will pick a chip up at the same time.'

2 Now read the article again and decide if the following statements are True or False. Make a note of the part of the text which helps you decide.

1 Greta and Freda live in England.
2 They speak nearly at the same time.
3 They feel the need to look exactly the same.
4 Local people are generally very kind and supportive towards the twins.
5 Their father's name is Jack.
6 Their mother tried to help them grow up with their own identities.
7 They have different characters.
8 Dr Bryan isn't surprised by the idea of telepathy between Greta and Freda.
9 Dr Bryan is concerned with the psychological aspects of multiple births.

Little is known about the childhood of the sisters, except that they grew up on a housing estate in York. From babies their mother treated them as one and encouraged their dependence on each other. Everything in their life was identical down to the twin dolls they played with. 'She told us always to stick to each other,' say Freda and Greta in unison. 'She said when you go to the shops always ask for two of something and if they've only got one, don't take it.'

As Jack Davenport remarks, 'They do have different personalities although they won't admit it. Greta is the softer, more sensible one. Freda is the one who tends to dominate her sister and lose her temper more quickly. In the last few years they have become quieter and much more intelligent company. All they want is love, friendship and understanding, which they have never had.'

Dr Elizabeth Bryan, Director of the Multiple Births Foundation says, 'These two are an extreme case, but I'm quite sure there is often telepathy between twins. If you shared the womb and your life together, there is bound to be.'

Having dealt with more than 3,000 sets of twins, she says, 'My concern is to help parents with the emotional stress of having two babies or more at the same time. The mother of Freda and Greta Chaplin tried to bring them up as a single child and didn't give them the chance ever to be separated. So they never had the opportunity to develop as individuals.'

3 Find words or phrases in the text with the following meanings.

1 at the same time *(para. 1)*
2 to hold tightly *(para. 2)*
3 a very short time *(para. 2)*
4 to exchange *(para. 2)*
5 part of your body, above your hips *(para. 3)*
6 a flat surface in a shop where you go to be served *(para. 3)*
7 to keep together *(para. 4)*
8 to agree that something is true *(para. 5)*
9 to become angry suddenly *(para. 5)*
10 part of a woman's body where a baby develops before it is born *(para. 6)*
11 certain, sure *(para. 6)*
12 anxiety, pressure *(para. 7)*

4 Discuss the following questions.

1 Do you think the writer of the article:
   a) dislikes the twins?
   b) feels sorry for the twins?
   c) admires the twins?
   Why?

2 What do you feel about the twins? Do you know any twins? Are they like the twins in the article?

Vocabulary: phrasal verbs (family)

1 Listen to sentences that contain the following phrasal verbs and make a note of what you think each verb means.

1 to grow up
2 to bring (someone) up
3 to look after
4 to get on (with someone)
5 to look up to (someone)
6 to take after (someone)
7 to get up to (something)
8 to tell (someone) off

2 Use some of the phrasal verbs to describe yourself and your own family situation.

EXAMPLE: *When I was about nine, I used to **get up to** all sorts of things. Once I ...*

from *Today* newspaper

27

Exam focus

Paper 3 Use of English (error correction)

In Part 4 of Paper 3 of the exam you are required to read a short text and decide if each line is correct or whether there is an extra word that should not be there.

Here is a procedure for doing this task:

- Read the text through quickly to get the general idea of what it is about.
- Look at each line and decide if it is correct or if there is an extra word that should not be there. If there is an extra word, decide what it is.
- Remember that the extra words are often grammatical words e.g. prepositions (*in, on, at,* etc.), articles (*a, an, the*), pronouns (*it, that,* etc.), auxiliary verbs (*do, will, am,* etc.), and determiners (*some, much,* etc.)

In this text seven lines are correct and seven lines contain a word that should not be there. (You are not given this information in the exam!) Decide which lines contain an extra word and correct them.

1	My brother Pete is quite a bit younger than I am.
2	We are look pretty similar, but he's a little
3	shorter and slimmer. He isn't as careful with
4	money as I am, and generally spends it on without
5	thinking. We play squash together from time to
6	time, but I'm much worse than he is. He can to run
7	a lot more quickly than I can. I get on very well
8	with my sister Sarah, but she is a lot of more
9	sociable than I am. She really prefers having her
10	head in a book to being with the people. She is
11	probably the most intelligent of all of us. I
12	think Kate is the nicest and most easy-going
13	person in the all family. I would say she is
14	generally a much more happier person than Sarah.

Grammar: making comparisons

1 Look again at the Use of English text and complete the following rules about making comparisons.

COMPARISONS

One-syllable adjectives

a) The comparative and superlative of one-syllable adjectives e.g. *young (line 1)* are generally made by ....

b) An exception is adjectives which end with a vowel plus a consonant e.g. *slim (line 3)* in which case you

....

c) Another exception is adjectives which end with *-e* e.g. *nice (line 12)*, in which case you ......

....

d) There are a number of one-syllable adjectives which have irregular comparatives and superlatives, including ....

....

Two and three-syllable adjectives

e) The comparative and superlative of two and three-syllable adjectives e.g. *sociable (line 9)* and *intelligent (line 11)* are generally made by ....

....

f) However, the comparative and superlative of two-syllable adjectives ending in *-y* e.g. *happy (line 14)* are generally made by ....

....

Extra information

g) Use *as ... as* to compare things which are ....

....

and *not as ... as* to compare things which are ....

....

h) Put *a bit/a little* before the comparative to show there is .... difference.

i) Put *a lot/much/far/a great deal* before the comparative to show there is .... difference.

j) To make the comparative and superlative of adverbs e.g. *quickly*, you generally use ....

....

Grammar reference p.164 (4)

2 Look at the pictures and decide which of the following sentences are true.

Wayne

Chuck

Floyd

1 Floyd isn't quite as tall as Chuck.
2 Floyd isn't nearly as tall as Chuck.
3 Floyd is as tall as Chuck.
4 Chuck isn't as tall as Wayne.
5 Chuck is much taller than Wayne.
6 Chuck is a bit taller than Wayne.

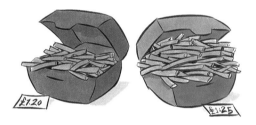

£1.20

£1.25

7 There aren't nearly as many french fries in the red box as in the blue box.
8 There are slightly fewer french fries in the blue box than in the red box.
9 There are a lot more french fries in the blue box than in the red box.
10 The french fries in the red box are far more expensive than those in the blue box.
11 The french fries in the red box are a little less expensive than those in the blue box.

3 Each of the following pairs of sentences should mean approximately the same. However, in every second sentence there is a word missing. Decide what the missing word is in each case.

1 My father is the hardest-working person I know.
   No one I know works as hard my father.
2 I've never met such an intelligent person.
   She is most intelligent person I've ever met.
3 We don't have nearly as much money as they do.
   They have lot more money than we do.

4 Simon is much older than I am.
   I am nearly as old as Simon.
5 I can't play tennis as well as she can.
   She plays tennis better I can.
6 Last time the ticket wasn't quite as expensive.
   Last time the ticket was a little expensive.

4 Work in a group with two other students. Student A and Student B should choose one of the alternatives from the list below to 'sell' to Student C.

Student A	Student B
1 a holiday in England	a holiday in the USA
2 a motorbike	a sportscar
3 an evening at a local disco	an evening at a local restaurant
4 a book	a film (of the same story)

Student A and Student B should each try to convince Student C that what they are 'selling' is better than what the other person is 'selling'. Use appropriate language for making comparisons. Student C will finally decide which is the best.

Before you start, listen to an example and decide who you think is the better 'salesperson'.

5 Below are some world records. Look at the pictures and decide what each world record is for. Then compare your ideas with other students.

1 55.8 cm   4 1,009,152,000
2 35m 55cm   5 8.61 seconds
3 92 hours

HIC....HIC...HIC....

Pronunciation: /ʌ/

1 Which of the words in the box have the sound /ʌ/ (as in *son*).

> mother   uncle   nephew   cousin   company
> bank   money   love   drunk   trouble   drank
> enough   young   blood   won   Monday   cup
> home   cough   shut   butter   much   London

2 Listen and make a note of the words above that you hear. Then turn to page 184 and look at the sentences you heard. Try saying them with good pronunciation.

Vocabulary: describing people (1)

1 Look at the following relations and decide which ones:

1 can be either male *or* female.
2 cannot be related to you by blood.

> stepmother   twin   niece   sister-in-law   nephew
> great-grandfather   half-sister   uncle   cousin

2

1 Look at the adjectives for describing people and match each one to the definitions 1–14 opposite.

a) hard-working   h) open-minded
b) generous   i) thoughtful
c) stubborn   j) naughty
d) self-confident   k) attractive
e) reliable   l) sensitive
f) loyal   m) modest
g) strict   n) ambitious

2 Try to think of one person you know who is like each adjective. Tell a partner who it is and give examples of their behaviour.

EXAMPLE: *My brother's very **hard-working**. He sometimes doesn't get home from the office until midnight.*

3 Work in a group with other students and think of an opposite for each adjective. Use a dictionary where necessary.

1 *adj* **1** showing that you are thinking deeply **2** paying attention to the feelings of other people

2 *adj* willing to give money, help, and kindness

3 *adj* having a strong desire to be successful, powerful, or rich

4 *adj* willing to consider new ideas and opinions

5 *adj* determined and having a strong will

6 *adj* severe in demanding obedience to rules of behaviour

7 *adj* **1** that may be trusted; dependable **2** that you can trust to perform well at all times

8 *adj* behaving badly, or not obeying a parent, teacher, or set of rules (used of children)

9 *adj* having a belief in one's own value and abilities

10 *adj* **1** pretty or HANDSOME (used of a person) **2** pleasant to look at

11 *adj* faithful to people, places, or things

12 *adj* having or expressing a lower opinion of your own abilities than you deserve (a word used to express approval)

13 *adj* showing delicate feelings or judgement

14 *adj* dedicating a lot of time and energy to work

3 Describe the different members of your family to a partner. Compare yourself with the members of your family using appropriate language for describing people and making comparisons.

Watch Out! *sensible/sensitive*

1 He's a rather *sensible/sensitive* child. He gets very upset if people get angry.
2 Be *sensible/sensitive* and put on some warm clothes. It's freezing!

Which is the correct alternative in each sentence?

Listening: Grimble

1 Look at the pictures and describe what is happening in each one.

A

B

C

D

E

2 You are going to hear an extract from a story called *Grimble*. Listen and put the pictures in Exercise 1 in the correct order.

3

1 Listen to the story again and make notes about what happens.
2 Now work with a partner. You should take it in turns to tell the story again by referring to your notes and the pictures.

4 Discuss the following questions.

1 How do you think you would feel if you were Grimble?
2 Does your family, or another family you know, have any strange or special habits that you think are different from other families?

Writing: drafting and redrafting

You are going to write the next part of the *Grimble* story. You should follow this procedure:

- Work with a partner and note down ideas of how the story continues. Divide these ideas into paragraphs.
- Write a first draft of the story together in 120–180 words.
- Exchange stories with another pair of students. Read their story and mark parts that you do not understand and where you would like some more information.
- Rewrite the story with your partner, responding to the comments from the other students.
- Go through your final version and check carefully for mistakes of grammar, spelling, punctuation, word order and vocabulary.

Reading

1   Read the following opening paragraphs to an article. What are the two families in the photos below going to do to make themselves very well-known?

Open House

*Families Reveal Their
Real-Life Secrets To Millions*

1   Thanks to the <u>telly</u>, we all know how the rich and famous live. But who knows what our friends and neighbours get up to behind closed doors?

For the first time, the inside secrets of four ordinary families are revealed in Sunday's *Frame the family*. In this 30-minute special the families open their hearts and homes using a camcorder to record the essential ingredients of their daily lives.

At times it's more like watching a video nasty! Huge rows, dad's unpleasant habits and secretly filmed confessions make
10   the show a uniquely revealing documentary.

Here, two families who took part, the Chiappis and the Gibsons, introduce themselves and give us a taste of things to come in the programme.

the Chiappis

the Gibsons

2   Look at the photos of the two families and talk about how you imagine them to be. Think about the following questions:

- How do the various brothers and sisters get on?
- What jobs do the parents do?
- Are the parents strict with their children?
- Are they a very close family?

3   Now read about the two families and check if your ideas were correct.

The Chiappi Family

Loud laughter and even louder arguments can be heard from the Chiappi's house. Italian-born Luciano, his wife Diane and three daughters Enza, 18, Daniela, 15, and Claudia, 13, changed nothing for the camera to reveal themselves as a fiery but
20   fiercely loyal family.

'There was one point when I wished the camera had been turned off,' admits Daniela. 'Claudia and I had a massive <u>row</u>. I was really angry and forgot Enza was filming. I was worried about it because I didn't want to be seen as hot-tempered and horrible.'

At that, the rest of the family <u>yell</u>, 'But you are hot-tempered and horrible!' and
30   the laughter and shouting begin again.

In the middle of it all is Luciano, 48, a garage owner. The four women admit they gang up on him. 'He can be a real pain in the neck! He's often <u>grumpy</u> and thinks he's never wrong,' says his 42-year-old wife Diane, a teacher. 'Everything we've shot is very true to life, except Luciano and I <u>fall out</u> much more than you see on the film.'

40   Claudia, who does a wicked impression of her dad, says, 'His jokes are really bad and he tells them a hundred times. Ever since we've been filming he has said, "You must talk to my agent first." and he still thinks it's funny!'

The girls kept the programme a secret from their dad until the very last moment. 'The irritating part is they didn't ask me, they have no respect. It's always the
50   same,' he <u>moans</u>.

The whole family is in for some surprises when the film is shown – they've all said privately what they think of the others.

'Sometimes it all became annoying when you didn't want to be filmed,' says Enza. 'But the best bit was finding out what irritated dad – long hairs in the plug hole!'

The Gibson Family

When 13-year-old Mark Gibson and 15-year-old sister, Suzanna volunteered their family for the programme, the television team knew they were going to have some fun.

'My family's mad, absolutely crazy,' says Suzanna seriously. 'I'm the sensible one,' she insists as dad Jack, 42, and mum Pauline, 38, burst into laughter as they listen to their daughter.

Jack, a Geography teacher, and Pauline, a doctor's receptionist, agree with their children's opinion of them. Pauline says, 'The most ridiculous things make us laugh – especially other people's <u>downfalls</u>. Our friends are amazed that we're letting complete strangers see our home-life by doing this. But I can't see why not. We've got nothing to be ashamed of.'

Jack, who once lived in a tree-house for a month in aid of charity, adds with a <u>grin</u>: 'Anyway, the kids and teachers at work already know I'm crazy, so it makes no difference to me.'

The fun-loving family obviously had a fantastic time with their camcorder. 'At first we really tried to be on our best behaviour and we even tidied up the house a bit,' laughs Pauline. 'But that only lasted a week, it was impossible to <u>keep up</u>.'

Water fights in the garden, when everything – including the camera – got completely <u>drenched</u>, were a regular feature of the hours of tape the Gibsons made. Mark loved the recording they made of an outing to the local zoo, while Suzanna hated the film her mother secretly took of her as she was doing her aerobic exercises in front of the bedroom mirror. Suzanna retaliated by lying in wait at 7.30 a.m. for her mum to come out of the shower. The family doesn't know which bits of film will actually make it to the screen until the programme is shown on television. But Mark's quite certain that the bit he took of his mum and dad getting ready to go to a party one night will be there.

'They're worse than teenagers, they take absolutely ages to get ready,' he complains. 'Dad stands there trying to decide what tie to wear and Mum spends hours putting on her make-up!'

4 Now read about the two families again and answer the following questions.

1 In which family did two of the children not always enjoy being watched by the camera?
2 Which husband and wife argue a lot?
3 Which father likes to try and make people laugh?
4 Which family seemed to really enjoy the whole experience?
5 Which family sounds particularly noisy?
6 Which daughter used the camera to get revenge on her mother?
7 Which husband and wife take a long time getting ready to go out?
8 Which father isn't treated the way he would like by the rest of the family?

5 Look at the words in the table which come from the text.

1 Decide what part of speech (noun, adjective or verb) each word is as they appear in the article.
2 Look at the suggested meaning of each word and decide if it is appropriate in the context. Two of the meanings are incorrect.

Word	Part of speech	Meaning
telly (line 1)	noun	television
row (line 24)		noisy argument
yell (line 28)		shout, cry out loudly
grumpy (line 34)		in a good mood
fall out (line 38)		quarrel, argue
moan (line 50)		complain, grumble
downfall (line 75)		bad luck, misfortune
grin (line 82)		wide smile
keep up (line 91)		continue to do something
drench (line 94)		break

6 Discuss the following questions.

1 Which family do you like the sound of most? Why?
2 Are either of the two families similar to your family? How?
3 How would you feel about your family being filmed for a programme like *Frame the family?*
4 What parts of your family life would you want/not want recorded?

from *TV Times* magazine

Vocabulary: describing people (2)

📼 **1** Enza Chiappi is showing some photos of her family to her new boyfriend. The photo they are talking about was taken in the same room as the one that goes with the article on page 32, but there are eight differences between the two photos. Look at the photo of the Chiappi family again, listen to the conversation and make a note of the differences.

2 Now listen again and decide which of the following words and expressions are mentioned in the conversation.

Age
She/he ...

is about (nineteen)
has just turned (sixteen)
is in her/his early/mid/late (forties)
is (quite) young/middle-aged/old

Hair
She/he ...

Length
is (going) (a bit) bald
has got short/shoulder-length/ long hair
Style
has got curly/straight hair

Build
She/he is ...

Size
thin   slim   wiry   stocky
well-built   overweight
Height
short   of medium height   tall

Face
She/he has got ...

a beard   a moustache
(long) eyelashes
a round/long face
a (pointed) chin
Body marks
a scar

Accessories
She/he is wearing .../has got ...

an earring
glasses   sunglasses
a (silk) scarf   (leather) gloves
a belt
a (gold) chain
a ring

Attitude
She/he looks ...

annoyed
bored
depressed
excited
as if she/he is having fun

3 Now put these words and expressions in the correct columns in the table.

1 (thin/thick) eyebrows
2 a fringe
3 a ponytail
4 a tattoo
5 contact lenses
6 high cheek-bones
7 wears it in a bun
8 teens
✓9 freckles
10 pleased with herself
11 plump
12 fed-up
13 frail
14 getting on   — age
15 wavy
16 wrinkles

4 Look again at the photo of the Gibson family and write a description of the people using words and expressions in the table.

5 Work with a partner. Student A should look at the picture on page 184 and Student B should look at the picture on page 189. There are ten differences between the two pictures. Describe the people in your picture and find the differences.

1 Fill in the gaps in the following sentences with an appropriate particle (*to*, *up*, *off*, etc.).

1 Would you mind looking .... our cat while we are on holiday?
2 I wouldn't want to bring my children ......*up*....... in a big city.
3 If I have to tell you ....*off*......... again, I will be very angry.
4 I can't believe how quickly Derek's children have grown ....*up*...... .
5 I get ....*on*...... very well with my two younger sisters.
6 He takes .....*after*..... his father. He really is very good with children.
7 I don't know why, but I've always looked up ....*to*..... my Aunt Sandra, probably because she is so beautiful and successful.
8 What have you been getting up ......*to*.......... ? Why is there mud all over the kitchen floor?

2 A man and woman were seen running away from a post office which had just been robbed. This is the report that an eye-witness wrote for the police. Fill in the gaps with an appropriate word from the box. You do not need to use all the words.

> at looking moustache well-built as much like contact lenses wavy lot bald in wearing putting looked ponytail sunglasses

DATE: 18/3/96

CRIME: Robbery of Mare Street Post Office

WITNESS: M. Stewart

I was just getting out of my car, when I saw these two people, a man and a woman, running fast down the other side of the street from me. They were being chased by one or two people who ran out of the post office.
The man was **(1)** .... taller than the woman. He was wearing black **(2)** .... and he had a long **(3)** .... He was carrying a red leather bag. He had long black hair, a beard and a **(4)** .... He had on a green anorak with badges on the sleeves. He was quite **(5)** .... and muscular. The woman was quite small and very slim, but she could run just as fast **(6)** .... the man. She had
(7) ...., shoulder-length hair and was probably **(8)** .... her late teens. She was **(9)** .... a dark blue T-shirt and jeans. They both **(10)** .... quite scared.

3 Compare three of the following things. Write a short paragraph for each using as many words and expressions for making comparisons as possible.

1 Two similar shops that you know well.
2 Two people that you know well.
3 Two pop groups/singers that you know well.
4 Two towns/countries that you know well.
5 Two computer games that you know well.
6 Your house/flat and somebody else's house/flat.

4 Say who the following people are.

1 Your mother's husband. *My father.*
2 Your brother's wife.
3 Your grandfather's mother.
4 Your mother's new husband.
5 Your father's sister.
6 Your mother's brother's son.
7 Your husband/wife's mother.
8 Your sister's daughter.

5

1 Choose one adjective to describe each of the following people.

a) Once Hans has decided to do something, it's impossible to make him change his mind.
b) Tom is very keen to do well in his job. He wants to get to the top of the company by the time he is thirty.
c) Anna is not fixed in her opinions. She is always ready to consider new ideas.
d) Anita is the sort of person that if she says she will do something, you know she will do it.
e) Once you are a friend of Paul's, you are a friend for life.
f) Maria never does any work. She just sits around doing nothing all day.
g) Eleni came top in all her exams, but she didn't tell anyone.
h) When you go out for a meal with Pierre, he always insists on paying.

2 Now form the noun of each of the adjectives. Mark the position of the stress on both the adjective and the noun.

EXAMPLE: *adjective: 'stubborn*
noun: 'stubbornness

Seeing is believing

Speaking

Look at the cartoon and discuss the following questions.

1 What is the point the cartoon is trying to make? Do you agree with it?
2 Which things in the cartoon do you have? Would you find them difficult to give up? Why?/Why not?
3 What technological developments in the home do you think there will be over the next twenty or thirty years?

Reading

1 Read the following article through quickly and answer these questions.

1 What is VR?
2 What different things is VR being used for at the moment?

Hype or hyper-reality?

Virtual reality will connect your senses up to a computer – and take you to the realms of dreams. Discover how virtual reality will revolutionise your world.

Looking for a new thrill? Perhaps you'd like to meet Madonna or Harrison Ford; wander the marbled halls of a palace that was destroyed a thousand years ago; go climbing up Olympus Mons on Mars, the Solar System's highest mountain. Virtual reality (VR) promises to make it possible.

(1 ———)
It aims to be more than just 'like' being there. It is claimed that it will be impossible to tell the difference. Indeed, the boundaries between real and virtual are already breaking down, thanks to technological improvements such as touch-sensitive body suits, and 3-D surround sound. The hope is that one day we will be able to do 'virtually' the things we cannot do in real life – because in VR we won't be bound by boring restrictions like the law of physics.

2 Now read the article again and choose the most suitable heading below for each numbered paragraph.

1 How 'real' can you get?/Who invented VR?
2 The problems of simulated flying./The early days of VR.
3 The Japanese VR revolution./Some practical applications.
4 The long-term effects./VR and drug abuse.
5 Enthusiastic response from psychologists!/Losing touch with reality?

3 Look at paragraphs 4 and 5 in the article again. Discuss the following questions and give examples to support your ideas.

1 Is there a danger of young people becoming 'addicted' to computer games?
2 Is there a danger that people will become unable to function properly in the real world because they spend too much time in virtually real worlds?
3 Do you think VR will become popular in a big way? Why?/Why not?

(2 ———)

Current VR technology grew out of developments in the flight-simulator industry. The skills needed to fly a plane are incredibly complicated, and the ability to land at different airports requires careful practice. The dangers of practising in real aeroplanes have been avoided for a long time by building an artificial cockpit with controls linked to a simulation of the real plane. Pilots in the simulator see and feel nothing but the artificial world and have direct control over it.

(3 ———)

Today's still quite limited technology is now quietly being used for all kinds of projects – planning telecommunication systems, designing drug molecules, and, in Japan, a scheme has already been successfully developed to use VR in furniture showrooms so customers can plan the layout of new kitchens. The plan is to integrate this with a complete computerised system – so the virtual kitchen designed by the customer goes through an automated process until delivery to the home.

(4 ———)

Iain Brown, a psychologist from Glasgow University, is worried that virtual reality will be extremely addictive. He has studied children whose dependence on computer games makes them behave like drug addicts. They spend all their money on arcade games and sometimes turn to crime to pay for their habit.

(5 ———)

Some psychologists think computers can be addictive because they are so predictable. Real life is often hard to control, but a computer will always do exactly what you tell it to. For some, to sit in front of a screen is to be secure. Brown worries that people who spend a lot of time in simplified, virtual worlds might not develop many of the skills they need to deal with the uncertainties of real life. But VR enthusiasts prefer to talk of the exciting possibilities like becoming a musical instrument or a robotic insect on Neptune.

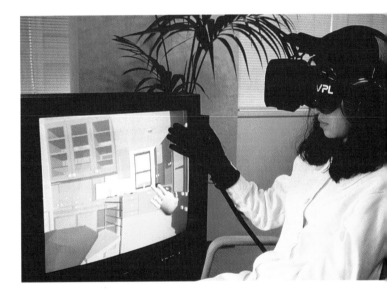

Watch Out! *so/such*

1 He is so predictable.
2 He is such predictable.
3 He is such a predictable person.
4 He is such predictable person.
5 He is a so predictable.

Which of these sentences are grammatically possible?

Grammar reference p.177 (19.3)

from *Focus* magazine and *The Guardian* newspaper

Vocabulary: science and technology

1 Work with a partner and make a list of all the useful information that a dictionary can give you.

2 Look at the dictionary entries below from the *Longman Active Study Dictionary of English* to see if they give you more or less information than you have in your list.

3 Now fill in the gaps in the following sentences with an appropriate word from the dictionary entries.

1 Please try and be *realistic*. We have no chance of arriving by 8 p.m.
2 This is an incredible discovery. It is going to *revolutionize* the way we treat our patients.
3 I'm afraid there's been a small explosion in the *lab* and it can't be used at the moment.

4 If you mix these two *chemicals* together, you will *produce* a very nasty smell.
5 I suppose, *theoretically* speaking it's possible, but it will never work in practice! *Personally*
6 There have been some important *discoveries* in *developments* the search for a cure for cancer.
7 I think the dishwasher is the best *invention* ever!
8 We need to increase the rate of *production* of this new drug. Demand is very high.

4 Look again at the words you used to fill in the gaps. Check how many syllables each word has in natural speech and where the main stress falls. Then say the words, with good pronunciation, to a partner.

EXAMPLE: *realistic: 4 syllables - re . a . 'lis . tic*

chem·i·cal /ˈkemɪkəl/ *n* any substance used in or produced by chemistry
chem·is·try /ˈkeməstri/ *n* [U] **1** the study of the substances which make up the universe and the way in which they change and combine with each other: *She's got a degree in chemistry.*

dis·cov·er /dɪsˈkʌvə/ *v* to find or learn about something for the first time: *Columbus discovered America in 1492.* | *The stolen goods were discovered in their garage.*
dis·cov·ery /dɪsˈkʌvəri/ *n* **discoveries 1** [U] the action of finding something: *The discovery of oil on land made the family rich.* **2** [C] something that is found out: *He made an important archaeological discovery.*

pro·duce /prəˈdjuːs ‖ -ˈduːs/ *v* **produced, producing** [T] **1** to have as a result or effect: *Gordon's jokes produced a great deal of laughter.* **2** to make something, especially in large quantities: *Gas can be produced from coal.* | *The factory produces 500 cars a week.* | **3** to grow or supply: *Canada produces good wheat.*
prod·uct /ˈprɒdʌkt ‖ ˈprɑː-/ *n* **1** something that is produced or made somewhere: *a new range of kitchen products* -see PRODUCTION (USAGE). **2** the result of experiences or certain situations: *Criminals are sometimes the product of bad homes.*
pro·duc·tion /prəˈdʌkʃən/ *n* **1** [U] the act of producing something, especially for sale: *This factory specializes in the production of larger cars.* **2** the amount of something which is produced: *Oil production is falling world-wide.*

de·vel·op /dɪˈveləp/ *v* [I] **1** to grow: *The fighting could easily develop into a full-scale war.* | *This flower developed from a tiny seed.* **2** [T] to improve something or make it grow: *a campaign to develop the local economy*
de·vel·op·ment /dɪˈveləpmənt/ *n* **1** [C] a new event: *There has been an important new development in the political situation.* **2** [C] a new invention, or an improvement to an existing machine or process: *recent developments in the treatment of cancer*

la·bor·a·tory /ləˈbɒrətri ‖ ˈlæbrətɔːri/ *n* **laboratories** (also lab *infml*) a building or room which contains scientific apparatus and in which a scientist works

real /rɪəl/ *adj* **1** not imaginary but actually existing: *a story of real life.* **2** true or actual: *What was the real reason for absence?*
re·a·lis·tic /rɪəˈlɪstɪk/ *adj* **1** sensible and reasonable: *Our income has got smaller, so we must be realistic and give up our car.* opposite **unrealistic**. **2** life-like (used of art or literature): *a realistic drawing of a horse* - **realistically** / -kli / *adv*

the·o·ry /ˈθɪəri/ *n* **theories 1** [C] an explanation for something which is reasonable or scientifically acceptable, but which has not yet been proved to be true: *Darwin's theory of evolution* | *The detective's theory is that the murderer was well known to the victim.* **2** [U] the general principles for the study of an art or science as opposed to practical skill in it: *musical theory* | *There will be two chemistry exams: one on theory and one will be practical.* **theoretical** /θɪəˈretɪkəl/ *adj* : *theoretical science* | *a theoretical possibility* -**theoretically** / -kli / *adv* : *Theoretically it's my job, but in fact I don't do it.*

in·vent /ɪnˈvent/ *v* [T] **1** to make up, think of, or produce something for the first time: *Alexander Graham Bell invented the telephone in 1876.* **2** to make up something unreal or untrue: *The whole story was invented.* | *I tried to invent an excuse.*
in·ven·tion /ɪnˈvenʃən/ *v* **1** [U] the act of inventing something: *The invention of the telephone was the start of modern telecommunications systems.* **2** [C] something that has been invented: *The telephone is a wonderful invention.*
in·ven·tor /ɪnˈventə/ *n* a person who invents something new

rev·o·lu·tion / revəˈluːʃən/ *n* **1** [C;U] great social change, especially the changing of a ruler or political system by force: *the Russian revolution.* **2** [C] a complete change in ways of thinking or acting: *The invention of the aeroplane caused a revolution in travel and communication.*
rev·o·lu·tion·a·ry[1] /ˌrevəˈluːʃənəri ‖ ʃənəri/ *adj* **1** connected with revolution (1): *a revolutionary leader* | *revolutionary ideas*
rev·o·lu·tion·ize /ˌrevəˈluːʃənaɪz/ (also **revolutionise** *BrE*) *v* **revolutionized, revolutionizing** [T] to cause a complete change: *The discovery of the new drug has revolutionized the treatment of many diseases.*

Grammar: *like*

1 The two people below have just come out of a new Virtuality Centre. Look at what they say and answer the following questions.

1 Who was impressed? Who wasn't?
2 What is the meaning of *like* in each case?

It was amazing. It felt just like the real thing.

It wasn't so great. It was a bit like standing very close to a computer screen.

2 Look at the following sentences with *like* and decide which ones you think are correct. Correct those sentences in which you think there is an error.

1 What's the weather like in Lisbon today?
2 My brother is the same age *like* me. ~~as~~ *as well as*
3 I am just like my father.
4 He *is* look like a banker. *looks like, is like*
5 What *are* you like doing at the weekends?
6 I like to get up very early on Sunday mornings.
7 That sounds like the postman.
8 Let's do something fun, *like* going ice-skating.
9 Would you like me *making* some tea? *to make*
10 I'll go and buy some bread if you like.

Grammar reference p.177 (19.1)

Watch Out! *like to do/like doing*

- Gavin *likes getting up* early because it's so quiet.
- Pete *likes to get up* early so he can get to work before the rush hour starts.

Who **enjoys** getting up early? Who **chooses** to get up early, but may not particularly enjoy it?

3

1 Make questions for the following answers using *like*. *What do you like doing?*
a) Playing football and seeing my friends.
b) About 7.30 a.m. so that I can use the bathroom before my brother gets up!
c) She's very funny. She makes me laugh all the time. That's why I like her.
d) The weather forecast on TV said that it's going to be warm and sunny. *What*
e) It's quite big with plenty of cinemas and places to go in the evening. The only problem is that there is quite a lot of pollution.
f) Just like me, except I have long hair and he has very short hair.

2 Now ask a partner the same questions.

4 Look at the picture below and try to imagine as much as possible about the man. Answer the following questions and then compare your ideas with other students.

1 What do you think he does?
2 What kind of family do you think he has?
3 What do you think he is like?
4 What do you think he likes doing in his free time?

Now turn to page 184 to see if your ideas were correct.

Exam focus

Paper 4 Listening (multiple matching)

In Part 3 of Paper 4 you will listen to a number of short extracts of people talking about a similar subject. You must then match sentences or prompts to each of the different extracts. You will hear the extracts twice.

Here is a procedure for this task:

- Read the prompts before you listen.
- Predict what you think each of the people will say.
- Make brief notes on what each person actually says.

1   You are going to hear five people talking about lies they have told. First look at the following sentences and discuss with a partner what you imagine the situation will be for each one.

EXAMPLE: *In A maybe someone went for dinner at a friend's house and the food was awful.*

A She/he didn't want to hurt someone else's feelings.
B She/he feels lots of people tell similar lies.
C As a result, she/he has decided never to lie again.
D She/he didn't report a crime.
E She/he was put in a difficult position by a friend.
F She/he pretended to know more than she/he did.

2   Listen to the extracts and make brief notes on each one.

3   Now listen again and match each extract to one of the sentences above. (One of the sentences is not needed.)

Speaking

1   Discuss the following questions.

1 What do you think about the behaviour of the people who told lies in the listening extracts? Would you have done the same thing in each situation or not?

2 a) Do you ever tell lies? If so, in what situations?
   b) Is it the same to lie by not saying anything as it is to lie by saying something?
   c) Are you a 'good' or a 'bad' liar (is it obvious or not to other people)?
   d) Do you generally know when other people are telling lies?
   e) Can the truth ever be a bad thing?
   f) What is a 'white lie'? In what situations might you tell a white lie?

2   Work in a group with three or four other students. Think of a strange or funny experience which happened to you, either real or imaginary, and tell the other members of the group your story. The other students should listen and decide whether you are lying or telling the truth. Then listen to the other students tell their stories.

Vocabulary: phrasal verbs (*take*)

- *They were completely **taken in** and told me to take it easy.*

1   What do you think the phrasal verb in **bold** taken from the last listening extract means?

2   Match a phrasal verb with *take* in Column A with its correct meaning in Column B.

A	B
1 You need to *take* a few days *off* work.	a) to imitate another person to make people laugh
2 I am thinking of *taking up* golf to get some exercise.	b) to occupy space or time
3 He's very good at *taking off* famous politicians.	c) to employ
4 I really should *take on* one or two more waiters. The restaurant is so busy.	d) to suddenly increase, to do well
5 This table *takes up* too much room in the kitchen. Let's put it somewhere else.	e) to have a holiday or a change
6 Sales of the new BMW have *taken off*.	f) to take control
7 He's so bossy. Whenever I try and work with him, he just *takes over*.	g) to start a new hobby

3 Now write a response for each of the following sentences using the phrasal verb in brackets.

EXAMPLE: Has there been much interest in that new computer game? *(take off)*
Oh yes, it's really taken off in the last month!

1 I feel terribly overweight at the moment. *(take up)*
2 How is your new secretary getting on? *(take over)*
3 I'm very tired and fed up at work just now. *(take off)*
4 Why have you stopped playing football on Saturdays? *(take up)*
5 Have there been any changes at work while I've been away? *(take on)*
6 Did you realise that he wasn't really a policeman? *(take in)*
7 Why is Mike being kept behind after class? *(take off)*

I tost you in

always : gullible
trusting

Watch Out! *actually*

1 A: Hi, Suzanne! How are you?
   B: *Actually*, my name is Susan!
2 Peter was in the living room, but I don't know where he is *actually*.

In which sentence is *actually* used correctly? What should the speaker have said instead of *actually* in the incorrect sentence?

Grammar: narrative tenses

1 Read the first part of the story opposite and answer the following questions.

1 What did the people of America think was happening?
2 What was actually happening?

2 Look at the text again and at the words which are underlined. Find examples of the Past Simple, Past Continuous and Past Perfect tenses.

3 Which tense is used to refer to:

1 an action which happened before another past action?
2 a finished (single or repeated) action or situation in the past?
3 an action in progress at a definite time in the past?

Grammar reference p.176 (17.5/17.6/17.7)

The Martians Have Landed

A few minutes after eight o'clock on the night of Sunday, October 30, 1938, a sombre voice <u>interrupted</u> a radio broadcast to warn Americans, 'Ladies and gentlemen, I have a grave announcement to make …'

The words that followed, beamed out in a programme networked across the United States, caused remarkable scenes of panic. For the announcement was that Martians <u>had landed</u> in North America and <u>were moving</u> across the country at great speed. Nothing seemed able to stop them, all resistance was useless. The USA was being taken over by men from outer space.

The announcement was part of a radio play, but one so realistic and produced by such a genius of the theatre that most people who heard it took it for fact.

The programme <u>had started</u> undramatically enough. At 8 p.m listeners <u>heard</u>, 'The Columbia Broadcasting System presents Orson Welles and his Mercury Theatre Of The Air in *War of the Worlds* by H.G.Wells'. Then came the unmistakable voice of Orson Welles: 'We know now that in the early years of the twentieth century, this world was being watched closely by intelligences greater than man's.' He was interrupted by a news announcer apparently reading a routine bulletin: 'Tonight's weather … For the next 24 hours there will not be much change in temperature …'

Nothing to cause alarm at this stage. But the atmosphere was being cleverly built up. Listeners who <u>had tuned</u> in from the start were already beginning to forget that what they <u>were listening</u> to was really a radio play.

4 Now read the rest of the story about the Orson Welles radio play and fill in the gaps with the correct form of the verbs in brackets.

Scene from the film 'War of the Worlds'

By chance, on the main rival network there (1) .... (be) a new singer being featured. He was an unknown. He (2) .... (come) on at ten minutes past eight and bored listeners (3) .... (begin) turning their dials to find out whether there was anything better on CBS. They (4) .... (join) War of the Worlds after all the preliminary announcements had been made. They had no idea that a play was in progress. All they knew was that strange things (5) .... (happen) along the eastern coast. The CBS announcer continued:

'Ladies and gentlemen, I have an important announcement to make. The strange object which fell in New Jersey earlier this evening was not a meteorite. Incredible as it seems, it (6) .... (contain) strange beings who are believed to be part of an army from the planet Mars.'

Soft music followed. A subtle touch to get people anxious. What (7) .... (go) on?

The announcer broke in again. There was a nervous, panicky tone to his voice. The Martians, hideous, leathery-skinned creatures (8) .... (spread) out. New Jersey police (9).................... (race) to stop them.

There was more music, more urgent announcements, chilling silences. People were glued to their sets. Earlier they (10) .... (phone) their relatives and warned them about what (11) .... (happen). Across the whole of America, people were beginning to panic.

Then the announcer (12) .... (come) on to the air again: 'We take you now to Washington for a special broadcast on the national emergency by the Secretary of the Interior.' A solemn voice was heard asking people not to panic – but at the same time telling them that the Martian landing was not only in New Jersey. Space vehicles (13) .... (fall) to earth all across the States. The beings from outer space (14) .... (already/killed) thousands of troops and civilians with death-ray guns.

One of Welles' actors (15) .... (pretend) to be the President of the United States and warned the American people against the dangers of panic. The show ended with an announcer screaming from the top of CBS skyscraper that Manhattan was being taken over. His feverish commentary finished in a strangled scream.

In New Jersey, where the Martians were first reported to have landed, the roads were filled with cars racing for the hills. Families fled from their homes with wet towels over their heads, believing this would save them from the nauseous space gases the radio (16) .... (tell) them about. The panic (17) .... (begin).

Sailors in the US Navy were recalled to their ships in New York harbour to be ready to defend America against the Martians. From Los Angeles to Boston there were reports of 'meteors'. Some people actually claimed to have seen Martians.

After it was all over, Welles, already a well-known actor at the age of 24, was fiercely criticised for throwing half the USA into terror. Dozens of people took legal action against CBS, but in the end the complaints were all withdrawn and, instead of taking Welles' show off the air, CBS bosses congratulated themselves for having hired the most talked-about actor in America.

5 Discuss the following questions.

1 Do you think something like this could ever happen in your country? Why?/Why not?
2 Do you think that there is intelligent life on other planets in our universe? If so, what do you think it is like?
3 Do you believe that people have actually seen UFOs?
4 What other evidence is there that life exists on other planets?

One person in the group should summarise and report back the main views of the group to the class.

6

1 Divide into two groups. Students from Group A should complete Joke A by filling in the gaps with the correct form of the verbs in the box. Students from Group B look at Joke B on page 185 and do the same.

Joke A

(ever) knew	ask	come	decide	go	have	pay	receive	send
sit	telephone							

Pete (1) .... at home trying to think what present to buy for his grandmother's ninetieth birthday. Finally he (2) .... to buy her a parrot because he thought it would be nice for her to have someone to talk to.

Pete (3) .... to a pet shop and (4) .... for a parrot with a large vocabulary. In the end he (5) .... £1000 for a beautiful parrot and the shop assistant said it was the most talkative parrot she (6) ....

Pete (7) .... the parrot to his grandmother and then (8) .... her on the day of her birthday to ask if she (9) .... it and if she liked it.

'Yes', she said. 'It (10) .... this morning when I opened my cards and I (11) .... it for lunch. It was delicious!'

2 Now tell a student from the other group your joke using appropriate narrative tenses.

Listening: extracts

1 Listen to five short extracts and decide which one:

A involves a joke.
B is part of a discussion about visitors from outer space.
C takes place in a school.
D involves a policeman.
E takes place in a hotel.

2 Now listen again and choose the correct alternative for each extract.

1 The two people speaking are
   A pupils.
   B parents.
   C teachers.

2 The hotel receptionist is
   A rude.
   B helpful.
   C confused.

3 The boy in the joke
   A has just been punished by his teacher.
   B is worried the teacher will be angry.
   C has made a lot of mistakes in his homework.

4 The woman
   A has something in the restricted area.
   B is a journalist.
   C has got information for the police.

5 The two people in the conversation
   A don't seem to agree.
   B agree in part.
   C completely agree.

Writing: narrative

In Paper 2 of the exam you may be asked to write a short story. You will probably need to write this in the past. The key elements for this are:

- correct use of past tenses
- linking expressions
- interesting and varied vocabulary
- imagination!

1   Read the following story and put the different parts in the correct order. Then compare your answers with a partner and say which words helped you to decide.

A They included maps with distant stars which were not known to astronomers at that time, but which have since been discovered.

B Few people believed the Lawsons until some astronomers were shown the pictures the Lawsons had drawn of the inside of the spaceship.

C Suddenly[1], an enormous[2] spaceship with flashing lights landed right in front of their car and a strange[3], glowing figure got out.

D They say that they were well-treated and that the aliens just wanted to find out about human beings.

E After that[4], the Lawsons claim they were taken aboard the spaceship and given a series of tests.

F Bill and Betty Lawson had been driving along a lonely road in New Hampshire when an amazing thing happened.

G In the end, the Lawsons were left on the same road unharmed but thirty kilometres further on.

2   The following words and phrases can help to make your narrative writing more interesting and clearer to read. Decide if they are similar to words [1], [2], [3], or [4] in the story in Exercise 1.

a) gigantic
b) following this
c) weird
d) all of a sudden
e) afterwards
f) without warning
g) odd
h) huge

i) out of the blue
j) vast
k) massive
l) some time later
m) from out of nowhere
n) after a while
o) peculiar

3

1 Read the following question which asks you to write a short story.

You have decided to enter a short story competition. The competition rules say that the story must begin or end with the following words:

They left Planet Earth surprised and rather disappointed by what they had found.

Write your story for the competition.

2 Now work with a partner and write the story together in 120–180 words. Follow this procedure:

- First decide whether you want to begin or end your story with the words provided.
- Then write a series of questions such as: *Where did they come from? Why did they come to Earth?*
- Next make notes to answer your questions. Arrange your notes in paragraphs.
- Now write your story. Try to include appropriate linking expressions e.g. *then, next* and interesting vocabulary e.g. *all of a sudden*.
- Finally check your work very carefully, particularly for errors with narrative tenses.

1 Fill in the gaps in the following text with the correct form of the words in capitals.

I always wanted to be a great (1) ....
I had these dreams of discovering a (2) _revolutionary_ new drug that would save the lives of hundreds of people. Unfortunately, I was never very good at (3) .... at school and I kept producing these horrible smells and the teacher used to get very cross with me.
  After a while, I decided I would become an (4) .... and design an amazing new (5) .... which would become a household name. My parents were quite encouraging, but told me to be a little more (6) .... and not quite so (7) .... A few weeks later I had a brilliant idea for a pen that, at least (8) _theoretically_, would write upside down. To my (9) _disappointed_ a friend of mine pointed out that it was not a new (10) _discovery_ .

SCIENCE
REVOLUTION

CHEMIST

INVENT
PRODUCE

REAL
AMBITION

THEORY
DISAPPOINT
DISCOVER

2 Put the words in the following sentences in order. The first word in each sentence has been underlined.

1 year off much you have time <u>how</u> taken this?
2 things really to soon going <u>I</u> off think are take.
3 on staff moment <u>we</u> any just can't more take the at.
4 time football on too much Saturdays takes <u>playing</u> up.
5 Bill tennis so <u>why</u> after many up has taken again years?
6 money taken gave I before been the <u>I</u> realised in had him I.
7 well off amazing how is history <u>it</u> he teacher take can his.
8 I'm take <u>could</u> you while over lunch me from at?

3 Read the following sentences and choose the correct tense.

1 I *was doing/did* my homework when I *heard/had heard* someone knock loudly on the door.
2 We *didn't see/weren't seeing* Paul because nobody *had told/was telling* us he was there.
3 Louise *painted/was painting* the bathroom at the same time as I *was cleaning/had cleaned* the kitchen.
4 I suddenly *was realising/realised* that I *left/had left* my wallet at home.
5 I *was having/had* a shower, *ate/had eaten* my breakfast and *was going/went* to work.
6 Everyone *had stood/was standing* around talking when she *walked/had walked* into the room.

4 Look at the pictures and write a short story in 120–180 words entitled *The hare and the tortoise*. Use appropriate narrative tenses.

5 All you need is love

Speaking

1 Look at these photos of famous singers. Do you recognise them? What do you know about them? What famous songs have they sung?

A

B

C

D

E

F

G

H

2 Discuss the following questions.

1 What kinds of music do you like?
2 Do you have any favourite singers/musicians/groups at the moment? Why do you like them?
3 Do you ever go to see them in concert?
4 Do you ever watch pop videos? What makes a 'good' pop video?
5 Do you play/Have you ever played any musical instruments? Which ones? Do you/Did you enjoy playing them? Are there any instruments that you would like to learn?

Listening: song

1 You are going to hear a song. As you listen think about the following questions.

1 Which of the singers in the photos is it?
2 What is the singer singing about?

2 Look at the words of the song opposite and fill in the gaps with an appropriate word from the box. Then listen again and check your answers.

blue	gift	world	funny	show	simple	roof
kind	sculptor	live	sweetest	hide	cross	

3 Discuss the following questions about the song.

1 What *feeling* is he talking about? *(line 2)*
2 What can't he *hide*? *(line 3)*
3 What word is missing in *line 4*?
4 Why does he say 'No' in *line 8*?
5 What is another word for *potions* in *line 9*?
6 Why does he say *I hope you don't mind* in *line 15*?
7 Why is he *cross* in *line 19*?
8 What do you think *turned on* in *line 21* means?
9 ... *these things I do* (line 22): what things is he talking about?
10 What does *they* refer to in *line 23*?

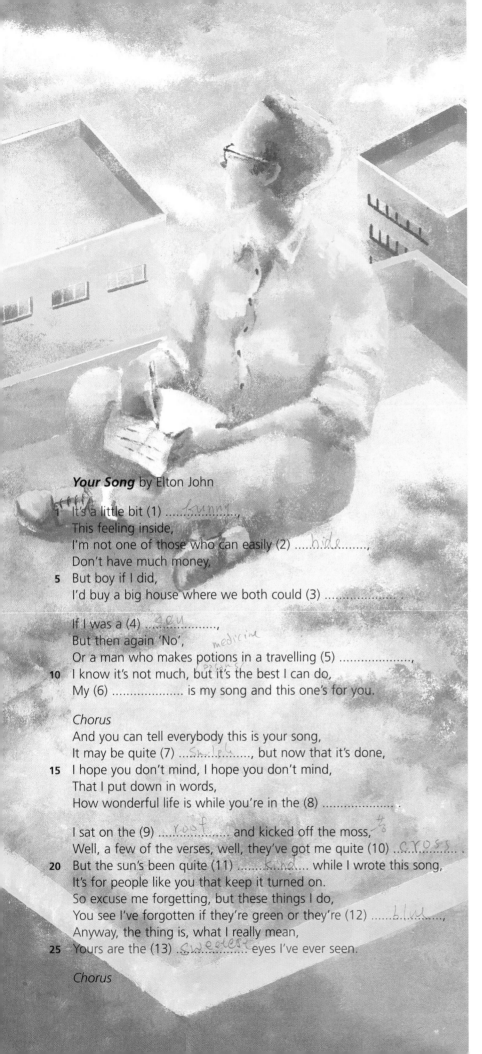

Your Song by Elton John

1   It's a little bit (1) .....funny......,
This feeling inside,
I'm not one of those who can easily (2) .....hide........,
Don't have much money,
5   But boy if I did,
I'd buy a big house where we both could (3) ....

If I was a (4) ....scu...........,
But then again 'No',   *medicine*
Or a man who makes potions in a travelling (5) ....,
10   I know it's not much, but it's the best I can do,
My (6) .... is my song and this one's for you.

Chorus
And you can tell everybody this is your song,
It may be quite (7) ....simple......, but now that it's done,
15   I hope you don't mind, I hope you don't mind,
That I put down in words,
How wonderful life is while you're in the (8) ....

I sat on the (9) .....roof....... and kicked off the moss,
Well, a few of the verses, well, they've got me quite (10) ....cross..... .
20   But the sun's been quite (11) .....kind..... while I wrote this song,
It's for people like you that keep it turned on.
So excuse me forgetting, but these things I do,
You see I've forgotten if they're green or they're (12) .....blue......,
Anyway, the thing is, what I really mean,
25   Yours are the (13) ....sweetest...... eyes I've ever seen.

Chorus

Vocabulary:
phrasal verbs (*down*)

1 Read the following general meanings of *down* when used in phrasal verbs and then match each meaning to one of the pairs of sentences below.

1   destruction, bringing to the ground
2   reduction, decreasing
3   stopping, completion
4   writing, recording

a) I *put down* in words how wonderful life is ...
4   Could you *take down* this letter as I dictate, please?

b) Will you *slow down*? You're going too fast.
2   You must cut down on the amount of chocolate you eat.

c) I know he's in there. We'll have to *break* the door *down*.
1   Lots of trees *came down* in last night's storm.

d) I'm afraid John is going to be
3   late. His car has *broken down*.   *ha-ha*
She waited for the laughter to *die down* before continuing.

2 Imagine the context for each of the sentences and decide who is speaking and what they are speaking about.

3 Now add the following sentences to the appropriate pair of sentences above.

1   If we *cut* that tree *down*, we'll let a lot more light in here.
2   We will have to *close* the mine *down*. There just isn't the demand for coal anymore.
3   Have you finished *getting* all the details *down*?
4   I think the price of bread will *go down* soon.   *cut down*

47

Reading

1   Read the extract below from a book called *The Go-between* and decide who the four people in the pictures below are.

2   Summarise briefly the answers to the following questions.

1 Why was Leo looking for Marian?
2 Where will Marian be the next day?
3 What does she want Leo to do?
4 How does he feel about this?

3   Discuss the following questions.

1 From what you have read, who do you imagine:
   a) Hugh loves?
   b) Leo (the narrator) loves?
   c) Marian loves?

2 Why do you think the book is called *The Go-between*?

3 How do you imagine the story ends?

4   Do you know any examples of stories with complicated 'love triangles' (think about books/ films/soap operas that you know). What happened?

---

1   Then I saw Marian. She was walking rather quickly up the path. When she saw me, she did not smile.

'What are you doing here?' she said.

'Hugh asked me to tell you ...,' I began, and then stopped.

'Yes? What did he ask you to tell me?'

'He asked me to find you,' I said.

I waited for her smile, but it did not come. She looked up and down the path and seemed annoyed about something.

'But what did he say? Have you forgotten?' she asked.

10   It was the first time her voice had sounded unkind to me. My face probably showed that I was hurt. And her manner changed then.

'I know it isn't easy to remember everything,' she said. 'But what does Hugh want?'

'He wants you to play a game with them.'

'What time is it?' she asked.

'Nearly seven o'clock.'

'We don't have dinner until half past eight, do we? There's plenty of time. I'll go.'

20   We were friends again, and we walked back together.

'He told me to bring you dead or alive,' I said.

'Oh, did he? And which do you think I am?'

I thought that was a good joke. Then she said: 'We're going to have lunch with some neighbours tomorrow. They're old people, as old as the hills. Mother thinks you might not be interested. Do you mind staying here?'

'Of course not,' I replied.

'What will you do to amuse yourself?' she asked.

'I'm not sure yet. I might do several things.'

30   'Tell me one of them.'

'Perhaps I'll walk somewhere.'

'Where?'

I had an idea then that she was guiding the conversation. I wondered what she wanted me to say.

'I might slide down a straw stack. It's great fun.'

'Whose straw stack?'

'Perhaps Farmer Burgess's.'

'Oh his?' She sounded very surprised. 'Leo, if you go to his farm, will you do something for me?'

40   'Of course. What is it?' But I knew before she told me.

'Give him a letter.'

'I hoped you'd say that!' I exclaimed.

'Why? Is it because you like him?'

'Yes. But I like Hugh more, of course.'

'Ah, that's because he's a Viscount, perhaps.'

'Yes, that's one reason,' I said, without any false shame. I had real respect for Hugh's rank. 'But he's gentle, too. He doesn't give orders to people. I thought a Viscount would be proud.'

She considered my remarks.

50   'And Mr Burgess,' I continued, 'is only a farmer.' I remembered his angry remarks to me at the straw stack. He did not know then that I was a guest at the Hall. 'He's rather a rough man, I think,' I added.

'Is he?' she said. 'I don't know him very well. We sometimes write notes to each other, on business of course. You said you'd like to take them.'

'Oh, yes, I would,' I said eagerly.

'Is that because you like T— Mr Burgess?'

'Yes. But there's another reason.'

60   'What is it?'

This was my chance to tell her the truth. It was not easy, but at last I said it.

'Because I like you.'

She smiled beautifully and said, 'That's a very sweet thought.'

Grammar: reported/direct speech

1 Look at the following examples of reported speech and find their direct speech equivalent in the text from *The Go-between*.

1 She asked me what I was doing there.
2 He said that Hugh had asked him to tell her ...
3 She asked him if he had forgotten.
4 She said she would go.
5 She told him that they were going to have lunch with some neighbours the next day.
6 She asked him if he minded staying there.
7 He said he might do several things.

2 Compare the reported speech and direct speech forms from Exercise 1 and answer the following questions.

1 What changes are made each time?

2 What rules about changing direct speech to reported speech can you make based on these examples? Think about:
- tenses of verbs e.g. Past Simple, etc.
- modals e.g. *will*, *might*, etc.
- questions
- time and place words e.g. *tomorrow*, *here*, etc.

3 Now turn to page 173 and check your ideas against Grammar reference 15.2/15.4.

3

1 Listen to a conversation between two friends. What is Tom's problem?

2 Now listen to the conversation again and write a summary of what you hear using reported speech.

   EXAMPLE: *Mike saw Tom and **asked him how he was**. Tom **said** ...*

3 Compare what you have written in reported speech with a partner.

Watch Out! *to suggest*

He suggested {
going
that they go
that they went
them to go
that they should go
} to an Italian restaurant.

One of the above patterns is not possible. Which is it?

Reporting verbs

4 Match the verbs in the box to a pattern below according to how they are used in reported speech.

accuse   admit   advise   agree   apologise   blame
congratulate   decide   deny   encourage   explain
insist   invite   offer   promise   recommend
refuse   remind   suggest   threaten   warn

a) verb + object + infinitive e.g. *He asked me to go.*
b) verb + (that) e.g. *She said (that) he had to go.*
c) verb + object + (that) e.g. *He told us (that) he had to go.*
d) verb + gerund e.g. *He admitted stealing her bag.*
e) verb + object + preposition + gerund e.g. *He accused me of stealing the money.*
f) verb + infinitive e.g. *He decided to lend her the money.*
g) verb + preposition + gerund e.g. *He insisted on lending her the money.*

5 Report the following statements using one of the reporting verbs above.

1 'I'm so sorry that I was late.'
2 'Don't touch that chair. It's just been painted!'
3 'I will do my homework after the film, honestly!'
4 'Why don't we go to the beach for a swim?'
5 'I'm *not* going to the party.'
6 '*You* stole that money.'
7 'Don't forget to get Paula a birthday present.'
8 'I'll take you to the airport if you like.'
9 'Yes, it's true. I did lie about my age.'
10 'I'll tell a teacher if you don't put it back.'

6 Work in small groups and write a short story in 120–180 words. The story must:

- be on the theme of love.
- use a mixture of direct and reported speech, including at least five of the verbs in Exercise 4.
- include reference to each of the following objects:

Speaking

1 Discuss the following questions.

1 What is the best book you have read recently? Who was it by? What was it about? Why did you particularly like it?
2 Have you read any books or graded readers in English?

2 Now look at these back cover blurbs taken from various readers and match them with the following book titles.

1 *Brave New World* (Aldous Huxley)
2 *A Passage to India* (E.M. Forster)
3 *Crime Never Pays*
4 *Rebecca* (Daphne du Maurier)
5 *Pygmalion* (Bernard Shaw)

3 Discuss which of the books you think would be suitable for:

1 someone who likes mysteries and solving problems
2 someone who likes reading about love and relationships
3 someone who is interested in political issues
4 someone who is interested in language and accent
5 someone who is interested in cross-cultural differences

4 Put the books in order according to which ones you would be most/least interested in reading. Compare your order with other students. Is it the same or different? Explain the reasons for your order.

A

MURDER: the unlawful, intentional killing of a human being. A terrible crime.

But murder stories are always fascinating. Who did it? And how? Or why? Was it murder at all, or just an unfortunate accident? Who will triumph, the murderer or the detective? This collection contains a wide range of murder stories, from the astute detections of the famous Sherlock Holmes, to the chilling psychology of Ruth Rendell.

B

AFTER THE DEATH of his beautiful wife, Rebecca, Maxim de Winter goes to Monte Carlo to recover. There he marries a quiet and ordinary young woman who is very different from his first wife. Maxim takes her back to England – to Manderley, his lovely country house.

The new Mrs de Winter finds that at Manderley Rebecca is still in everyone's thoughts – including Maxim's – and she begins to feel that she will never be able to equal Rebecca as a wife or as mistress of Manderley.

Then one day a discovery is made – and the young Mrs de Winter begins to understand why Rebecca is still so important to all those at Manderley.

C

'You see this creature with her kerbstone English: the English that will keep her in the gutter to the end of her days. Well, sir, in three months I could pass that girl off as a duchess at an ambassador's garden party.'

❀ ❀ ❀ ❀

Can Professor Henry Higgins *really* turn flower-girl Eliza Doolittle into a lady?

D

East meets West in this intriguing story. Or does it? Why should Miss Quested accuse Dr Aziz of assaulting her on an outing to the Marabar Caves? How can Dr Aziz defend himself against such an unfair charge?

Will the trial cause a bloody battle between the Indians lined up behind Dr Aziz and the British community solidly behind Miss Quested?

E

ALL human values have change. What in the past were seen as virtues hav been wiped out. Family life ha disappeared, human beings are produce in bottles instead of being born in th natural manner. People do not suffer; bu they have no ideas of their own, their live are planned for them from start to finish and they know nothing of the passions, th joys and sorrows, the triumphs or th defeats of the great figures of the past. I spite of the light and often amusing way this book is written, here is a warning to u all to think carefully about the way the world is developing before it is too late.

Writing: background reading texts

1

In Paper 2 of the exam, Question 5 will refer to various set books. There will be one or two general questions which you can answer by referring to one of these books. You may be asked to write your answer in the form of a composition, an article, a report or a letter.

Here is a procedure to follow when reading a set text:

- Read the book once all the way through to get a general idea of the story and the main characters.

- Explain the basic story to another student (in English!).

- Read the book again, more carefully this time. As you go through each chapter, underline key words which you do not know the meaning of and look them up in your dictionary.

- Read the book one last time and make notes in a notebook under headings.

  EXAMPLE: **Characters   Relationships   Places   Events**

  You may want to add other headings depending on the content of the particular book.

- Make a list of questions that you might be asked about your book and discuss them with other students.

2 When you have done all of the above, write an answer to one of the following questions in 120–180 words.

---

1 What do you think is the most important event that takes place in the book you have read? Write an account of it and why it is important for a student who has not yet read the book.

2 Who do you think is the most interesting person in the book you have read? Write a report for your school magazine, explaining why this person is interesting and how she/he contributes to the story as a whole.

Vocabulary: ways of talking

1

1 Complete the following table on the use of *say, tell* and *speak*.

	say	tell	speak
a lie	✗	✔	✗
'Yes'			
English			
a story			
something			
loudly			
me his name			

2 Translate the verbs into your language. Do they go with the same words and phrases as in English?

2

1 Read the following short text and decide if it comes from:

a) a newspaper article.
b) a diary.
c) a letter to a friend.

I went to a party the other night at Jo's. Do you remember I was telling you about her the other day. She's Paul best friend. It was great. I got (1) .... to these really interesting people. We started (2) .... various things and I really felt they were on my wavelength. One guy (3) .... me he had done the same course (Spanish) that I want to do at university but dropped out after a year. I (4) .... him why. He (5) .... that they never actually (6) .... much Spanish on the course, and that most of the time they (7) .... in English about Spanish literature.

2 Now choose the correct alternative to fill each gap.

1 **A** saying   **B** telling   **C** chatting
2 **A** speaking   **B** discussing   **C** talking
3 **A** told   **B** asked   **C** said
4 **A** discussed   **B** told   **C** asked
5 **A** said   **B** spoke   **C** told
6 **A** told   **B** discussed   **C** spoke
7 **A** said   **B** talked   **C** told

Use of English

1 Look at the picture below and describe what you can see in as much detail as possible. Think about:

● what year it might be
● where it might have been taken
● who the people are

2 Fill in the gaps in the following text with the words in the box. You will need to use three more words that are not in the box.

was	being	still	that	to (x 2)	has	when	will	be	their

Sweethearts claim share of picture profits

by ALISON JAMES in Paris

TWO lovers steal a kiss on a busy Paris street, oblivious to everything around them, including a photographer. Forty-two years on, the same pair stand in the same spot, (1)................... very much in love. At least, Denise and Jean-Louis Lavergne claim they are the lovers in the world's most romantic picture taken (2)................... a spring morning in 1950. Photographer Robert Doisneau, 80, says otherwise. The dispute over 'The Kiss by the Hotel de Ville' will now (3)................... settled in court. The Lavergnes are demanding £50,000 plus a share of the millions the famous shot (4)................... made for Doisneau and his picture agency Rapho, since it (5)................... made into a poster in the 1980s.

Denise, 64, (6)................... runs a small Paris printing company with her 66-year-old husband, said, 'It was a romantic time, we were young, engaged, so in love and oblivious to the people around us. We didn't even see that our picture was (7)................... taken. We got married on July 8 that year.'

It was only (8)................... they saw the picture on the cover of a magazine – on (9)................... 38th wedding anniversary – that they realised their kiss (10)................... been captured forever. They tracked down Doisneau and met him in 1990. 'He was very friendly and told us other people, but no couples, had come forward claiming (11)................... be in his picture.'

Last night Doisneau's lawyer Julien Hay said he had proof (12)................... models posed for the picture. He said the photographer humoured the Lavergnes (13)................... let them believe they were the romantic subjects. 'They (14)................... not get a franc,' he added.

from *Today* newspaper

Exam focus

Paper 5 Speaking

1 Read the following information on the two ways in which the interview part of the exam can be organised.

A Candidates take this paper in pairs and there are two examiners at the interview. One of them will ask you both questions, show you pictures, etc. The other will be silent, but will be listening to the quality of your English. This part of the exam will last about 15 minutes.

B Candidates take this paper individually and there is only one examiner. Otherwise the format of this paper will be approximately the same.

2 Now read the following information on the four different parts of Paper 5.

1 In Part 1 the examiner will spend a few minutes encouraging you to give information about yourselves such as where you live, your free-time activities, etc.
2 In Part 2 you are given two photos to look at and talk about.
3 In Part 3 you will be given a visual prompt such as a picture or drawing and you will have to do some kind of task (with the other candidate), such as problem solving, speculating, etc.
4 In Part 4 you will discuss questions (with the other candidate) which relate to the subject of the task in Part 3.

3 You are now going to practise Parts 3 and 4. Imagine that two friends of yours in their early twenties have just got married and are about to move into their own unfurnished flat. Below is a plan of the living room and the furniture they are going to put into it. Work with a partner and decide on the best arrangement for the furniture in the room.

4 Discuss the following questions.

1 What are the advantages/disadvantages of young married couples living with their family?
2 Is there an ideal age to get married?
3 Do you have a 'dream place' where you would like to live?

53

Vocabulary: love and marriage

1 Explain the difference between the following pairs of words.

1 to go out with someone/to live with someone
2 to be infatuated/to fall in love
3 to get engaged/to get married
4 to get pregnant/to have a baby
5 to have an anniversary/to have a birthday
6 to have rows/to have discussions
7 to chat/to flirt
8 to get a divorce/to split up

2 Look at the words in the box and discuss:

1 the meaning of each one.
2 the significance of each one when people get married.

| a wedding   a registry office   a church   the aisle |
| a vicar   the bride   the bridegroom   the best man |
| the bridesmaids   the ring   the reception |
| the organist   the choir   a bouquet   a veil |
| a honeymoon |

Listening: wedding upset

1 You are going to hear a description of an unusual wedding. Listen and answer the following questions.

1 What happened as the bride and groom were about to be married the first time?
2 What happened just after they were finally married?

2 Now listen again and decide which of the people in the box the following statements apply to. You will need to refer to some of the people more than once.

| the vicar   the groom   the wedding guests |
| the bride   the bride's mother   the best man |
| the bride's parents   the bride's uncle   the organist |
| the groom's relations |

1 They arranged the wedding.
2 Most of them were from London.
3 He was looking very handsome.
4 They were extremely surprised.
5 She fainted.
6 He shouted in church.
7 They were all talking to one another.
8 He was feeling very insecure.
9 He had had too much to drink.
10 He asked the same question twice.
11 He changed his mind.

Speaking

Discuss the following questions.

1 What happens when people get married in your country? Are there any special activities or customs?
2 Describe the last wedding that you went to. Whose wedding was it? Who was there? What happened?

1 Choose the most suitable alternative below to fill in the gaps in the following text.

For their honeymoon they went on a (1) .... in the Greek islands. It was a very modern (2) .... and there was even a swimming pool on one of the (3) .... . They had an enormous (4) .... with a bathroom and a bedroom. Julia was a bit (5) .... about travelling by ship because she'd seen the film *The Titanic* a few weeks before. She wanted to check that there were enough (6) .... and lifeboats before they left the port just in case anything (7) .... wrong.

For some reason James found this very (8) .... and they started to (9) .... the most terrible rows on the very first day. Julia could hardly believe that this was the same man she had (10) .... in love with a year before. He had never shown any sign of being so (11) .... when they were just going (12) .... together. She began to (13) .... ever having married him.

To make matters even worse, James started to (14) .... with some of the other young women on board. He danced with one of these women all evening on the last night and that made Julia decide that the only solution was to split (15.) .... with James and start her life all over again.

1   **A** voyage   **B** cruise   **C** travel   **D** journey
2   **A** ferry   **B** tanker   **C** liner   **D** yacht
3   **A** decks   **B** docks   **C** storeys   **D** floors
4   **A** compartment   **B** flat   **C** apartment   **D** cabin
5   **A** irritated   **B** nervous   **C** fed up   **D** relieved
6   **A** lifeguards   **B** life jackets   **C** lifelines   **D** lifesavers
7   **A** did   **B** made   **C** had   **D** went
8   **A** irritation   **B** irritated   **C** irritating   **D** irritate
9   **A** fight   **B** do   **C** make   **D** have
10   **A** felt   **B** fallen   **C** found   **D** fault
11   **A** impatient   **B** unconscious   **C** surprising   **D** thrilling
12   **A** away   **B** over   **C** through   **D** out
13   **A** repent   **B** regret   **C** relieve   **D** respect
14   **A** flit   **B** flight   **C** flirt   **D** float
15   **A** away   **B** out   **C** up   **D** apart

2 Write questions for the following answers.

1   Teresa? She'll be twenty-four next birthday.
2   Quite like me, actually. She's rather shy when you first meet her, but once you get to know her she's very friendly.
3   A boyfriend? Yes, his name's Nelson. He's from Brazil.
4   She studies journalism and works part-time in a boutique.
5   She goes swimming a lot and plays the violin with a local orchestra.
6   No, she hasn't, but she'd like to. She's been to the United States, though.
7   Yes, she enjoyed it very much.
8   In New York with some relatives.
9   Yes, she learnt a lot. Her English is much better now.
10   Yes, she has. She got a 'B' and she's going to do the Certificate of Advanced English next year.

3 Fill in the gaps in the following text with an appropriate word.

Though they are very different in all sorts of ways cricket and baseball are also quite similar. (1) .... they are both played with very hard balls, some of the players have to wear (2) .... to protect their hands and to help (3) .... catch the ball. Golfers wear them too, but (4) .... need them to stop their hands slipping on the (5) ....

In racket sports (6) .... tennis, squash and badminton a good grip is essential as well (7) .... strength, speed, stamina and, in the case of modern tennis, height. Tall players have a tremendous advantage when they serve because they can hit the ball at (8) .... great speed that their opponents are lucky to get the ball back over the (9) .... It's (10) .... important to keep your cool. Lots of players lose concentration if a linesman says a ball they have returned is (11) .... Occasionally the (12) .... will overrule the decision and say that the ball was in after all.

There's not often any doubt whether someone (13) .... scored a (14) .... or not in football, but players sometimes disagree (15) .... the referee over penalties.

4

1 Match a prefix in Column A with a word in Column B. Use each prefix and word once only.

EXAMPLE: *il + legal > illegal*

Column A

1 il
2 re
3 dis
4 over
5 under
6 post
7 ex
8 sub
9 im
10 un
11 ir
12 in

Column B

a) significant
b) mature
c) write
d) responsible
e) natal
f) line
g) wife
h) legal
i) titles
j) eat
k) organised
l) comfortable

2 Now fill in the gaps in the following sentences with an appropriate word formed in 1 above.

a) You wouldn't be so .... if you had a diary and wrote down all the things you have to do.

b) This letter is very badly written. I'm afraid you'll have to .... it.

c) I prefer to see American films in English with .... in my own language.

d) If you .... like that, you'll get indigestion.

e) This sofa is really .... It makes my back ache.

f) In most countries it is .... to open a bank account in a false name.

g) It was very .... of you to go out and leave your younger brothers and sisters alone in the house.

h) After you've read the book once straight through, read it again and .... some of the words you want to look up in your dictionary.

i) He has been divorced for ten years now, but he still has a good relationship with his ....

j) She really is very .... – she always gets upset when she doesn't get her own way.

5 Rewrite the second sentence so that it has a similar meaning to the first sentence using the word in **bold** and other words.

1 Nobody in our class is as good at basketball as I am.
   player
   I am .... in our class.

2 My older brother is a social worker in one of the big hospitals.
   works
   My older brother .... in one of the big hospitals.

3 My friends left before I arrived at the meeting point.
   when
   My friends .... at the meeting point.

4 'Alright, I stole the money. I admit it,' she said.
   that
   She admitted .... the money.

5 Susan plays the piano better than Jacky.
   as
   Jacky doesn't play .... Susan.

6 Badminton and tennis are similar in some ways.
   like
   Badminton .... in some ways.

7 'Would you like to stay for dinner?' she asked.
   invited
   She .... for dinner.

8 The Nigerian beat the Moroccan by 2.5 seconds.
   faster
   The Nigerian ran .... the Moroccan.

9 'What's the time?' he asked.
   tell
   He asked me .... the time.

10 Are you saying I'm lying?
   accusing
   Are you .... lying?

6 Read the following text and look carefully at each line. Some of the lines are correct and some have an extra incorrect word that should not be there. If a line is correct, put a (✔) at the end of it. If there is a word that should not be there, circle it. There are two examples at the beginning (**0** and **00**).

0	I was absolutely delighted when I found out my sister and I	✔
00	had (to) won a big prize in the national lottery. But when I	
1	tried to find the ticket, I started to worry. I had	
2	thrown away a lot of the old bus tickets and receipts just a	
3	few days before and I had nearly thrown it away the lottery	
4	ticket as well. Luckily I have realised just in time and put	
5	it away safely. Now that I knew our lucky number was the	
6	winning number the problem was that I couldn't remember	
7	exactly where did I put it. I was looking through the papers	
8	on my desk when I remembered it had been a very windy	
9	the night before it. Some of my papers had blown off the	
10	desk and I was very relieved when I found the ticket amongst	
11	them on the floor. I checked the numbers carefully in the paper	
12	and immediately phoned to my sister to tell her the good	
13	news. She could hardly believe it and just kept	
14	asking me if I was sure. We arranged her to meet	
15	that evening to decide how to spend the money.	

7 Read the following text and use the word in capitals at the end of each line to form a word that fits in the gap in the same line.

I get a lot of (1) .... from my job. Advertising	**SATISFY**
can be very (2) .... because you have to think of	**CREATE**
new ways to attract people's (3) .... . The best	**ATTEND**
way to do this is by surprising them. (4) .... is	**FAMILIAR**
boring and people soon get fed up with an (5)	**ADVERTISE**
they have seen many times before. (6) .... they	**CONSCIOUS**
want to be shocked. Apart from (7) .... , the other	**ORIGINAL**
really important (8) .... of a good campaign is	**CHARACTER**
(9) .... . After all if people don't remember what	**MEMORABLE**
was being advertised, they won't buy the (10)	**PRODUCE**

8 Fill in the gaps in the following sentences with an appropriate particle (*in*, *at*, *through*, etc.) or verb in the correct form.

1 I was feeling very unfit so I decided to take .... aerobics

2 Sorry we're late. The car .... down on the way.

3 He tells really funny jokes and makes us all laugh by taking .... our dad.

4 .... down! You're driving much too fast.

5 Mobile phones have really taken .... here. Everyone seems to have one.

6 It took several days for the fire to .... down after it had been burning for so long.

7 We'll have to get rid of that old sofa. It takes .... too much space and it's very uncomfortable.

8 I think it's terrible the way they've cut .... all the lovely trees in this street.

9 Whenever she joins in our games, she just takes .... and starts telling us all what to do.

10 That new supermarket is taking .... over one hundred people to work as cashiers.

11 My boss threatened to sack me if I .... on making mistakes.

12 Her parents died when she was ten and she .... up by her aunt.

It's all in the mind

Reading

1 You are going to read an article about the brain and intelligence. Before you read, discuss the following questions.

1 What is 'intelligence'?

2 Is an 'intelligent' person someone who:

- is good at passing exams?
- is imaginative?
- gets what she/he wants in life?
- understands new ideas quickly?
- has a good memory?
- deals with people well?
- is sensible?
- reads a lot?
- is good at crosswords?

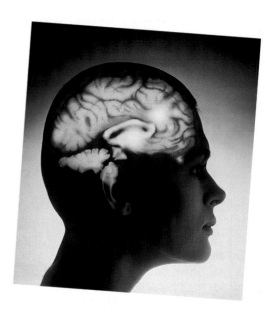

2 The following words all appear in the article. Match each one with its correct definition on the right.

1 brain	a) a natural form of sugar found in fruit
2 myth	b) the bone of your head which encloses your brain
3 IQ	c) a measure of how clever someone is
4 skull	d) a tool with a narrow blade at one end, used to put screws into something or remove them
5 addicted	e) the organ in the top part of your head which controls thought, feeling and physical activity
6 glucose	f) instructions for cooking a particular dish
7 screwdriver	g) a false story which many people may believe
8 mental	h) unable to stop taking or using something
9 recipe	i) concerned with the brain or thinking

3 Read the article quickly and decide which one of the following subjects it does *not* refer to.

a) improving your brain power
b) men and women
c) psychological illness
d) brain weight
e) old age
f) the physical needs of the brain

4 Read the article again and choose the most suitable heading from the list below for each numbered part of the article. The first one has been done for you.

A A horrifying history.
B Bloodthirsty.
C Is bigger better?
D Make your brain work.
E How much do we know?
F The battle of the sexes.
G The super computer.

5 Make a note of two things you did not know before reading the article which you found interesting. Tell a partner.

6 If you would like to try some IQ puzzles to develop your mental agility, turn to page 185.

The Mind Machine?

(0 —— E ——)

Although intelligence has been studied, and the brain has been studied, there is little understanding of how the brain works to produce intelligence. This has something to do with the fact that the brain contains around 100 billion cells (about the number of stars in the Milky Way).

(1 ————)

One of the continuing myths about the relationship between intelligence and the brain is that the brains of very clever people are somehow physically different from those of ordinary people. At the beginning of the century an American scientist called E.A. Spitzka produced a list of the weights of the brains of important, well-known men. The heaviest brain on the list was that of Turgenev, the Russian novelist, at 2000g. However, the brain of another great genius, Walt Whitman, weighed only 1282g.

(2 ————)

There are no significant differences between the intelligence levels of males and females. However, girls under seven score a little higher than boys in IQ tests and the highest IQ recorded is that of Marylin vos Savant at 230. However, men and women do differ in the way they think. Generally, women are more skilled verbally and men do better on visual-spatial tasks.

Interestingly, the fibres which join the two halves of the brain have been found to be larger in women than in men. This supports the theory that women can change from 'practical' to 'emotional' thinking more quickly than men.

(3 ————)

People with mental problems have often been treated extremely badly. Two hundred years ago, the mentally ill were swung around in revolving chairs, or holes were drilled in their skulls to release evil spirits. From the 1930s, the mentally ill were subjected to electric shock therapy and lobotomy – the removal of part of their brain. In the 1960s and 70s, thousands of people were given drugs to cope with anxiety and then became addicted to them.

(4 ————)

The brain needs ten times as much blood as other organs of the body, as it can't store glucose for later use. This is different to muscles and other organs and although the adult brain makes up only two per cent of the body weight, its oxygen consumption is twenty per cent of the body's total.

(5 ————)

There are similarities between brains and computers. Computers can do complicated calculations at incredible speeds. But they work in a fixed way, because they can't make memory associations. If we need a screwdriver and there isn't one, we will think laterally and use a knife or coin instead. Computers can't do this. In fact, it is claimed that when it comes to seeing, moving and reacting to stimuli, no computer can compete with even the brain power of a fly.

(6 ————)

Most of our mental processes are deeply formed habits. Challenging your brain to do things differently helps it develop. Try changing routines as often as you can: take a bus instead of going by car, sit in a different chair. An extreme but useful exercise is to read something upside down – you can actually feel your brain at work.

Exercise more. Good health and fitness levels give you overall improved energy which leads to better concentration.

Cooking is a good all-round mental exercise. It needs mathematical, organisational and scientific skills as well as challenging memory and creative ability. Use recipes at first and then learn to guess amounts, combinations, reactions of ingredients and timing.

Do puzzles and play games. Teach yourself to work out codes and expand your vocabulary at the same time.

from *Esquire* magazine

Vocabulary: word formation

1   Look back at the article on the brain and find the following words.

1   the noun from *intelligent (part 0)*
2   a verb from *different (part 2)*
3   the noun from *similar (part 5)*
4   a noun from *to calculate (part 5)*
5   the positive adjective from *useless (part 6)*
6   the noun from *healthy (part 6)*
7   the noun from *energetic (part 6)*
8   the adjective from *science (part 6)*

2   Mark where the main stress falls in the pairs of words in Exercise 1. In which pairs is it the same and in which pairs is it different?

EXAMPLE: *in'telligent, in'telligence (same)*

3   Now complete the following sentences with the correct form of the word in brackets. Use your dictionary if necessary.

1   My mother was such an .... person, always busy, always in a hurry. (ENERGY)
2   I made a stupid .... and so things didn't turn out as planned. (CALCULATE)
3   I'd like to do it .... this time. I hope you don't mind. (DIFFERENT)
4   There is one important .... between Sean and Katie. They both really enjoy discussing politics. (SIMILAR)
5   If you ate more ...., you wouldn't have all these problems with your skin. (HEALTH)
6   I want to be an important .... when I grow up. (SCIENCE)
7   It's almost impossible to actually measure .... (INTELLIGENT)
8   He's .... at mending things. I'll just have to do it myself. (USE)

Speaking

1   Discuss the following questions.

1   What do you think is the purpose of going to school? Is it to make you more intelligent? Is it to learn information? Is it to pass exams? Is it to develop social skills when dealing with others?
2   How successful are the schools you have been to in achieving these aims?

2   What are the five most important characteristics that make:

a) your ideal teacher?
b) an ideal student?

List the characteristics in order of importance.

Vocabulary: education

1   Fill in the gaps in the following sentences with the words in the box.

playground   truant   cheat   heart   correct
term   give   absent   hard   degree   break
university   headmaster   report   board

1   Our teachers .... our homework in the evening and .... it out the next day.
2   My brother tried to .... in the exam, but he was caught and sent to the ....
3   I like to play football in the .... with my friends during the lunch ....
4   She got a very good school .... because she worked so .... this ....
5   I'd like to go to .... when I finish school and do a .... in Economics.
6   The teacher wrote the rules on the .... and told us to learn them by ....
7   Were you .... for a good reason yesterday or were you playing .... ?

2   Read the following text and choose the correct alternative in each case.

I started school when I was five and I went to the local (1) *nursery/primary school*. I liked it very much; the (2) *classes/lessons* were small and the (3) *teachers/professors* were very friendly. At eleven I changed and went to (4) *sixth form college/secondary school*. Things didn't go so well here. I hated studying (5) *subjects/courses* like Biology and Physics and I got terrible (6) *points/marks* in tests. My parents tried to (7) *teach/learn* me the things I didn't understand, but it was no good. I used to get very worried about my end-of-year exams and one year, even though I spent a lot of time (8) *revising/reviewing*, I knew I wouldn't (9) *pass/succeed*. In the end I was right – I (10) *failed/missed* all the exams and had to (11) *retake/remake* them all a few months later. That was the worst year of my school life, but it didn't stop me having a good (12) *course/career* as an engineer.

> **Watch Out!** *take/pass/fail*
>
> 1 He *passed* the exam.
> 2 He *took* the exam.
> 3 He *failed* the exam.
>
> What did he do first? Which is a good result? Which is a bad result?

3   Read the following sentences and match each phrasal verb in *italics* to a meaning below.

1 Please *speak up*! We can't hear you at the back.
2 If you don't know what it means, *look* it *up* in a dictionary.
3 Why do you always *pick on* me? It's just not fair!
4 Paul is having problems *keeping up* with the other children in his class.
5 You need to try and *get across* your ideas better.
6 He *catches on* very quickly. You never have to explain anything twice.
7 I'll *let* you *off* this time, but I don't want to catch you two fighting again.
8 I can't *work out* how to do this maths problem.
9 He *picked up* a lot of Italian by just chatting to people in cafés.

a) learn	f) talk more loudly
b) not punish	g) find information in a reference
c) understand	book
d) treat badly	h) communicate
e) calculate	i) maintain the same level

4   Think about the different schools you have been to in the past or which you go to now and discuss the following questions.

1 How did/do you feel about each of them? Did/do you enjoy them?
2 What would you (have) change(d) about your school in order to improve it?
3 Were/Are they single-sex or mixed? Do you think it is better to have single-sex or mixed schools?
4 Were/Are they strict?
5 Did/Do you have any special friends?
6 Did/Do you play any sports/musical instruments at school?
7 Did/Do you have any teachers or subjects that you especially like(d)/dislike(d)?
8 How often did/do you have to take exams? How did/do you feel about exams? Did/Do you enjoy them/hate them/get nervous about them?

Listening: exam fever

1   You are going to hear three students talking about exams. Listen and answer the following questions.

1 Which person doesn't mind exams?
2 Which person doesn't like exams?
3 Which person doesn't give his/her opinion?

2   Now listen again and decide which of the students (1, 2 or 3) talk about the following things.

a) oral exams	d) writing speed
b) coursework	e) revising for exams
c) competitive exams	f) failing exams

3   Make a note of what each student says about the above points.

Function: giving opinions, agreeing/disagreeing

1

1 Look at the following ways of giving opinions and fill in the gaps.

> I think (that)
> .... my opinion
> .... my point of view } exams are a good thing.
> As .... as I'm concerned }

2 Mark where you think the main stress usually falls in the expressions on the left.

3 Now listen to someone saying the sentences and check that you put the stress in the right place.

2

1 Put the following ways of agreeing and disagreeing in order from strong agreement to strong disagreement. Decide which two are similar in strength.

  a) I don't really agree.
  b) I completely agree.
  c) I agree up to a point, but ...
  d) I couldn't agree more.
  e) I don't agree at all.
  f) That's right.

2 Listen to the phrases being used in conversation and check your answers. Then say the sentences/phrases imitating the pronunciation of the people you heard.

Watch Out! *agree*

• I'm sorry, but I am not agree with you.

What's the mistake in this sentence?

---

3 Work with a partner and briefly give your opinion about each of the following. Your partner should say if she/he agrees or disagrees and why.

1 the weather at the moment
2 smacking young children
3 banning smoking in restaurants
4 the need to look after the environment
5 the quality of the programmes on TV

4 Work in a group with other students and discuss whether you agree or disagree with the following statements. Give reasons.

1 Exams are not an accurate measure of a person's ability.
2 A mixture of exams and coursework is a good idea.
3 You should repeat a school year if you fail your exams.
4 You should be told the questions a little time before you go into the exam.
5 Exams should involve an oral and a written part.
6 Competitive exams are a good idea.

Writing: discursive (1)

In Paper 2 you may be asked to give your opinion on a particular question. Here is an example of the type of question you may have:

> An international young people's magazine is investigating the question:
>
> *Should students only be judged by their results in end-of-year exams?*
>
> Write a short article for the magazine on this topic, based on your own experience.

1 You are going to read a sample answer to this question, but first look at the following sentences and say what the names are of the different punctuation marks.

> How do you spell 'competitive'?
>
> "It's time to stop writing," she said.
>
> Stop throwing those paper-clips!

2 Now look at the following sample answer to the question above.

1 In the first and second paragraphs there are ten mistakes of punctuation. Find and correct them.
2 In the third paragraph there is no punctuation. Rewrite it, putting in the correct punctuation as necessary.

more and more in my country, student achievement is being based on a mixture of continuous assessment and end-of-year exams some people claim that this is leading to lower standards in schools' but I don't believe this is true.

In my opinion, it is much fairer to allow the work students do during their school year to count towards their final result for various reasons. Firstly, it is possible to have a bad day when you take your exams and not show your true ability secondly, exams don't encourage real learning as students just memorise lots of information for the exam and then immediately forget it all as well as this, it is much more realistic to spend time thinking about a question or problem discussing it with other people and researching it in books. This is, of course something you cannot do in an exam.

in conclusion then i believe that we should make coursework an increasingly important part of students final marks this will give a fairer and more accurate picture of each students real ability

3 Now read the sample answer again and decide:

1 what the purpose of each paragraph is.
2 if you agree in general with the views of the person who wrote it.

4 You are going to write your own answer either to the question preceding Exercise 1 or the one below in 120–180 words.

You should follow this procedure:

- Work with a partner and think of ideas to include.
- Organise your ideas into sensible paragraphs.
- Write a rough draft.
- Read through the draft and make sure you have included appropriate linking expressions.
- Check your punctuation.
- Show the draft to another student and ask them if everything is clear and easy to understand. If not, discuss how you might reword it.
- Write a final version.

> An international young people's magazine is investigating the view that:
>
> *There is no point in making students repeat a school year if they fail their exams.*
>
> Write a short article for the magazine on this topic, based on your own experience.

Exam focus

Paper 1 Reading (multiple choice)

1 In Part 2 of Paper 1 you will have to answer multiple choice questions about a text. Here is some advice on how to approach this task, but it is in the wrong order. Work with a partner and put the advice in the correct order.

a) If in doubt, check that the other possible answers are either not referred to in the text or that they are contradicted by the text.

b) Read the text more carefully, so that you feel confident you have a clear picture of what is being said.

c) Read the text quickly to get the general idea of what it is about.

d) Go back to the text and find the part which justifies your answer.

e) Choose the one of the four multiple choice answers closest to your original idea.

f) Look at the multiple choice questions one by one and decide what you think the answer to each one is. If possible, do this without looking at the suggested answers.

2 Read the opposite text through quickly to get the general idea of what it is about. Then read it again more carefully and answer this question.

● In what ways, if any, does this person sound like you?

3 Think carefully about the answers to the following questions.

1 Why does the student in fact read the newspaper?
2 When does the student start planning his first break?
3 How many programmes does the student finally watch?
4 After he finishes the first TV programme, what then delays the student?
5 What does the student actually eat?

101 WAYS TO AVOID STUDYING

1 The Six-o'clock-In-The-Evening-Enthusiastic-Determined-And-Well-Intentioned-Studier-Until-Midnight is a person with whom you are probably already familiar. At 6 o'clock he approaches his desk, and carefully organises everything in preparation for the study period to follow. Having everything in place he next carefully adjusts each item again, giving him time to complete the first excuse: he remembers that in the morning he did not have quite enough time to
10 read everything of interest in the newspaper. He also realises that if he is going to study, it is best to have such small items completely out of the way before starting.

He therefore leaves his desk, has a quick look through the newspaper and notices as he looks that there are more articles of interest than he had originally thought. He also notices, as he turns the pages, the entertainment section. At this point he decides to plan his first break – perhaps an interesting
20 half-hour programme between 8 and 8.30 p.m.

He finds the programme, and it inevitably starts at about 7.00 p.m.

At this point, he thinks, 'Well, I've had a difficult day and it's not too long before the programme starts, and I need a rest anyway and the relaxation will really help me to get down to studying ...' He returns to his desk at 7.45 p.m, because the beginning of the next

programme was also a bit more interesting than he thought it would be.

At this stage, he remembers that phone call to a friend which, like the articles of interest in the newspaper, is best cleared out of the way before the serious studying begins.

The phone call, of course, is much more interesting and longer than originally planned, but eventually the studier is back at his desk at about 8.30 p.m.

At this point in the proceedings he actually sits down at the desk, opens the book with a display of physical determination, and starts to read (usually page one) as he experiences the first pangs of hunger and thirst. This is disastrous because he realises that the longer he waits to satisfy his pangs, the worse they will get, and the more interrupted his study concentration will be.

The obvious and only solution is a light snack. This, in its preparation, grows, as more and more tasty items seem necessary to satisfy the hunger. The snack becomes a feast.

Having removed this final obstacle the desk is returned to with the certain knowledge that this time there is nothing that could possibly interfere with the following period of study. The first couple of sentences on page one are looked at again ... as the studier realises that his stomach is feeling decidedly heavy. Far better then to watch that other interesting half-hour programme at 10 o'clock, after which the digestion will be mostly completed and the rest will mean he can really get down to work.

At 12 o'clock we find him asleep in front of the TV.

from *Use your Head* by Tony Buzan

4   Now look at the complete questions and multiple choice answers below and follow the suggested procedure in Exercise 1. Choose the correct alternative in each case.

1 The student in fact reads the newspaper in order to
   A find out what is on TV.
   B avoid beginning work.
   C be able to work continuously without a break later.
   D keep up-to-date with world events.

2 The student starts planning his first break
   A half an hour before he actually starts work.
   B more than forty-five minutes before actually starting work.
   C around 8.00 p.m.
   D when it is too late.

3 The student finally watches
   A one complete programme only.
   B parts of two programmes.
   C at least one complete programme and part of another.
   D at least two complete programmes.

4 His study period is delayed because
   A he decides to phone a friend.
   B he starts thinking about an interesting phone call.
   C a friend calls him.
   D he finds an interesting article about telephones in the paper.

5 What does the student actually eat?
   A A snack and then a large meal.
   B A large meal only.
   C Only a snack, but he would like a large meal.
   D Nothing at all, but he would like a snack.

5   Discuss the following questions about how you study and what you do to learn more effectively.

1 How much English homework do you do/should you do every night/week?
2 How often do you find you need breaks from work?
3 When do you work best: in the morning, afternoon or evening?
4 Do you prefer studying alone or with friends?
5 Do you like listening to music while you study? If so, what kind of music?
6 What do you do to help you remember new information you have learnt in class?
7 What different ways have you found helpful in learning new vocabulary?
8 Do you have a good dictionary? If so, what is it? Why do you like it?
9 Have you used any good grammar books? If so, what were they? Why did you like them?
10 What contact with English do you/could you have outside the classroom? (Think about the skills of listening, speaking, reading and writing.)

Grammar: gerunds and infinitives

1 Look at the following sentences and decide which are grammatically correct and which are not. Correct those which you think are wrong.

1 He <u>decided</u> planning his first break.
2 I <u>like</u> to study with friends.
3 I <u>hate</u> revising for exams.
4 She <u>wants</u> buying a good dictionary.
5 He <u>promised</u> to work all night.
6 He <u>keeps</u> failing his exams. It's terrible.
7 Have you <u>considered</u> to leave school at sixteen?
8 Simon <u>admitted</u> cheating in the exam.
9 He <u>began</u> to answer the question without making a plan.

2 Look at the verbs in Exercise 1 that are underlined and how they are used. Then put each of them into one of the following categories.

Verbs + infinitive (with *to*)	Verbs + *-ing* form	Verbs + infinitive or *-ing* form

Grammar reference p.167 (7)

3 Here are some more verbs. Make sure that you understand the meaning of each one and then put them in the correct category above.

agree   arrange   avoid   can't stand   choose
continue   deny   enjoy   expect   fail   hope
intend   manage   mind   offer   plan   prefer
pretend   promise   refuse   remember   seem
stop   suggest   try

— **Watch Out!** *to mind* ◄

A: Would you mind closing the window?
B: No, not at all.

Is B happy to close the window?

4 Look at these pairs of sentences and decide if there is a significant difference in meaning. If you think there is a difference, say what it is.

1 She stopped to have lunch.
  She stopped having lunch.

2 I'd like to have a coffee at 11a.m.
  I like to have a coffee at 11a.m.

3 I began to read that book last night.
  I began reading that book last night.

4 I remembered to lock the front door.
  I remembered locking the front door.

5 She prefers working in the evenings.
  She prefers to work in the evenings.

6 He tried learning ten new words every day.
  He tried to learn ten new words every day.

5 Look at the words in Columns A, B and C and write five complete sentences using one word from each column.

EXAMPLE: *She agreed to marry her boyfriend.*

A		B		C
admit	agree	buy	give	elephant
arrange	avoid	go	have	boss
begin	continue	kill	like	boyfriend
decided	denied	marry	start	business
offered	refused	stay	steal	new Rolls Royce
suggest	try	wash	school	

6 Now look back at all the verbs that you put into categories in Exercises 2 and 3 and invent a story as a class. The story begins:

It had been a very exciting day for George ...

Each student should add one new sentence which includes one of the verbs you have studied. Each verb can only be used once.

1 Punctuate the following sentences.

1 we need eggs tomatoes and some rice
2 how do you say teacher in italian
3 do you think hes good looking she asked
4 first of all in my opinion we should ban smoking in all public places
5 sarah has lived in argentina since she was a child
6 dont give him the gun she screamed

2 What words are being defined in each of the following sentences?

1 A child who misses school without a good reason.
2 The qualification you get if you succeed at university.
3 The school year is divided into three of these.
4 Where school children can play during breaks.
5 The opposite of 'to pass an exam'.
6 What you should do before an exam to help you remember information.
7 The type of school for children between three and five years old.
8 A phrasal verb which means 'to learn'.
9 To try and see another student's answers during an exam.
10 The piece of paper a school sends parents which contains a child's grades and the comments of the teachers.
11 A phrasal verb which means 'not to punish'.

3 Write a short description of your experience of school like the one in Vocabulary Exercise 2, page 61.

4 Complete the following sentences using an appropriate past tense.

EXAMPLE: He/agree/meet/us/7.00 last night.
    He agreed to meet us at 7.00 last night.

1 They/pretend/not/notice him.
2 She/offer/give him/lift/airport.
3 He/deny/steal/woman's bag.
4 She/enjoy/sing/local rock band.
5 He/plan/leave/school/when/he/be sixteen.
6 They/promise/bring/car/back/the weekend.
7 I/remember/see/her/as/I/leave/disco.
8 They/suggest/go/back/Mike's house.
9 She/decide/be/nicer/him.
10 They/admit/cheat/the exam.

5 Look at the underlined words and decide if they are used in the correct form. Correct those that you think are wrong.

1 I'm very <u>unhealthy</u>. I don't do any exercise and I only eat junk food.
2 She's not <u>dissimilar</u> in appearance to her mother. They're both tall and fair.
3 I just don't have any <u>energetic</u>. I'm tired all the time.
4 I don't believe it's possible to measure <u>intelligent</u>.
5 We need more <u>scientific</u> equipment for the Physics department.
6 Could I borrow your <u>calculation</u>? The battery in mine has run out.
7 This pen is <u>useless</u>. It doesn't write properly.

6 In the following conversation the speakers have made five mistakes with the language of giving opinions and agreeing/disagreeing. Find the mistakes and correct them.

A: Did you hear the government is going to introduce national exams for seven-year-olds?
B: Yes, I did and from my opinion it's a big mistake. Children should be learning at school, not worrying about passing exams.
A: I'm not really agree with you. Don't you think it's important for parents to know how well their children are doing at school? And it's also a way of judging how well the teachers are doing.
B: I don't agree on all. Firstly, parents get reports every term about the progress of their child. And secondly, just because the pupils of some teachers don't do very well, this does not mean that the teachers aren't doing their job.
A: I suppose I agree down to a point, but I still don't think it's such a bad idea.
B: Well, as far I'm concerned, it's the worst idea this government has ever had.

The price of fame

Reading

1 Discuss the following questions.

1 Who is your favourite actress/actor? Why do you like her/him?
2 Do you know the actor in this photo? What films is he famous for? Do you know anything else about him?

2 Read the following text and make a note of one thing that you did not know which surprises you.

Super-Brats

1 Macaulay Culkin is now undisputed king of the Hollywood super-brats, the cute kids who are making a fortune at the box office.

He has played Nintendo games with Michael Jackson and has dated a supermodel. 'Mack' as he is known to his friends, helped 20th Century
10 Fox take an incredible $507 million for *Home Alone*, which went on to become one of the biggest grossing films of all time. Culkin played Kevin McCallister, the angelic child who's mistakenly left behind by his parents when they go off to Europe for Christmas. Both hands clapped to his cheeks, eyes and mouth wide with fright, Mack's signature
20 'Aaaaaaaaaahhhh!' scream face was copied by children across the world months after the movie had left town. Writer/producer John Hughes says, 'Kids really liked it because Kevin was like them. He didn't have

superhuman powers. He foiled the burglars with plain old stuff from around the house.'

Macaulay's personal fortune is
30 now valued at around $1m for every year he's spent on earth, but ... 'I'm just like every other kid,' claims Mack. 'When I'm not doing movies I go out with my friends and do things any normal kid would do: go to a video arcade or go get pizza. I don't get an allowance, but whenever I need money I go, "Mom, Mom, can I get ten bucks for pizza?" She goes,
40 "Sure, sure, sure.", but it's not always "Sure, sure, sure." I have chores, I wake up every day at seven. Then I try to wake up for half an hour. Then I walk the dog for twenty minutes, that's my favourite. I miss my family when I'm away filming. My younger brothers and sisters love *Home Alone*, but I don't think they realise I'm in it.'
50 However, as LA-based psychologist Dan Rosenthal points out, 'Showbiz children are under an

incredible amount of pressure to achieve. First off there's the auditions. Parents push their kids into attending way too many of them, often when they should be in school or doing their homework or playing baseball or whatever.'
60 Rosenthal claims he has often seen children pushed to nervous breakdowns by starstruck parents. 'The most disturbing aspect of all this is when parents make a child feel inadequate when they fail to get parts. Kids can't cope.' He also describes how plastic surgery is becoming increasingly common among pre-teens. 'Foolish parents or
70 unscrupulous casting agents sometimes believe that if only little Mary had a nose job, she could have any part she wanted. The long-term psychological effects show that it's simply not worth it. In fact, I often advise child clients to choose a nice risk-free career like insurance instead.'

from *Time Out* magazine

3 Now read the text again and choose the correct alternative for each question. (See page 64 for advice on how to do multiple choice questions.)

1 In *Home Alone* Macaulay Culkin plays a child who

A goes to Europe on holiday with his parents.
B is deliberately deserted by his parents.
C has nightmares.
D finds himself on his own by chance.

2 John Hughes thinks children liked the film because the main character

A was just a typical everyday kid.
B wasn't very clever.
C got on well with burglars.
D was very strong.

3 Macaulay Culkin

A earns $1m a year.
B has over $5m.
C earns $1m a film.
D has under $5m.

4 When he needs money, Macaulay Culkin just asks his mother and

A she gives him what he wants.
B she gives him what he wants as long as it is for food.
C she gives him what he wants if he does some work around the house.
D she may or may not give him what he wants.

5 The psychologist Dan Rosenthal thinks

A showbiz children are generally too ambitious.
B the children's fame has a bad effect on their relationships with their parents.
C the children's parents are often largely to blame for the children's problems.
D parents feel inadequate if their children don't do well.

6 Rosenthal thinks plastic surgery

A should be avoided by everyone.
B can help children get parts, but that it's not worth the expense.
C is a waste of time for showbiz children.
D is not only a waste of time, but will also have a bad effect on the children in later life.

7 *unscrupulous* in *line 70* means

A not hard-working.
B not caring about honesty or fairness.
C not interested in financial gain.
D not patient.

8 *it* in *line 74* refers to

A a nose job.
B a psychological effect.
C a part in a film.
D life in general.

4 Discuss the following questions.

1 What feelings do you have about Macaulay Culkin – envy/admiration/pity/irritation? Do you think he is 'just like every other kid'?
2 What problems do you think that being a child star can cause the individuals concerned?
3 Do you think it is right that individual film/pop/sports stars can earn so much money?

Vocabulary: entertainment

1 Fill in the gaps in the following sentences with an appropriate word. You have been given the first part of each word and the number of letters.

1 I like sitting in the front r–– in the cinema because I like to be really near the scr–––.
2 The best sc––– in the film is where she escapes.
3 He is a great dir–––––– and really inspires his act–––.
4 In general the pl–– was quite original, but the en–––– was terrible. Everyone got married and they all lived happily ever after!
5 It's the first Shakespeare pl–– I have seen in the th–––––.
6 My aud––––– went very well. They gave me the pa––. Reh–––––––– start on Monday. It's all very exciting!
7 The first per–––––––– is in eight weeks' time.
8 Some of the cri––––– from the top newspapers were there. I hope the rev––––– will be good. They should be. The aud––––– app–––––– for ages.
9 We went to a wonderful con–––– last night. It was a new sym––––– by that Russian com–––––. He actually con–––––– the orc–––––– himself.
10 They are my favourite pop gr–––. I've got their last album on cass––––. I really like the lead sin––– and the bass guit––––– in particular.

2 Describe the last film/concert/opera/play that you went to. What was it like? Did you enjoy it? Why?/Why not?

Function: giving advice

- *In fact, I often advise child clients to choose a nice risk-free career like insurance instead.*

1 Read the sentence above taken from the text on Macaulay Culkin and decide which of the following are possible 'direct speech' versions. Correct any grammatical errors that you find.

You should to You ought to If I were you, I would You really must You would better It would be a good idea if you	choose a nice risk-free career like insurance instead.

2 Look at the following situations and write one or two sentences of advice for each of them, using some of the different forms above.

1 A friend of yours wants to learn English as quickly as possible, but needs advice about what to do to be most effective.
2 A friend of yours wants to lose a lot of weight very quickly.
3 A friend, who is a parent, has a 10-year-old daughter who has just starred in a successful film and looks like she will do more film work.
   or
4 Choose your own situation in which you have to give a friend advice.

3 Divide the following expressions into two groups according to whether they are used to:

a) accept advice
b) reject advice

1 That's a really good idea.
2 Actually, I've already tried that.
3 Yes, you're quite right, I should.
4 I'm not sure that's such a good idea.
5 I couldn't possibly do that!

4 Now work with a partner and roleplay one or two of the situations in Exercise 2. Use a variety of expressions for giving and accepting/rejecting advice.

Grammar: Present Perfect

1 Discuss the following questions.

1 What famous person/people do you like/admire? Why?
2 Who is the most famous person you have ever met or seen 'in the flesh'?
3 What films have you seen recently? Describe the plot of one of them and say what you liked/disliked about it.

2 In general we use the Present Perfect to refer to things that have happened between some time in the past and now.

Match each of the following examples of the Present Perfect Simple with a definition of its use below.

1 I have met one famous person in my life, and that was Tom Cruise.
2 I have just spoken to Linda. She wasn't very happy.
3 I have known Pete for ages.
4 I have lived here since 1993.
5 I have watched every match they have played since I was a boy.
6 Oh no! Someone has spilt Coca-Cola all over the living room carpet.

a) With 'state' verbs e.g. *be, believe,* etc.
b) When we can see a present result of past actions.
c) When we talk about experience, that is things that have happened at some time in our lives.
d) When we are describing situations that have continued from some time in the past until now.
e) When we are describing repeated actions that have continued from some time in the past until now.
f) When we are describing recent events (but we don't say exactly when they happened).

Grammar reference p.175 (17.3)

3 Opposite is a letter that a student studying in London wrote back to an English friend living in his country. This student is still having problems with tenses, particularly the Present Perfect. Find the mistakes so the student can correct the letter before he sends it!

43 Belvedere Mansions,
Kensington,
London SW3.
20/1/98

Dear Robin,

Well, as you can see, I finally got to England. I am here now since January 10th and it was all being wonderful!

I have stayed with a very nice family who are looking after me very well. I have had my own room with an ensuite bathroom and a comfortable chair, a desk to work at and even a TV (very good for my English!).

I did lots of things since I arrived. I was visited Buckingham Palace, been to Camden Market (where I bought lots of clothes!) and seen the waxworks at Madame Tussaud's, which were incredible (so life-like!).

The other great thing is the school where I have studied. My teacher is very friendly and the other students are also very nice. We have all been out together a couple of times to a restaurant, which was great.

I watch TV every night since I arrived. It's quite difficult to understand but I'm getting used to it. Something I am <u>not</u> getting used to is the weather, which had been crazy. One minute it is raining, the next minute, brilliant sunshine. You never know what to wear!

Well, that's about it for now. I'll write again soon.

Best wishes,
Ahmet

4

1 Practise using the Present Perfect Simple to find out about another student. Look at the shapes below. Student A should follow the instructions on page 186, and Student B the instructions on page 190.
2 Look at what your partner has written in each of the shapes and guess what the significance of what they have written is. Your partner should say if you are right.
3 Now ask questions beginning *How long ...?*, *What ...?*, *Why ...?*, *Where ...?*, etc. to find out more about what they have written.

5 Discuss the following questions.

1 What is in the News at the moment?
2 What important things have happened in your country and abroad recently?

6 Look at the following pairs of sentences. What is the difference in meaning between a) and b)? Why is the Present Perfect Simple or Continuous used in each case?

1 a) I've read that book.
   b) I've been reading that book.
2 a) He's cut down that tree.
   b) He's been cutting down trees.
3 a) They've lived in Athens all their lives.
   b) They've been living in Athens for the last two years.
4 a) I've written six letters this morning.
   b) I've been writing letters all morning.

7 Look again at the example sentences above and decide which one of the following rules about the Present Perfect Continuous is not true.

We use the Present Perfect Continuous when we want to:

a) indicate that a situation or activity has been temporary.
b) emphasise the continuation of an activity, that is not yet finished.
c) describe a repeated activity.
d) describe a completed action (something that has finished).

Grammar reference p.176 (17.4)

8 The following dialogue contains a number of examples of the Present Perfect Simple. Which of them should be changed to the Present Perfect Continuous to make the conversation sound more natural?

HELEN: Hi! How are you? I haven't seen you for ages. What have you done?

ANNE: Oh, not much, but I did get a job!

HELEN: Really! Where?

ANNE: At the big supermarket near the church. I've worked there for about six weeks now ... But what about you? You look great, really fit!

HELEN: Yes, well, I've played a lot of sport recently and I had a week's holiday in the south of Spain.

ANNE: Have you heard from Alan at all?

HELEN: No, it's funny. I've tried to contact him, but I keep getting an answerphone message. It's very irritating. I've phoned him at least five times.

9 Work with a partner and roleplay the following situation. Use the Present Perfect Continuous where appropriate.

Student A *is a tenant in a block of flats. She/he is not at all happy because of the behaviour of one of the other tenants.*

Student B *is the landlady/landlord of the block of flats.*

Student A should go and see Student B and explain what has been happening and why she/he is not happy. Here are some examples of what she/he might want to complain about:
- loud music late at night
- DIY noises (hammering, sawing, etc.) on Sundays
- constant rows and shouting
- rubbish left in the corridors
- children drawing graffiti on the walls

Student B should listen to Student A's complaints and then say what she/he can or can't do about each one.

Exam focus

Paper 2 Writing (a report)

In Paper 2 you may be asked to write a report of some kind. This may involve you assessing good and bad points of something and making a recommendation. To answer this question well it is particularly important that you:

- organise your report appropriately.
- do exactly what the question asks.
- use appropriate linking expressions.

1

1 Before you write a report, join the following two clauses in as many different ways as possible. You should use the linking words and expressions below, paying attention to word order and punctuation.

> he is rich and famous/he isn't happy

- but
- even though/although
- however
- in spite of/despite
- on the one hand ..., but on the other hand ...

Grammar reference p.169 (9.4/9.5/9.6)

2 Complete the following sentences in an appropriate way.
   a) The seats in the theatre were comfortable, but ...
   b) He wanted to be a famous actor. However, ...
   c) She refused to star in his new film despite the fact that ...
   d) On the one hand he enjoyed being recognised in the street, but ...
   e) Although the film received good reviews in the press, ...
   f) In spite of needing a holiday, she decided to ...

3 Now write each of your sentences again, using one of the other linking expressions.

2

1 Read the following question which asks you to write a report.

> You recently started to work in local tourism and you had to visit a new tourist attraction (for example, theatre, museum or disco) in your area. Now you must write a report for your boss.
>
> Write your report in 120–180 words describing the attraction, what it has to offer to tourists and commenting on its good and bad points.

2 Look at the following answer to the question and fill in the gaps with appropriate linking words.

To: Michael Fenton
From: Sandra Woods
Re: The Leicester Square Disco Palace

As requested I visited the new disco, which is becoming increasingly popular with young foreign tourists. Below is a summary of the most important relevant points with some recommendations.

1. The general facilities in the disco are extremely good. There is a large dance area with a video screen, adjoining bar and upstairs restaurant. (1) _____, given the large numbers of customers, the number of toilets (at present one men's and one women's) needs to be increased.

2. (2) _____ the actual music is played at a reasonable volume and seems to be appreciated by the audience, I was concerned that it was very limited in range (only current hit singles).

3. The restaurant was rather expensive, but (3) _____ this, the quality of the food was not at all good and the service was slow and occasionally rude.

Conclusion
This is a generally well-run and attractive disco. I predict it will become increasingly popular in time. I do recommend, (4)_____, that we speak to the director about:
a) the range of music (perhaps suggest a '60's night' or a '70's night')
b) the prices and general standard of the restaurant.

3 Now you are going to write a report on a local tourist attraction in your area. Follow this procedure:

- Note the key points in the instructions. (Remember you were asked what it has to offer to tourists and to comment on its good and bad points.)
- Think of the various areas to consider (for example, if it's a theatre, how close to the centre of town, general condition of theatre, price of tickets, frequency of performances, types of plays performed, comfort of seats, interval facilities, etc.)
- Note the good and bad points under each area.
- Write your report in 120–180 words following the layout in the report opposite. Start each numbered paragraph with a general point and use the various expressions you practised above to link good and bad points. Finish with your conclusion and recommendations.
- Check to see that you have covered the main points in the instructions and that you have written about the right number of words.

Speaking

MOMI is the *Museum of the Moving Image* in London. Imagine you have gone to the Museum with some friends. You have seen the first part of the Museum (sections 1–10), but there are still thirty sections that you have not seen. Unfortunately, there is only an hour left before the museum closes. Work with a partner and choose eight more sections to go and see.

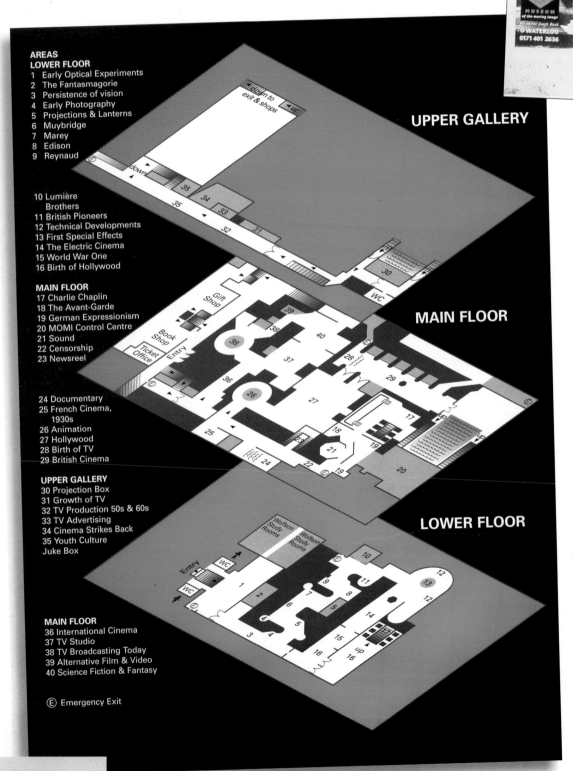

AREAS

LOWER FLOOR
1 Early Optical Experiments
2 The Fantasmagorie
3 Persistence of vision
4 Early Photography
5 Projections & Lanterns
6 Muybridge
7 Marey
8 Edison
9 Reynaud

10 Lumière
    Brothers
11 British Pioneers
12 Technical Developments
13 First Special Effects
14 The Electric Cinema
15 World War One
16 Birth of Hollywood

MAIN FLOOR
17 Charlie Chaplin
18 The Avant-Garde
19 German Expressionism
20 MOMI Control Centre
21 Sound
22 Censorship
23 Newsreel

24 Documentary
25 French Cinema,
    1930s
26 Animation
27 Hollywood
28 Birth of TV
29 British Cinema

UPPER GALLERY
30 Projection Box
31 Growth of TV
32 TV Production 50s & 60s
33 TV Advertising
34 Cinema Strikes Back
35 Youth Culture
Juke Box

MAIN FLOOR
36 International Cinema
37 TV Studio
38 TV Broadcasting Today
39 Alternative Film & Video
40 Science Fiction & Fantasy

Ⓔ Emergency Exit

UPPER GALLERY

MAIN FLOOR

LOWER FLOOR

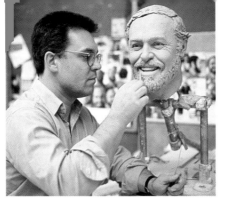

Use of English

1 Work with a partner and describe what you can see in the photos opposite.

2 Read the text below to find out where the photos were taken.

3 Read the text again and fill in the gaps with an appropriate word. Seven of the words you need are in the box below.

| the | enough | to | on | with |
| had | by | | | |

Madame Tussaud's is London's

(1) .... visited tourist attraction, with over two and a half million visitors a year. There are over 400 models (2) .... display. Each one is worth £20,000, so security is tight. However, (3) .... the monitors and eagle-eyed staff, visitors can't resist picking up souvenirs and someone even went off (4) .... Marie Antoinette's head.

Making the wax models is a highly skilled and lengthy process. From start to finish (5) .... takes months of work for the artists and craftsmen who combine to produce the final figure. All the waxworks are life-size replicas of the real person, down to the last detail. Even Michael Jackson's inside trouser leg (6) .... been measured and recorded. This is considered highly classified information, of course.

Stuart Williamson, a sculptor here for fifteen years, says, '(7) .... they come to the museum or we go to them. We went to Buckingham Palace to do the Royal Family and the Neverland Ranch for Jackson. They sit on a turntable where they (8) .... measured and photographed from every angle possible.

I then sculpt the clay, trying to get a feel for their personality, which is (9) .... important as what they look like.'

The most nerve-racking part of the job can be when the real person meets their wax double. Bob Geldof thought that he wasn't scruffy (10) .... and proceeded to ruffle his twin's hair. The Dalai Lama thought the whole thing was hilariously funny.

Clothes for the models are often chosen (11) .... the famous themselves. Madame Tussaud's has the only exact replica of Princess Diana's wedding dress. Sometimes clothes (12) .... given to the museum. John Haigh, the acid bath murderer, donated his suit (13) .... day before he was executed. And when comedian, Lenny Henry, revisited Madame Tussaud's, he was horrified to see his wax double wearing his favourite pink suit – he (14) .... been looking for it for two years.

The public's fascination with fame and fortune means Madame Tussaud's will continue to be a popular venue for many years (15) .... come. ■

Listening: stagefright

1   You are going to hear an extract from a radio programme looking at the problem of stagefright. Before you listen, discuss the following questions.

1   What is stagefright?
2   What are some of the physical symptoms of stagefright?

2   Look at the following statements and listen to the programme. Which of the four people interviewed, Helen, Steve, Gavin and Colin, does each one refer to? There is one extra statement which does not apply to any of them.

1   She/he has no memory of what exactly happened in one performance.
2   She/he thought about saying 'Sorry' to the people watching.
3   She/he generally feels ill before a performance.
4   She/he actually fainted at the beginning of a performance.
5   She/he was so nervous that she/he tried to think of a way to stop the performance.

3   Fill in the gaps in the following sentences with the correct form of the word in brackets. All the words are in the interview you have just listened to.

1   I have never felt such .... – I thought I was going to faint. (TERRIFIED)
2   Just because it is a .... problem, it does not make it any easier to live with. (PSYCHOLOGY)
3   She always has these terrible .... attacks, just before an exam. (ANXIOUS)
4   You shouldn't be .... of the dog. He's very friendly really. (FRIGHT)
5   In one .... I was in, the star of the show fell off the stage. (PRODUCE)
6   She's a very experienced .... She's been doing it for years. (PERFORM)
7   He's a .... football player and has been one for many years. (PROFESSION)
8   It was so cold and we didn't have any blankets so we .... at night. (FREEZE)

Speaking

Discuss the following questions.

1   What things make you afraid?

2   Do you have any memories of bad experiences with any of these things? What happened?

   • looking down from a great height
   • spiders
   • small, enclosed spaces e.g. lifts
   • the dentist
   • exams
   • snakes

3   Choose one fear that you have talked about. What advice would you give to someone who wanted to overcome this particular fear?

1 Read the following text and choose the correct alternative to fill each gap.

As a child my parents were very keen to take me to lots of classical (1) .... playing all the great (2) .... like Beethoven and Bach. I used to hate them. We usually used to sit right in the front (3) .... and to stay awake I would mentally choose one member of the (4) .... and stare at him until he went red with embarrassment. The best time was when one (5) .... was getting so excited that his wig slipped off!

Nowadays I much prefer going to the cinema. I hope to be a great film (6) .... one day or at least a (7) .... for a good film magazine. My girlfriend is an actress and at the moment has got a small (8) .... in a (9) .... in London. They had their first night last week. It was really exciting and the (10) .... applauded for ages.

1 **A** musicals **B** concerts **C** shows
   D performances
2 **A** composers **B** writers **C** artists
   D musicians
3 **A** line **B** aisle **C** row **D** queue
4 **A** band **B** soloist **C** group **D** orchestra
5 **A** conductor **B** inspector **C** manager
   D leader
6 **A** manager **B** production **C** director
   D organiser
7 **A** critic **B** criticise **C** criticism **D** critical
8 **A** section **B** bit **C** part **D** scene
9 **A** play **B** theatre **C** stage **D** act
10 **A** supporters **B** viewers **C** onlookers
   D audience

2 Choose the correct alternative in each sentence.

1 I like him *although/in spite of* he is often mean with money.
2 You can watch TV now, *but/however* you must do some homework later.
3 He's good-looking, but *on the other hand/ although* he is very selfish.
4 *In spite/Despite* the fact that it was raining, they decided to go to the park.
5 He really liked the film. *However/Even though*, he couldn't afford to buy the video.
6 *Although/In spite of* training really hard, he didn't get chosen for the team.

3 Fill in the gaps in the following sentences with a correct form of the verbs in brackets. Use the Present Perfect Simple, Present Perfect Continuous, Past Simple or Present Simple.

1 I .... *(be)* in this school for one and a half years now.
2 He .... *(play)* football regularly for many years when he was younger.
3 Where have you .... *(play)*? You're covered in mud!
4 He .... *(not/give)* me back the money he borrowed yet.
5 We .... *(visit)* her whenever we can.
6 I .... *(know)* them since I was a child.
7 I .... *(lift)* heavy boxes all morning and now I need a rest.
8 When .... *(you/get)* my letter?
9 She .... *(live)* in my flat since June.
10 That man .... *(watch)* us for the last twenty minutes.

4 Read the following reply to a letter sent to the problem page of a magazine.

1 Decide what the original problem was.
2 Decide if each line of the letter is grammatically correct or if there is an extra incorrect word that should not be there.

1 Clearly at your age, this kind of rule seems quite
2 unreasonable. Despite of this, it is important to realise
3 that your father is just being a concerned parent. He is
4 obviously worried so that you might not be safe if you
5 stay out so late. On the other hand, he really must
6 be understand that he can't treat you like a child all your
7 life. It might be a good idea if you could to find some sort
8 of compromise. For example, you could go and come back
9 with a good friend who your father knows and trusts. If I
10 were being you, I would have a quiet word with your
11 mother about this as well she is clearly sympathetic to how
12 you feel if even though she seems to be supporting your father.

Looking good

Speaking

1 Look at the photos and discuss the following questions.

1 What do you think of the styles in the photos?
2 What decades do you think they come from (the 1920s, the 1930s, etc.)?

2 You are going to hear a famous song. Listen and answer these questions.

1 Which photo would you associate with this type of music?
2 What do you think the title of the song is?

3 Listen to the song again and put the lines of the verses in the correct order. You have been given the first line of each verse.

Verse 1
Well, you can do anything
But don't you step on my blue suede shoes
Two for the show
Now go, cat, go
Well, it's one for the money *(1)*
But stay off my blue suede shoes
Three to get ready

Verse 2
And don't you step on my blue suede shoes
Step on my face
But uh-huh honey lay off* them shoes
Slander** my name all over the place
But stay off my blue suede shoes
Well, do anything that you want to do
Let's go, cats
Well, you can knock me down *(1)*
Well, you can do anything

*lay off = don't touch
**to slander = to say bad things about

4 Discuss the following questions.

1 What kind of clothes do you generally wear to school or work/to go out with friends in the evening/around the house at weekends?
2 Do you prefer any particular kind of clothes?
3 Do you have a piece of clothing that you particularly like wearing?

Vocabulary: clothes

1 Put the words in the box below into one of the following categories.

Types of clothes	Types of shoe	Accessories	Patterns

> belt sandals jacket anorak pullover skirt cardigan trainers
> plain slippers brooch T-shirt vest tights socks shorts
> Wellington boots earrings bow-tie waistcoat striped suit
> raincoat bracelet checked blouse dress high-heeled shoes
> dungarees sweatshirt leggings pyjamas braces scarf

2 Describe some of the items above to a partner, who should tell you their names.

EXAMPLE: A: *You wear it around your neck to keep warm or to look nice.*
B: *A scarf.*

3 Look around the class. Can you name what the other students are wearing?

Watch Out! *suit/fit/go with*

1 This coat doesn't *fit/suit/go with* you. It's the wrong colour.
2 The tie doesn't *fit/suit/go with* this shirt. It needs to be plain.
3 The sweater doesn't *fit/suit/go with* me. I need a larger size.

What is the correct alternative in each sentence?

---

4 Work with a partner.

Student A: look at the pictures opposite. They are in a jumbled order. Listen to Student B describe each picture and then number them according to the description you hear.

Student B: look at the pictures on page 186. Say the number of the picture and then describe it for Student A.

Reading

1 Look at the woman in the picture. Who is she and why is she famous?

2 Read the introduction to the article opposite. What two things has the woman in the picture done in addition to being a model?

3 Divide into two groups, A and B. Group A should read Part A of the article and Group B should turn to page 186 and read Part B. Answer as many of the following questions as you can from the information in your part of the article.

1 How old was Naomi when she became a model?
2 What surprises Terry O'Neill about supermodels?
3 What does Naomi have in common with Jackie Onassis and Princess Diana?
4 How long has Naomi been interested in dance, music, etc.?
5 What are Naomi's main free-time activities?
6 What are some of the negative characteristics people say Naomi has?
7 Why does James Collard think that Naomi cannot be stupid?

SUPERMODEL SENSATION

Following her runaway success as supermodel, her infamous debut as novelist and her decision to make an album, Naomi Campbell, it seems, can turn her hand to anything ...

by JAMES COLLARD

> Part A

1 As **I** walk to my date with Naomi Campbell at the Halcyon Hotel, I reflect on the oddity of this girl's life – a model at 15, a success in New York at 16 and now, at the tender age of 23, touring the major European capitals promoting her novel *Swan* and her album *Babywoman*. Naomi, like Jackie and
10 Diana, has joined that tiny elite club of women so famous and so talked about that **they** need only be known by their first names.

Sure enough, everyone I consult is happy to give an opinion about **her**, and in the same tones of absolute certainty people use when they're telling you the time. 'Naomi is always late.', 'She must be very
20 stupid.', 'I bet she's really pushy.' and so on. **She** must, however, be able to charm even at long distance, because I was already wanting to defend her before we'd even met.

Naomi may have a fiery temper at times (who doesn't?), but it is universally accepted that she can be delightful – when she wants to be, some might add. But I'm greeted
30 with a dazzling smile and quiet, almost old-fashioned courtesy. Eager to put her at her ease, I tell her that I enjoyed her novel (it is unputdownable!) and that I found the album impressive. 'I was surprised,' I add, 'to find myself thinking that maybe models aren't all stupid, you know what I mean?'

'Yeah, absolutely. The idea that us models have no brains at all, no
40 intelligence, that we can't make decisions, we can't even speak – that's just ridiculous. I don't care because I'm not like **that**, and what they say mustn't stop me from doing what I want to do.'

I, for one, don't see how anyone who so clearly knows how to work the system can be considered stupid. And to have survived so well, she
50 must indeed have had to have been very strong. There may have been heated debate about the authorship of *Swan*: how much is Naomi, how much is the ghost writer, Caroline Upcher. But much of **it** is recognisably Naomi's voice, especially when it describes the shock of a young, black model plucked from obscurity in south
60 London and obliged to get smart quick in the New York fashion world at an age when most of us are feeling shy at the school disco. Naomi agrees **it** was a shock.

'But I loved it, I don't regret a day. I was very lucky. I've got nothing to complain about, and I wouldn't want to change it particularly. The only thing was I
70 had to grow up tremendously fast, to get the know-how. Yes, I maybe missed out on some of the 16–20 thing, but I wanted a career and you can't have both. Understood.'

from Attitude magazine

8 What was a shock for Naomi in the early days of her career?
9 Why doesn't Naomi want children yet?
10 What does Naomi say she had to give up in order to have a career?

4 Now work in A/B pairs and tell your partner about the answers to the questions in your part of the article.

5 Look through the complete article again (both Parts A and B) and identify what each pronoun in **bold** is referring to.

6 Discuss whether you feel the writer of this article is:

a) critical of Naomi Campbell.
b) sympathetic towards Naomi Campbell.
c) has no particular feeling towards Naomi Campbell.

Give reasons for your opinions.

Vocabulary: phrasal verbs (*give*)

- *I'll never **give up** travelling altogether.*

1

1 Match the two halves of these sentences containing phrasal verbs with *give*.

1	If you don't *give up* eating sweets,	a)	that eventually he *gave in* and said I could go.
2	I asked him so many times	b)	when you have finished with them.
3	That fire *gives off*	c)	all these old clothes to charity.
4	The teacher *gave out*	d)	the compositions they had written the night before.
5	The big smile on his face	e)	you are going to get terribly fat.
6	Don't forget to *give back* the keys	f)	*gave away* how happy he was.
7	I'm going to *give away*	g)	an incredible amount of heat.

2 Now match each phrasal verb with one of the following meanings.

1	to produce	5	to donate
2	to agree/surrender	6	to stop
3	to show/reveal	7	to return
4	to distribute		

Writing: describing people

1 In Paper 2 you may be asked to write a description of a person. Read the question below and then the answer opposite. In seven lines of the answer there is an extra incorrect word which should not be there. Find the extra word and correct the lines.

> A local radio station is running a *Best Friend of the Year* competition. To enter, you must write a short composition describing someone you really like.

1 I suppose the first thing one notices about Sarah is her long black hair and her dark brown eyes. She has a lovely smile and doesn't generally wear much make-up. She's not very much tall, but she is quite slim and has got some very slender arms and hands.

2 What I particularly like about her is the way she thinks of carefully about what she says and always makes interesting, intelligent comments. She's got a great sense of humour and when I'm with her I can never stop to laughing. Once you get to know her a little, however, you realise that she is not as quite as confident as she first seems.

3 She loves wearing clothes from the 60s and has lots of long dresses with 'hippy' patterns and bead necklaces to go with them. She's also got some silver bracelets which she wears all the time and you always know where she is because you can to hear them clinking together!

4 The most distinctive thing about her is her laugh. She is actually a very cheerful person and she has a very optimistic view of the world. After I've been with her for a little while I am always feel great!

2 Find words in the text which have similar meanings to the following words/phrases.

1	fairly (*para. 1*)	6	initially (*para. 2*)
2	especially (*para. 2*)	7	appears (*para. 2*)
3	remarks (*para. 2*)	8	adores (*para. 3*)
4	marvellous (*para. 2*)	9	numerous (*para. 3*)
5	a bit (*para. 2*)	10	in fact (*para. 4*)

3 Now write a description of someone you admire in 120–180 words. First, underline any words or expressions from the above text that you think you might find useful. Decide how you are going to organise your article in paragraphs. You may wish to include sections on:

- physical appearance
- special characteristics
- personality
- clothes

Grammar: *used to/would*

1   There is a mistake in each of the following sentences. Correct each sentence with an appropriate form of *used to* or *would*.

1   Dance use to be my main subject.
2   Did you used to play basketball?
3   I am not used to work such long hours.
4   He is getting used living in the city.
5   My father was played football with me every weekend.
6   I would to walk to church with my parents every Sunday.
7   I would really love playing tennis when I was younger.

2   Look at the sentences you corrected in Exercise 1 and decide which of the following rules apply to the structures below. More than one rule may apply to each structure.

1   We use it to talk about repeated or regular actions in the past which do not happen now.
2   We use it to talk about past states.
3   We use it to say how accustomed we are to a (new) situation.

a)   *used to* + infinitive (without *to*)
b)   *be/get used to* + *-ing* form
c)   *would* + infinitive (without *to*)

Grammar reference p.177 (18)

3   Fill in the gaps in the following sentences with <u>one</u> word. (Contractions count as one word.)

1   They used .... have a small house in the country.
2   She really isn't used to .... to school on her own.
3   I can't .... used to my new Maths teacher. She's so different from my last teacher.
4   We .... spend hours just drinking coffee and talking. But that was years ago.
5   I .... slowly getting used to these glasses, but they are still a little uncomfortable.
6   I .... use to have such long hair.
7   He .... never let me do the things that I wanted to do.

4   Choose five different years in your past, for example when you were seven, nine, eleven, thirteen and fifteen years old. Then write sentences to describe routines or states that were true then, but are no longer true now.

EXAMPLE: *When I was thirteen, I **used to play** a lot of volleyball, but I don't anymore.*

5   You are going to play *Lifeswap*. In *Lifeswap* you live another person's life.

●   First choose someone you would like to exchange lives with e.g. Superman/a famous pop star/a TV personality/a good friend/another student in the class.

●   Write down what you imagine their typical daily routine to be.

●   Now imagine a week has passed. Tell your partner:
    a)   who you have been.
    b)   their typical routine.
    c)   which parts of their routine you have found it easy/difficult to get used to.

    EXAMPLE: *I have been Superman. I **am getting used to** flying around and catching criminals, but I **can't get used to** constantly chang**ing** my clothes in telephone boxes!*

Exam focus

Paper 3 Use of English (key word transformations)

1 In Part 3 of Paper 3 you will be asked to change a sentence so that it keeps the same meaning but using different words.

EXAMPLE:
John found it difficult to adjust to his new school.
used
John couldn't . *get used to* . his new school.

It is important to remember:
- not to change the key word in any way.
- not to change the parts of the second sentence which are given.
- to put in only the number of words required (probably 2–5 words).

2 Now do the same with these sentences which use some of the language you have studied in previous units. You have been given the exact number of words needed in each case.

1 Flying frightens many people.
   afraid
   Many people — — — flying.

2 It's very rare for me to go to the cinema.
   hardly
   I — — — — the cinema.

3 Jim has done more work than you.
   as
   You haven't done — — — — Jim.

4 I had imagined there were going to be many more people.
   far
   There were — — — — I had imagined.

5 He is similar in appearance to his father.
   like
   He — — his father.

6 I was advised to start swimming by my doctor.
   take
   My doctor advised me — — — swimming.

7 'I'm sure you stole that money,' he said.
   accused
   He — — — — the money.

8 I thought it would be a good idea if I went home.
   ought
   I thought — — — — home.

Listening: designer row

1 Listen to a conversation and decide why the people in the picture above are upset.

2 Now listen again and answer the following questions.

1 Why was Julie's mum pleased with what she bought?
2 What was wrong with what she bought?
3 What is Julie worried will happen to her at school?
4 Why does Julie become angry with her dad?

3 Discuss the following questions.

1 How important is it to you to be fashionably dressed? What are current fashions at the moment? Do you like to wear particular brands/makes of clothes?
2 How much do you think you can tell about a person from the clothes they wear?
3 How far is it true in life that there is 'one rule for grown-ups and another for kids'?

Vocabulary: body and health

1   How quickly can you write down the names of fifteen parts of the body? Compare your answers with the rest of the class and see if anyone had a word that no one else thought of.

2   Fill in the gaps in the following sentences with an appropriate part of the body. Then decide what the completed underlined idiom means.

1 He retired last year and now he has lots of <u>time on his</u> ....
2 Don't <u>put words in my</u> .... That isn't what I was going to say.
3 What's his name? Oh, how frustrating, it's <u>on the tip of my</u> ....
4 I've got a terribly <u>sweet</u> .... – I love sweets and chocolates.
5 He<u>'s got a</u> .... – coming round here after everything he said!
6 Look, we seem to have <u>got off on the wrong</u> .... Can we start again and be friends?
7 Why don't you tell me what the matter is? You'll feel better if you <u>get it off your</u> ....
8 He may not be very clever, but at least <u>his</u> .... <u>is in the right place.</u>

3   Choose the correct alternative in each sentence.

1 There were lots of people waiting to see the doctor in her *theatre/ward/surgery*.
2 I've got a terrible *pain/sore/hurt* in my left leg.
3 The doctor gave me this *receipt/prescription/recipe* for some painkillers.
4 This cut should *heal/cure/recover* soon.
5 You are very hot. Let me take your *heat/ fever/temperature*.
6 I fell over and *twisted/turned/slipped* my ankle.
7 Before you go on holiday, you are going to need some *punctures/stabs/injections*.
8 She's got a very *sore/raw/rough* throat and won't be able to sing.
9 The ambulancemen carried him away on a *bed/stretcher/hammock*.
10 It took him a long time to get *over/by/off* his illness.
11 She was covered in *spots/freckles/bruises* after she fell down the stairs.
12 Have we got any *Sellotape/plasters/blu-tac*? I've cut my finger.

4   Work in small groups and discuss the last time you were ill/in hospital/had an accident. What happened? How did you feel?

Reading

1   Look at the title of the article opposite and try to predict what it will be about.

2   The following words all appear in the article. Match each one with its correct definition on the right.

1 to giggle	a) to reduce or lessen pain or some other unpleasant feeling
2 to monitor	b) funny, amusing
3 to relieve	c) what the body uses to defend itself against things that enter it and cause disease
4 research	d) the treatment of illnesses of the mind or body without drugs or operations
5 humorous	e) to watch, listen to or examine what is happening
6 to stimulate	f) to make something more active or develop more quickly
7 immune system	g) to laugh in a silly, childish way
8 therapy	h) detailed study of a subject to find out something new

3   Now read the article and answer the following questions.

1 Do doctors now understand exactly how laughter helps?
2 Do people generally laugh more or less than before?
3 Is there any real evidence to suggest laughter helps?

Why laughter is the best medicine

*Our unserious side is being taken seriously by doctors.
Laughing helps you fight illness – and gets you fit. But how it works
is still being puzzled out.*

group of adults are lying in a circle on the floor listening to a recording of 'The Laughing Policeman'. At first everyone feels ridiculous and there's only the odd nervous giggle, but suddenly the laughter becomes real. It quickly spreads around the room until everyone is infected by it. **(1 ———)**

Doctors are starting to believe that laughter not only improves your state of mind, but actually affects your entire physical well-being. The people lying in a circle are attending a workshop to learn the forgotten art of laughter. **(2 ———)**

Britain's first laughter therapist, Robert Holden says: 'Instinctively we know that laughing helps us feel healthy and alive. Each time we laugh we feel better and more content.'

(3 ———) A French newspaper found that in 1930 the French laughed on average for nineteen minutes per day. By 1980 this had fallen to six minutes. Eighty per cent of the people questioned said that they would like to laugh more. Other research suggests that children laugh on average about 400 times a day, but by the time they reach adulthood this has been reduced to about fifteen times. **(4 ———)**

William Fry – a psychiatrist from California – studied the effects of laughter on the body. He got patients to watch Laurel and Hardy films, and monitored their blood pressure, heart rate and muscle tone. He found that laughter has a similar effect to physical exercise. It speeds up the heart rate, increases blood pressure and quickens breathing. **(5 ———)** Fry thinks laughter is a type of jogging on the spot.

Laughter can even provide a kind of pain relief. Fry has proved that laughter produces endorphins – chemicals in the body that relieve pain.

Researchers from Texas tested this. **(6 ———)** The first group listened to a funny cassette for twenty minutes, the second listened to a cassette intended to relax them, the third heard an informative tape, while the fourth group listened to no tape at all.

Researchers found that if they produced pain in the students, those who had listened to the humorous tape could tolerate the discomfort for much longer.

Patch Adams is both a doctor and a performing clown in Virginia, America. **(7 ———)** 'There's evidence to suggest that laughter stimulates the immune system,' says Adams, 'yet hospitals and clinics are well-known for their depressing atmospheres.' Adams practises what he preaches. He wears his waist-length hair in a ponytail and also has a handlebar moustache. He usually puts on a red nose when seeing patients.

4 The following sentences have been removed from the article. Decide in which numbered gap each one should go. (There is one extra sentence which you do not need to use.) See page 23 for a suggested procedure for this task type.

A Somewhere in the process of growing up we lose an astonishing 385 laughs a day.

B It also makes our facial and stomach muscles work.

C He is convinced that humour should be a part of every medical consultation.

D Some have even been referred by their family doctors.

E They divided forty university students into four groups.

F This will also help improve your personal relationships.

G But we could be losing our ability to laugh.

H This is laughter therapy in action.

Grammar: *can, could, may, might*

1 Complete the second sentence in each of the following pairs so that it has a similar meaning to the first.

1 a) But we could be losing our ability to laugh.
   b) But it is possible (that) we ...
2 a) Laughter can even provide a kind of pain relief.
   b) Laughter is even able ...
3 a) Those who had listened to the humorous tape could tolerate the discomfort for much longer.
   b) Those who had listened to the humorous tape were ...
4 a) Anyone may attend the workshop.
   b) Anyone is allowed ...

2 Rephrase each of the following sentences using *possible, allowed* or *able to*.

1 You could be right.
2 You may go now if you wish.
3 They might be in the kitchen.
4 You can't smoke in here.
5 He might be home late tonight.
6 It could rain this evening.
7 I can swim.
8 Paul may know the answer.
9 He can't still be at the office.
10 I could play the piano when I was much younger.

3 Look at these pictures of everyday objects taken from strange angles and say what you think they could/might be.

4 Comment on your ability in relation to the following things. Say if you can/can't do them, when you began to learn how to do them, how you learnt to do them and how well you can do them now.

1 cook
2 drive
3 play a musical instrument
4 speak French
5 swim
6 paint

5 Work with a partner and roleplay the following situation. One of you is Student A and the other is Student B. You should use *can, could, may, might* as much as possible.

Student A: your teenage daughter/son has asked you if she/he can have a party in your house/flat. You have said 'Yes' but now must discuss the 'rules', that is what is allowed and what is not allowed. Think about the following questions:

– How many people will come?
– What food and drink will there be?
– How loud will the music be?
– Where will people stay overnight?
– Which rooms will be used?
– Who will tidy up afterwards?

In general you are a little nervous about the idea because last time a number of things were broken and your neighbours complained about the noise.

Student B: you have asked if you can have a party at home and your parents have agreed. Your mother/father wants to discuss now how it is going to be organised. You have a horrible feeling that they are going to make so many rules that it won't be any fun at all. Try and get your parents to go out, so you can organise it how you want.

A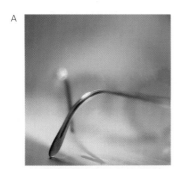
B
C
D

E
F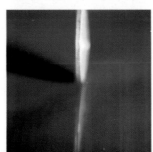
G
H

1 Fill in the gaps in the following text with an appropriate word. You have been given the number of missing letters in each case.

40 years in bed – with flu

A DOCTOR taking over a local practice visited a 74-year-old woman (1) – – – had been bedridden for 40 years. He wasn't (2) – – – – to find anything wrong with her. He discovered that the doctor before him (3) – – – ordered the woman to bed because she had influenza and had told (4) – – – not to get up again until he returned. Unfortunately, he had forgotten (5) – – return.

Within a (6) – – – days, the 34-year-old single woman had recovered. But she remained in her sickroom waiting for (7) – – – doctor's visit. Several weeks went by and he still did not call. By then the patient had discovered that she

enjoyed (8) – – – – – looked after so much that she refused to move.

At first she (9) – – – nursed by her mother. But when the old woman died, a brother-in-law took over. Finally, a new doctor to the area paid a routine call to (10) – – – patient's home in Taunton, Devon, and examined the woman, now (11) – – – – 74 and still determined to keep to her bed. It took seven months (12) – – sympathetic encouragement before the old lady was persuaded (13) – – leave her bed, but happily she was on her feet again (14) – – – three fairly active years before her death (15) – – the age of 77.

2 Choose the correct alternative in the following sentences.

1 He *used to/would* be very good at art when he was at school.
2 She *would/was used to* come up to my room before I went to sleep and tell me stories.
3 I can't *be/get* used to working on the night shift.
4 I *am used/used* to the weather now. I've been here for nearly a year.
5 We didn't use to *spend/spending* all our time working.
6 She *could/was able* play the piano very well when she was your age.
7 They *can/might* be away for the weekend, but I'm not sure.
8 You *may/might* leave now if you wish.
9 They *can't/couldn't* come over to see us until next Thursday.
10 *Could/May* you open the window a little?

3 Fill in the gaps in the following sentences with a correct particle (*up, in, out,* etc.).

1 She never gave .... hope that he would come back one day.
2 I couldn't decide whether to keep the money he left me or give it ....
3 He gave .... an air of importance as if he really knew he was special.

4 Under no circumstances will we give .... to threats.
5 Could you give .... the exam papers, please?
6 His hands were shaking and this gave .... how nervous he was.
7 Did you give me .... that book I lent you the other day?

4 Write a description of a famous person. Then read it out to the rest of your class and see if they can guess who you are describing.

5 Work with a partner and revise the phrasal verbs you have learnt so far. Look back at pages 17, 27, 40, 47, 61 and 81.

- Write five sentences, using phrasal verbs you have learnt.
- Then write the sentences again without the phrasal verbs but keeping the same meaning. (Underline the words which could be replaced by a phrasal verb.)
- Show the second set of sentences to another pair of students and see if they can rewrite them, this time using phrasal verbs.
EXAMPLE:

Pair A – *I* stopped *eating chocolate a month ago.*
Pair B – *I **gave up** eating chocolate a month ago.*

Too much of a good thing

Grammar: countables/uncountables

1 Divide the words in the box into two groups, countable and uncountable. If there are words which you think can be both countable and uncountable, decide what the difference in meaning is between the two.

apple	wood	bread	travel
flu	furniture	iron	
headache	information		
business	chicken	luggage	
coffee	advice	country	
news	weather	chocolate	
hair	trip	work	cold	toast
fruit	equipment	rubbish	

2 Look at the following sentences and decide why each one is wrong or unlikely.

1 He's got a short, black hair and a beard.
2 I'd like a chicken to start with, please.
3 The news are very bad, I'm afraid.
4 My trousers hasn't been cleaned yet.
5 Let me give you some advices.
6 The police was very helpful.
7 Can I have another bread, please?
8 Let's go for a walk in a country.
9 I'd like to make toast to the bride and groom.

3 Fill in the gaps in the following sentences with an appropriate word from the box. In some of the sentences more than one word is possible.

some	much	many	little	bit	lots	lot	few	deal	piece
sheet	lump	slice							

1 He's got .... of friends.
2 There are just too .... cars on the roads these days.
3 Could you cut me another .... of bread, please?
4 We've been to Italy .... of times.
5 That's an interesting .... of news.
6 He only has a .... sugar in his tea.
7 Could you lend me a .... of paper?
8 Oh no! A .... of coal has fallen on the carpet!
9 We've been having .... awful weather recently.
10 We spent a .... days with my mother in Spain.
11 We wasted a great .... of time looking for you.
12 There were a .... of people at the party last night.
13 Would you like another .... of cake?
14 Let me give you .... good advice.
15 I'm afraid I haven't got .... time.

Grammar reference p. 166 (6)

Reading

1 Read the text opposite and answer this question.

● Did they enjoy the meal?

IRISH STEW

by Jerome K. Jerome

1 WE ROAMED ABOUT SONNING for an hour or so, and then we decided to go back to one of the Shiplake islands, and put up there for the night. It was still early when we got settled, and George said that, as we had plenty of time, it would be a splendid opportunity to try a good, slap-up supper. He suggested that, with the vegetables and general odds and ends, we should make an Irish stew.

10 It seemed a fascinating idea. George gathered wood and made a fire, and Harris and I started to peel the potatoes. I should never have thought that peeling potatoes was such an undertaking. The job turned out to be the biggest thing of its kind that I have ever been in. The more we peeled, the more peel there seemed to be left on; by the time we had got all the peel off and all the eyes out, there was no potato left – at least none worth speaking of. George came and had a look at it – it was about the size of a peanut. He said, 'Oh, that won't do! You're wasting them. You must scrape them.'

20 So we scraped them, and that was harder work than peeling. They are such an extraordinary shape, potatoes. We worked steadily for five-and-twenty minutes, and did four potatoes.

George said it was absurd to have only four potatoes in an Irish stew, so we washed half-a-dozen or so more, and put them in without peeling. We also put in a cabbage and some peas. George stirred it all up, and then he said that there seemed to be a lot of room to spare, so we went through the hampers, and picked out 30 all the odds and ends and added them to the stew. There was half a pork pie and a bit of boiled bacon left and we put them in. Then George found half a tin of potted salmon, and he emptied that into the pot.

He said that was the advantage of Irish stew: you got rid of such a lot of things. I found a couple of eggs that had got cracked, and we put those in. George said they would thicken the gravy.

I forget the other ingredients, but I know nothing was wasted; and I remember that towards the end, 40 Montmorency, who had shown great interest in what was going on, went away and then reappeared a few minutes afterwards with a dead water-rat in his mouth, which he evidently wished to present as his contribution to the dinner.

We had a discussion as to whether the rat should go in or not. Harris said that he thought it would be all right, mixed up with the other things, and that every little helped; but George said he had never heard of water-rats in Irish stew, and he would rather be on the 50 safe side, and not try experiments.

Harris said, 'If you never try a new thing, how can you tell what it's like? It's men such as you who prevent the world's progress.' And so the rat went in.

It was a great success, that Irish stew. I don't think I have ever enjoyed a meal more. There was something so fresh and tasty about it. Here was a dish with a new flavour, with a taste like nothing on earth.

And it was nourishing, too. As George said, there was good stuff in it. The peas and potatoes might have 60 been a bit softer, but we all had good teeth, so that did not matter much: and as for the gravy, it was a poem – a little too rich, perhaps, for a weak stomach, but nutritious.

from Three Men in a Boat

2 Now read the story again and choose the correct alternative for each of the following questions.

1 The group decided

A to eat in a restaurant.
B to cook for themselves in the open air.
C to go and buy some food.
D to get Montmorency to cook for them.

2 Who was mainly in charge of cooking the Irish stew?

A Harris
B Montmorency
C George
D the narrator

3 They found peeling potatoes

A difficult at first but they got used to it.
B quite easy.
C difficult but fun.
D hard work.

4 How many different ingredients does the narrator mention went into the stew?

A seven
B eight
C nine
D ten

5 Who was definitely in favour of including the water-rat in the stew?

A Montmorency and the narrator
B Harris and George
C the narrator and George
D Harris and Montmorency

6 What does *eyes* in *line 16* mean?

A dirt
B dark spots
C people watching
D knives

7 What does *that* in *line 60* refer to?

A The fact that they all had good teeth.
B The fact that they didn't all have good teeth.
C The fact that the peas and potatoes were soft.
D The fact that the peas and potatoes were hard.

Vocabulary: phrasal verbs (*put*)

- *We decided to go back to one of the Shiplake islands, and **put up** there for the night.*

1   Match each of the following sentences to a correct response below.

1   So what couldn't you *put up with*?
2   I'm afraid he's going to have to be *put down*.
3   Didn't you *put* any money *by*?
4   I hated the way you *put* me *down* at the party this evening.
5   Do you think you could *put* me *through* to the Managing Director?
6   I think we should *put* prices *up* again.
7   Why don't we *put* it *off* for a couple of months?
8   Could you *put* me *up* for a couple of nights?
9   How quickly can you *put* that fire *out*?

a)   Are you joking? We only just had enough to live!
b)   I'm really sorry, but we just don't have room.
c)   I'm terribly sorry, but he's in the middle of a meeting.
d)   I don't know. It depends how far it has already spread.
e)   The way he never came home. He was always in the bar with his friends.
f)   Our wedding! How could you suggest such a thing?
g)   I only said you were being a bit silly.
h)   Are you sure? But he's only broken a leg.
i)   But if we do, we'll lose all our regular customers.

2   Now decide what the meaning of the phrasal verb is in each sentence.

3   Choose one of the pairs of sentences from Exercise 1 and continue the conversation.

EXAMPLE:
A: **Could you put me up for a couple of nights?**
B: **I'm really sorry, but we just don't have room.**
A: *But I can't afford to stay in a hotel.*
B: *Well, I could give my brother a ring. He lives quite close.*
A: *Would you? That would be really kind! ...*

Vocabulary: food and cooking

1   Decide which is the odd one out in each of the following groups of words.

1   parsley/peas/thyme/basil
2   a wooden spoon/a penknife/a ladle/a spatula
3   to roast/to grate/to bake/to fry
4   a cooker/an oven/a cook/a grill
5   to slice/to chop/to roll/to cut
6   a frying pan/a saucepan/a sieve/a pressure cooker
7   to mix/to sprinkle/to stir/to whisk
8   sweet/sour/sharp/hard
9   a bowl/a plate/a course/a dish
10   tough/rare/medium/well-done
11   a starter/a second helping/a main course/a dessert
12   to crack/to fold/to scramble/to boil

2   Think of other words to add to some of the groups in Exercise 1.

'I'm sorry, sir, but you did ask for the chef's speciality.'

3   Fill in the gaps in the following sentences with an appropriate word from one of the word groups in Exercise 1. You may need to change the form of the words you use.

1   I'd like a .... egg for breakfast with some bread and butter.
2   Could I have my steak very ...., practically uncooked, please?
3   .... some chopped herbs on top of the pasta before serving.
4   Leave the meat in the .... for at least two hours to make sure it is properly cooked.
5   Put the rice in the .... and shake it to get rid of all the water.
6   They .... their own bread. It's absolutely delicious.

4 Discuss the following questions.

1 Do you enjoy eating meat? If so, what kinds of meat do you like? How do you like them cooked? How do you like your steak done? If you don't like meat, explain why and say what kinds of food you do particularly like to eat.
2 What are your favourite desserts?
3 Are there any particular herbs or spices that you like on your food?
4 How well can you cook? Do you enjoy cooking? Why?/Why not?
5 How many different ways do you know to cook:
   a) eggs?
   b) potatoes?
   Which do you prefer?

Watch Out! *lay/lie*

1 Could you *lay* the table for lunch please?
2 I think I'll go and *lie* on the bed for an hour.
3 He *lied* in the sun and read a book.
4 I can't understand why he *lied* to me. He normally tells the truth.

Which of these sentences is not correct?

---

5 You are going to mime some actions to a partner, who should try to guess what you are doing. Student A should look on page 187 for a list of things to mime, and Student B should look on page 190.

Exam focus

Paper 4 Listening (note taking/blank filling)

In Part 2 of Paper 4 you will hear either a monologue or a conversation between different people. You will be asked to summarise in notes what the speakers have said or write down specific pieces of missing information.

We are going to practise this now. You are going to hear a conversation between two friends, one of whom is telling the other how to make 'Tunisian Brik à l'oeuf'. Listen and complete the friend's notes with a word or short phrase.

Tunisian Brik à L'oeuf

1. _____ the onion.
2. Mix the onion with _____ and _____.
3. Add _____ and _____.
4. Put an egg in the _____ of the brik and put the _____ around the egg.
5. Prepare all this on the _____.
6. _____ the brik and place it in the _____, sealing down the edges.
7. Turn the temperature _____.
8. After _____ minutes, turn the brik over with a _____.
9. Serve with _____.

Speaking

1 Work in a group with other students and together decide on a particular dish that you know how to cook. Make a list of the ingredients you need and the instructions for how to cook it.

2 Now work in pairs with a student from a different group. Explain to your partner what ingredients you need and how to cook your particular dish. Your partner should listen and make notes. By the end she/he should have a complete recipe and a clear idea of how to cook the dish.

Reading

1 Discuss what you think it means to be an 'addict'.

2 Read the article opposite about different types of addicts and decide which person you think has the most serious problem.

3 Read the following sentences and decide which person (Becci, Janine, Tony Benn or Anne) each one refers to. One of the sentences does not refer to any of them.

1 Her/his addiction led to crime.
2 She/he became out of touch with the rest of her/his life.
3 She/he was addicted to getting things she/he never used.
4 She/he feels her addiction is a substitute for love.
5 She/he needs it to help her/him work effectively under pressure.
6 She/he is receiving professional treatment.
7 Her/his addiction may have had serious physical consequences.
8 She/he isn't convinced she/he should give it up.

4 Find words or phrases in the text with the following meanings.

1 the exception, the unusual person (*para. 1*)
2 a desire (*para. 2*)
3 to compensate (*para. 2*)
4 to change from solid to liquid (*para. 2*)
5 to destroy (*para. 3*)
6 to realise what is happening (*para. 3*)
7 to stop being under control (*para. 3*)
8 to make people worried (*para. 4*)
9 to fall down (*para. 4*)
10 too much (*para. 4*)
11 very difficult and painful (*para. 4*)
12 fashionable (*para. 5*)
13 to come to an end (*para. 5*)

Are you hooked?

No one likes to admit they're an addict. They are sad creatures ruled by deadly substances such as tobacco or alcohol. But there are others less damaging to the health. Like it or not, large numbers of us are addicts. Addictions can be chemical (caffeine), emotional (shopping), physical (exercise) or downright strange – such as picking your spots! You're the odd one out if you don't have at least one everyday addiction. What do you do when you feel under pressure, bored or depressed? Get lost in the world of TV? Go shopping? Eat one bar of chocolate after another?

Becci has been a chocaholic for ten years. 'I just get an urge for it – a need,' says Becci. 'I really don't know why, it's just so delicious. People say that chocolate can make up for lost passion – I don't know about that, but I love the way it melts in my mouth.' Every day, Becci gets through several bars of her favourite Cadbury's chocolate (the one with the soft caramel centre is the best). But it's not only the bars she goes for – hot chocolate drinks and chocolate cakes are also essentials. Towards exam time, Becci feels she has to increase her intake to cope with all the work. 'If I get up late, I'll have chocolate for breakfast, then more and more during the day. I am addicted. It's like smoking, I suppose, but I have no plans to give it up. If I like it so much, why should I?'

Addiction to exercise can ruin your life, Janine learnt to her cost. 'I was swimming at least fifty lengths a day, jogging to the gym and doing three aerobic classes a week. At home, I used an exercise bike and keep-fit videos. My husband said that I didn't have time for him, and he was right. But I couldn't believe it when he left me. Finally, I came to my senses, I wanted to get fit but it all got out of hand and my addiction ruined my marriage. Now, I'm seeing a counsellor and gradually reducing the amount of exercise I do.'

Well-known Member of Parliament, Tony Benn, just can't live without his favourite drink. He has on average eighteen pints of tea a day and his addiction has raised concern about his health. When he collapsed recently, some people blamed his excessive tea drinking. Mr Benn has calculated that, over the years, he has drunk enough tea (around 300,000 gallons) to displace an ocean-going liner. If he ever tried to stop, he would find it agonising.

Anne shopped for thirteen hours a day without leaving her living room – she was addicted to TV shopping. When she got home from her job as a nightcare worker at 8.30 a.m., Anne would immediately tune into a satellite TV shopping channel and buy everything in sight. Her home was soon an Aladdin's cave of household goods and trendy clothes she didn't need. When her cash ran out, she stole money from the elderly patients in her care and was charged with theft. 'It seemed so easy,' she says. 'I didn't realise I'd become so addicted.' Anne's family have now removed her satellite receiver.

from *Best* magazine

5 Discuss the following questions.

1 What advice would you give to the four addicts (and their families) in the article?
2 Would you say you were addicted to anything?

Grammar: future forms

1 Read the statements above and decide which of them is:

a) a prediction (no present evidence).
b) a decision made at the moment of speaking.
c) an intention or plan.
d) an arrangement (some of the details have been worked out).
e) a prediction (based on present evidence).
f) a description of something in progress at a definite time in the future.
g) a description of something which will be completed before a definite time in the future.

2 Name the different future forms used to express the concepts above.

Grammar reference p.176 (17.8)

3 Look at the following sentences and choose the most appropriate future form.

1 I'*ll apply/am going to apply* for a job at the local hospital. I've been thinking about it for ages.
2 I'm sure he *will leave/will have left* the company soon.
3 If he isn't careful, that little boy *is going to fall/is falling* and hurt himself.
4 This time next week we *are going to lie/will be lying* in the Australian sun!
5 I was talking to Paul and apparently the whole family *is going/will go* to his house for Christmas.
6 I hope you *are finishing/will have finished* the painting by the time we get back!
7 I tell you what. If you are getting him some CDs for his birthday, I'*ll get/am going to get* him a tie.

4

1 Now you are going to practise using the various future forms. First, write down in any order the following things.

- Something you are going to do in the very near future.
- Something you hope you will have done within five years.
- Something you will probably be doing at 3 p.m. on Sunday.
- Something you are definitely doing tomorrow.
- Something you think will happen to a member of your family in the near future.

2 Now look at what a partner has written and say which of the above categories you think each sentence goes into.

EXAMPLE: '***I'm playing tennis*** *with José.' That's something you're definitely doing tomorrow.*

5

1 Now make some resolutions. Write down two things that:

a) you do, but which you would like to stop doing.
b) you don't do, but which you would like to start doing.

2 Tell a partner about your resolutions. Say what you are going to do to help you achieve your goal.

EXAMPLE: *I want to get more exercise, so **I'm going to start going swimming** twice a week from tomorrow.*

Listening: an addict's story

1 You are going to hear an extract from a radio programme. Listen and answer the following questions.

1 What is Lawrence's problem?
2 Is he better now?

2 Now listen to the extract again and decide if the following statements are True or False.

1 The presenter at first doesn't think Lawrence is so different from anybody else.
2 Lawrence would only buy food, tapes, clothes or dolls' houses.
3 Lawrence found the experience of buying in this way very exciting.
4 Lawrence never received his bank statements.
5 The presenter is shocked by how serious Lawrence's problem became.
6 Lawrence believes his behaviour was a way of compensating for what he didn't get as a child.
7 Lawrence's wife left him.
8 Lawrence got professional help.
9 Marlene got a new job to try and pay some of the bills.
10 They sold a lot of the things that Lawrence had bought to help get money.

Vocabulary: shopping

1 Match each of the following statements to a shop below in which you might hear it being said.

1 I only bought these last week and already the heel has come off.
2 Could I have a dozen red roses, please?
3 Do you have anything to help with a sore throat and runny nose?
4 A large, brown loaf and a couple of jam doughnuts, please.
5 I'd like to send this first class – and do you have any of those special airmail letters?
6 I'm afraid this check-out is only for customers with fewer than ten items.
7 Could you give me a couple of those avocados and a pound of the mushrooms, please?

a) a florist's   e) a supermarket
b) a greengrocer's   f) a post office
c) a baker's   g) a shoe shop
d) a chemist's

2 Complete the missing words in the following sentences. You have been given the correct number of letters in each case.

1 There are always good bar–––––– in the January sa–––.
2 I had to qu––– for ages, but the food is very good va––– in that shop.
3 I'm afraid these trousers are too lo––– around the waist. Do you have a slightly smaller si–– ?
4 Do you know, I think the shop assi–––––– gave me £1 too much cha––– .
5 I'm afraid we can't give you a ref––– if you don't have your original rec–––– .
6 How much do you cha––– to have things deli––––– ?
7 Oh, that colour really su––– you. It mat–––– your eyes.
8 Did you see on the la––– that this shirt is made of si–– and has to be handwashed?
9 I'm sorry, we don't have any in st––– at the moment, but there are a number on or–––. They should be here next week.
10 Oh no! I've lost my wal––– and it's got all my cre––– cards in it.
11 If anything goes wr–––, all parts and labour are fully covered by the one-year guar––––– .

3 Discuss the following questions.

1 What are your favourite shops?
2 When was the last time you really enjoyed going shopping? What did you buy?
3 Have you ever had any bad experiences while shopping? (For example, have you ever had to complain?) If so, what happened?

Listening: a complaint

1 You are going to hear a conversation between a shop assistant and someone making a complaint. Listen and put the following pictures in the order in which they are referred to.

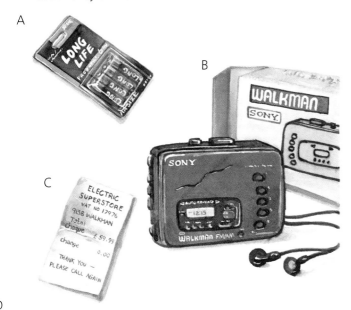

A

B

C

D

2 Now listen again and answer the following questions.

1 What does a) the customer b) the shop assistant say about each of the pictures above?
2 Is the shop assistant generally:
   a) sympathetic?
   b) aggressive?
   c) defensive?

3 Look at these incomplete sentences from the conversation between the customer and the shop assistant and try to remember who said each one. Then listen to the complete sentences and fill in the missing words.

1 I see. ....
   matter?
2 But you should ....
   .... bought it.
3 That's ridiculous. But anyway ....
   .... thing.
4 Well, you know it's ....
   .... for ten hours.
5 Look, it says here ....
   ....
   undetectable by other people.
6 We've certainly never ....
   .... before.
7 Well, I suppose ....
   .... model.
8 Well, if I ....
   receipt.

Speaking

1 Work with a partner and roleplay the situation you heard above, using your own words and/or some of the expressions from Listening Exercise 3.

2 Now roleplay two of the following situations, taking it in turns to be the person who is complaining.

a) You have just had a disgusting meal at an expensive restaurant. When you tried to complain, the waiter was rude to you. You have asked to speak to the manager.
b) You bought a new coat from a local shop. Soon after, you discovered that there is a tear under one of the arms and that two of the buttons have fallen off. You have taken it back to the shop.
c) You have just arrived at a hotel on holiday. Your room is not how it was described in the brochure. For example, there is no view of the sea and there is no bath, only a shower. Also, the sheets on the bed do not appear to have been changed since the last guest. You have gone down to reception.
d) You bought a board game from a shop. You gave it to a friend as a present but, very embarrassingly, some of the pieces and cards are missing. You have taken it back to the shop.

Writing: a letter of complaint

1 In Paper 2 you may be asked to write a more formal letter, for example a letter of complaint. Look at the following phrases/sentences and decide which ones you would normally expect to find in an informal letter and which you might find in a more formal letter. Mark them **I** (informal) or **F** (formal).

1 Dear Mr Jenkins,
2 Lots of love, Pierre.
3 See you on the 20th. I can't wait!
4 I am writing with reference to a purchase I recently made in your store.
5 I look forward to receiving a reply at your earliest convenience.
6 Yours sincerely, Maria Gonzales.
7 It was really great to hear from you after such a long time.
8 Thank you for your letter of 15 September.

2 Mike Harding, the customer who complained in the conversation you heard on page 95, was not happy about what happened in the shop, so he decided to write a letter to the Manager. Complete the middle part of the letter continuing with the formal style you can see at the beginning and end.

Dear Sir/Madam,

I am writing to complain about a Walkman that I bought from your shop last week and also about the treatment I received from one of the staff there.

When I got home, and took it out of its box, I was not very pleased to find

So, I am sure you will understand why I feel so annoyed and frustrated by the whole incident. I look forward to hearing from you in the very near future, either to offer me a complete refund or to exchange the original Walkman for one which is actually in a decent condition.

Yours faithfully,

M.Harding

3

1 You are going to write a letter of complaint as a follow-up to one of the situations you roleplayed on page 95. Before you write the letter, match up the two halves of the following sentences.

1 When I came to the main course, I found	a) that we couldn't actually play the game.
2 To my horror, the first time I wore it	b) that all the pieces were there.
3 I was shocked at the difference between the standard of the rooms in the hotel	c) I found a tear under one of the arms.
4 At the time the shop assistant assured me	d) by anyone in all my life.
5 I have never been spoken to so rudely	e) that all the vegetables were stone cold.
6 Even more embarrassing was when	f) but in fact I was facing out on to a motorway.
7 I had been promised a view of the sea,	g) compared to how they were described in the brochure.
8 My friend's children were extremely disappointed	h) two of the buttons came off as I was in the middle of a formal dinner.

2 Now write your letter of complaint in 120–180 words. You may use some of the phrases from Mike Harding's letter or from the sentences above.

1 Look at this picture of a kitchen and name all the items you can see.

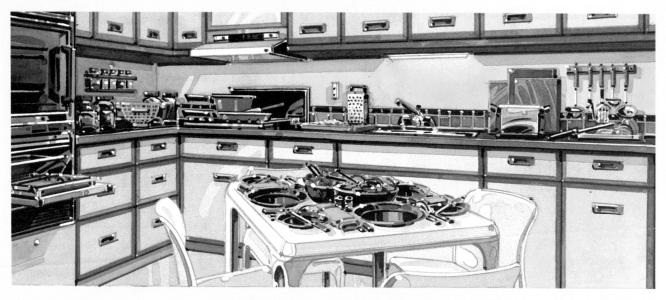

2 Look at the following pairs of words and decide what the difference is between them.

a) a ladle/a spatula
b) to fry/to boil
c) a bowl/a plate
d) a cooker/an oven
e) well-done/tough
f) tight/loose
g) a bargain/a sale
h) to suit/to fit
i) a receipt/a recipe

3 Fill in the gaps in each of the following sentences with an appropriate particle (*up*, *out*, *down*, etc.).

1 I can't believe it. The price of bread has gone .... again.
2 I can't put up .... his rudeness any longer!
3 My cat got very old and in the end he had to be put ....
4 Put that cigarette .... Can't you see this is a No-Smoking area?
5 If the weather doesn't change, we'll have to put the match .... until next Saturday.
6 I try and put about £25 .... every month in a special savings account.
7 I can't stand the way he's always putting her .... He thinks he's so clever.
8 She said she was going to put me .... to the Customer Services Department, but then I got cut off.
9 Come and stay with us. We can put you .... for as long as you like.

4 Read the following text and choose the correct alternative in each case. (–) means that no word is needed.

I had (1) *an/some* important business at the weekend and I had to go by plane. It was all a (2) *bit/piece* of a disaster. On (3) *a/the* news before I went, I heard that (4) *the/(–)* weather was going to be bad. It was, and (5) *the/(–)* flight was pretty unpleasant. Then, when I got to the airport, several (6) *pieces of luggage/luggages* were missing with all my notes in them.

When I arrived, I asked at reception for (7) *an/some* information about local restaurants and decided to have (8) *a/(–)* dinner in the hotel. I had (9) *a/(–)* chicken which was a big mistake. It was badly overcooked and the vegetables were as bad. I decided to go up to (10) *the/(–)* bed quite early. Unfortunately the bed was awful, like the rest of the (11) *furniture/furnitures* in my room. I didn't sleep well!

Next morning I got up early to wash my (12) *hair/hairs*, and then I went down to breakfast. I asked for (13) *a/(–)* toast and coffee for breakfast. Needless to say the toast was burnt and the coffee was undrinkable. I decided to just have (14) *a/a piece of* fruit instead. Finally I arrived at my meeting, but when I got there I was told it had to be cancelled because the president of the company was ill. It had all been (15) *a/(–)* waste of time.

5 Write a letter of complaint for another of the situations you roleplayed in Speaking on page 95.

How to make a fortune

£ Pound out of control

Reading

1 You are going to read an article about the man in the photo opposite. The following words appear in the article. Match each one with a definition on the right.

1 a benefactor	a) to employ someone
2 a speculator	b) a businessman with great wealth and power
3 to devalue	c) a person who helps other people by giving money
4 to hire someone	d) a person who buys and sells goods
5 to gamble	e) someone who tries to make money by taking business risks
6 a trader	f) to reduce the value of something (especially money)
7 a tycoon	g) to take a risk in the hope of gaining something

2 Read through the article quickly. What are your initial feelings about George Soros? Do you admire/dislike /or not feel strongly about him either way?

3 The following sentences have been removed from the article. Read the article again and put each sentence in the correct numbered gap. There is one extra sentence which you do not need to use. (See page 23 for a suggested procedure for this task type.)

A One of his strongest memories is of being envious of the cat because it got sardines for breakfast and he did not.

B Its initial investment of $4.8m has grown to nearly $6 billion, one third of which is the personal stake of Soros.

C Out of the $250m he plans to donate in the next two years, $100m has gone to set up an International Foundation for Science in Russia and $50m to the Humanitarian Initiative in Bosnia.

D His simple $60 watch and patterned tie could have been picked up at an airport shop.

E In 1978 he met Susan Weber, a 22 year-old art history documentary maker, at a dinner party.

F He and his elder brother were doted on by their parents, particularly by their father, who worked very little when he came back from the war, spending most of his time with his sons.

G That evening, in his Fifth Avenue apartment, he enjoyed a simple supper, cooked by his French chef, before retiring to bed.

H Some time later, in 1973, he parted company with his employers.

THE MAN WHO BROKE THE POUND

When George Soros was a child, he thought he was God. Today he is a legend: the Man who Broke the Pound, the ultimate gambler who bet $10 billion on Black Wednesday and won. Soros has also made his name as the billionaire benefactor of the eastern bloc.

At 5.30 p.m. (10.30 p.m. in London) on September 15, 1992, George Soros was sitting in his Manhattan office, perched on the 33rd floor of a mirrored skyscraper overlooking Central Park. Confident that sterling could not stay in the Exchange Rate Mechanism, Soros instructed his head trader, Stanley Druckenmiller, to sell $10 billion-worth of sterling, taking a giant gamble that it would have to be devalued overnight.

(1 ———) Next morning he was woken at 7 a.m. by a call from Druckenmiller telling him he had just made $958m. Later he learned he had made further gains by siding with the French authorities against speculators attacking the franc. All in all, from the events of what became known as 'Black Wednesday', he had made close to $2 billion.

Attractive, with thick wavy grey hair, apple cheeks and appraising eyes behind aviator glasses, Soros bears none of the accoutrements of a tycoon. (2 ———) 'I have a very, very abstract mind,' he says, 'and as a result I don't really take pleasure in material possessions. If I were a different person I'd buy old masters, but I don't like to collect.'

Born in 1930 in Budapest he was the beloved younger son of a Hungarian Jewish lawyer, Tivadar, who had been a prisoner of war in Siberia between 1917 and 1921. **(3 ——)** Soros often credits his success as a trader to the inflated sense of self his father gave him.

In 1947 Soros, aged 17, escaped the communist regime, leaving his parents behind in Hungary and emigrating to London. His only source of income was money given to him by an aunt who had already fled to Florida. It was a desperately lonely period: he made few friends, partly because he couldn't speak the language properly, partly because he had no money. **(4 ——)** In 1949 he became a student of economics at the London School of Economics and then, later, in 1956, aged 26, he moved to New York with $5000, his share of the profit he had made on £1000 given to him by a relative to invest. Then in 1957 George's parents also left Hungary for the States but, apart from one disastrous attempt to open an espresso stand on Coney Island, they did not work and George had to support them. He was still poor and when his father developed cancer in the early 1960s George was forced to ask the husband of a friend to help him find a surgeon who would treat him free of charge.

The turning point came in 1963. He was hired by Arnhold and S. Bleichroeder to advise American institutions on their European investments. **(5 ——)** It was then that he set up the Soros Fund which, by the late 1970s, was already beginning to make large profits. **(6 ——)**

Since 1979, Soros, a native Hungarian, has ploughed more than $100m of his speculation profits into funding an 18-strong network of foundations spanning central and eastern Europe and Russia. **(7 ——)** In 'The Man Who Broke The Pound', a Thames Television documentary shown in December, Soros said the money he had made represented the equivalent of £12 for every man, woman and child in Britain, who, he said, really ought to have contributed it to the transformation of eastern Europe. 'But I am happy to do it for them.'

Grammar: relative clauses and pronouns

1 Here is some important information on defining relative clauses. Read it and then do the exercise which follows.

DEFINING RELATIVE CLAUSES

a) *He is the man* <u>*who broke the Pound*</u>. The underlined part of this sentence is a **defining relative clause** and is essential to the meaning of the sentence.

b) *The person* (**who**) *I spoke to had red hair.* In this case **who** can be left out because it refers to the object of the verb 'speak', that is I spoke to *the person*.

c) *Have you got the money* **which** *I lent you?* **Which** is used to refer to things and places.

d) **Who** and **which** can both be replaced by **that**.

e) **Whom** is possible (instead of **who**) when it is the object of the verb in the relative clause. However, it is not very often used in informal English. For example, it would be much more natural to say **Who** *are you going to the party* **with**? than **With whom** *are you going to the party?*

f) *This is the house* **where** *I was born.* **Where** is used to refer to places.

g) *Are you the person* **whose** *car is blocking my drive?* **Whose** indicates possession.

h) Commas are not used to separate the clause.

Grammar reference p.173 (14)

Join a clause in Column A to a clause in Column B with an appropriate relative pronoun to make a complete sentence. Use each clause once only.

A	B
1 We went to the Italian restaurant	a) dog was barking all night.
2 Where's the book	b) I first met Andrew.
3 They are the people	c) had the biggest screen.
4 Could you tell me the nearest place	d) stole my bag.
5 That boy is the thief	e) has noticed my new haircut.
6 The disco over there is	f) I picked from the garden.
7 I bought the TV	g) they sell stamps?
8 You are the only person	h) you said you would lend me?
9 These are the flowers	i) they have fantastic pizzas.

2 Here is some important information on non-defining relative clauses. Read it and then do the exercise which follows.

NON-DEFINING RELATIVE CLAUSES

a) *Soros,* <u>*who was born in Hungary,*</u> *has lived in America for many years.* The underlined part of this sentence is **a non-defining relative clause** and this gives us extra information. This clause can be removed from the sentence without destroying the central meaning.

b) In non-defining relative clauses we use **who** for people and **which** for things. We cannot replace either of them with **that** and we cannot omit them. e.g. *His car,* **which** *broke down yesterday, is nearly ten years old.*

c) We use commas at the beginning and end of these clauses, unless they end the sentence. e.g. *Yesterday I spoke to Pete,* **who** *said he was going to leave the company.*

d) We can use **whose**, **whom** and **where**. e.g. *Richard,* **whose** *father is Greek, speaks both Greek and English fluently./The manager,* **to whom** *I spoke about my complaint, is going to give me a refund./ I'm going to spend a few days in Paris,* **where** *I first met José.*

Grammar reference p. 173 (14)

Join the following pairs of sentences to make one sentence with a non-defining relative clause. Use commas appropriately.

EXAMPLE: I lent my car to my next door neighbour. My car has a large boot.
I lent my car, **which has a large boot,** *to my next door neighbour.*

1 We went to Spain. There are fantastic beaches in Spain.
2 I'm looking forward to my birthday. My birthday is next month.
3 My present car is a grey Saab. It is three years old.
4 I'm seeing Carol this evening. Her parents are on holiday.
5 My boss wants to see me. I don't get on with him.
6 I read that new book by Iain Banks and I enjoyed it. Pete lent it to me.
7 Matt is going to be best man at my wedding. I've been friends with him since university.
8 Thank you for the birthday card. I got it on Friday.

3

1 Read the following sentences and decide which of the relative pronouns are essential and which can be omitted.

   a) <u>My best friend</u>, *who* <u>I've known for</u> ten years, now lives in Italy.
   b) <u>One thing</u> *that* <u>makes me really angry is</u> people *who* drop litter in the street.
   c) I rarely go back to <u>the town</u> *where* <u>I was born.</u>
   d) I've lost contact with all <u>the people</u> *who* <u>I was close to at school.</u>
   e) <u>The single object</u> *which* <u>I treasure the most is</u> a ring my girlfriend gave me.

2 Look again at the sentences and tell a partner something about yourself referring to the underlined part of each sentence.

Vocabulary: *do/make*

- *It was already beginning to* **make large profits.**

1 Divide the words in the box into two groups according to whether they are used with *do* or *make*.

business   an arrangement homework   a mistake money   a decision the washing-up   the bed a noise   a favour   one's best a complaint   harm   sure fun of   a test   an excuse a choice   an effort a phone call   a profit   peace

2 Work with a partner and write a short story about two friends, Derek Do and Martin Make, who share a flat together, but who are very different in character. Derek is nice, friendly and helpful (and uses expressions with *do*), but Martin is mainly concerned about getting more money (and uses expressions with *make*).

Begin like this and use as many expressions with *do* and *make* as possible:

One day Derek **was doing the washing-up** *in the kitchen. When he saw Martin, he asked him to help, but Martin* **made an excuse** *and said he* **had made an arrangement** *to meet someone for lunch ...*

Vocabulary: money

1 Divide into three groups, A, B and C. Each group should check that they know the meaning and pronunciation of the words in the appropriate box. Use a dictionary where necessary.

A

> a cheque (book)   a cashpoint machine
> to withdraw   a current account   economical
> a deposit account   interest   a bank statement
> to be overdrawn   an exchange rate   the economy

B

> cash   a coin   a £10 note   change
> a mortgage   to earn   a wage   a salary
> overtime   commission   a tip   to gamble
> a casino   a charity   to afford   well-off   hard up

C

> to be in debt   to owe   to lend   to borrow
> the stock market   to invest   shares   profit   loss
> tax   inflation   insurance   a fine   a pension
> a sale   a bargain   to inherit   an heir

2 Now work in groups of three, one student from Group A, one student from Group B and one from Group C. Explain the meaning and pronunciation of your words to the other students.

3 Discuss the following questions.

1 What do you enjoy spending money on?
2 How do you feel about borrowing money? Would you worry about being in debt?
3 Do you think pocket money is a good idea? Why?/Why not?
4 What do you think about people who deliberately avoid paying tax?
5 Do you have a bank account? Do you get interest? Do you get a monthly statement?
6 When do you tip and how much?
7 Are you cautious with money or do you tend to spend it when you have it?
8 Have you ever gambled? When? What happened?
9 Do you ever give money to charity?
10 Do you like looking for bargains in the sales?

> **Watch Out!** *earn/win/gain*
>
> 1 They've *earned/won/gained* £500,000 in the lottery.
> 2 He's *earned/won/gained* a lot of weight recently.
> 3 I need a job so I can *earn/win/gain* some money.
>
> Which is the correct alternative in each sentence?

4

1 Here are two well-known sayings. What do you think they mean? Do you agree with them? Why?/Why not?
   - *Money is the root of all evil*
   - *Money makes the world go round*

2 Do you have any sayings in your own language on the subject of money? If so, what are they?

Speaking

Imagine the following situation. A language school in London is offering two scholarships. All applicants are invited to write in and explain their situation. The scholarship includes three months of English courses, all food and accommodation and some pocket money. You and a partner have been given the task of selecting the two most deserving candidates. Read the list of candidates below and decide on the two who you think should be awarded the scholarship. You should be prepared to give reasons why.

First look at page 62 to remind yourself of the language of giving opinions and agreeing/disagreeing.

Ioanna comes from Greece. She is a teacher of English and already quite fluent. She wants to make her English perfect and is interested in being involved in the training of other English teachers.

Wang I-Hua comes from a small town in the south of China. She has never been outside her town, but has always dreamed of travelling. This would be the chance of a lifetime.

Mehmet is a very clever student who is brilliant at science, but keeps failing the English part of his university entrance exam. His teachers have written a letter supporting his case.

Carmen is a Spanish nurse working for a small charity. She is about to go out to a part of Africa currently suffering from disease and famine where English is widely spoken. She will work in a village hospital with local people.

Christiane is an excellent primary school teacher who has been told she must start teaching English to her pupils as well as everything else. At the moment she has no ability in English.

Javier is a refugee living in London. He can't go back to his country because of the political problems there. He is with his wife and two young children. He is having problems finding a job because of his English.

Wojtek is a young man from Poland who would like to set up an import-export business, but needs to improve his English to do so.

Writing: an application

In Paper 2 you may be asked to write an application. In this type of writing task you will often need to give information about yourself and say why you would be good for a certain thing, for example a scholarship or a job. The style of writing will be similar to that of a more formal letter.

1 Here is part of the application form for the scholarship on page 102 which one of the applicants has completed. Which of the applicants is it from?

Describe your reasons for wanting the scholarship and what you intend doing when you finish the course.

I arrived in London ago three months with my wife and two children young. Since then I very hard have tried to get a job (in my country I was a lawyer). However, isn't very good my English and I think this is the reason why I yet haven't found a job. I seem always to have problems when I have to speak at interviews. I am sure that if I could improve my English spoken, I would to get a job be able and my family support.

I have done my best to improve my English since I arrived. I have studied books of grammar and listened to the radio, but to meet people so that I can practise my speaking it is quite difficult. I think that having regular classes of language would really help me and as soon as possible I am very keen to start. I know what a reputation good has your school and very grateful I would be if seriously you would consider my application.

2 The applicant who wrote this has a problem with word order in English. Read the text again and correct all the word order mistakes that you can find.

3 Now write an application for the above scholarship. You can either take the part of one of the other applicants or you can apply yourself.

Vocabulary: numbers

- *He had just made **$958 million**.*

1 How do you pronounce the number in **bold** above?

2 Work with a partner. Take it in turns to say each of the numbers in the pyramid, starting at the top. Then make your own number pyramid for your partner to say.

58
958
7,958
47,958
647,958
3,647,958
13,647,958

3 Match the following numbers to a description on the right.

a)	¼	1	a speed
b)	0.25	2	a weight
c)	3–0	3	a telephone number
d)	40–15	4	a decimal
e)	0171 491 2598	5	a date
f)	30/6/95	6	a percentage
g)	1 m 65 cm	7	a temperature
h)	85 kg	8	a height
i)	78%	9	a price
j)	32°C	10	a fraction
k)	85 mph	11	a score (in football)
l)	£14.05	12	a score (in tennis)

4 How do you pronounce the numbers on the left? Listen and check your answers.

5 Work with a partner. Student A should look at the questions on page 187 and Student B at the questions on page 190. Ask your partner the questions and make a note of the answers. Then answer the questions your partner will ask you.

> **Watch Out!** '0'
>
> How many different ways can '0' be said?
> Think about: football, tennis, telephone numbers, decimal numbers, etc.

Exam focus

Paper 5 Speaking Part 2 (talking about photographs)

In Part 2 of the interview you will be shown two theme-related photographs (e.g. of types of holidays). You will be asked to describe them and to talk about them in relation to yourself for a short time. If you are taking the exam with another student, she/he will also be asked to react personally to the subject of your photographs. The examiner will then give her/him two different theme-related photographs (e.g. of people doing different jobs). She/he will be asked to describe them and to talk about them in relation to her/himself for a short time. Finally you will also be asked to react personally to this second set of photographs.

You are going to practise this now with a partner.

1 Both of you should look at photos 1 and 2 below. Student A should compare and contrast what she/he can see in the two photos and say how she/he feels about eating in places like these. Then Student B should say if she/he has ever eaten in places like these.

2 Both of you should look at photos 3 and 4 below. Student B should compare and contrast what she/he can see in the two photos and say how she/he feels about hobbies like these. Then Student A should say if she/he has ever done a hobby like these.

1

2

3

4

Listening: inventors

1 Read the following information on two inventions. Which of the numbers in the box do you think goes in each gap?

| 120 billion | 55 million | 6 | 45 | 15/9/79 |

Trivial Pursuit
Worldwide sales: (1) .... sets
● Invented by Scott Abbott, John and Chris Haney
● Date invented: (2) ....

Trivial Pursuit's inventors took just (3) .... minutes to come up with their bestselling game, but over three years to achieve mass distribution. Today, a box sells every (4) .... seconds in one of the thirty countries where the game is now available.

Post-it Notes
Worldwide sales: (5) .... since 1978
● Invented by Spencer Silver and Robert Oliveira
● Date invented: 1964

Post-its were invented by accident, when attempts to make new glues produced one that didn't stick very well. Silver thought it was a breakthrough; 3M, his employers, did not. Silver never gave up and the product became a sales sensation when it reached the marketplace in 1978.

2 You are going to listen to an extract from a radio programme called 'Money Matters'. What inventions are referred to in the programme?

3 Listen again and this time complete the notes below on what each speaker says. You will need to write a number, a word or a short phrase in each gap.

1 Making money from an invention is certainly not
....
2 Richard Payne's company aims to put together inventors and ....
3 The first thing he says you should do is to find
....
4 The two things that make an invention which makes money are that it is ....
5 The reason why Parkhouse invented the wire coat-hanger was because he didn't want to
....
6 Pemberton created Coca-Cola in the year
....
7 The original Coca-Cola logo was drawn by
....
8 Pemberton sold his claim to the Coca-Cola fortune for ....
9 Candler made a lot of money from Coca-Cola mainly because he was so good at
....

4 Look at the different inventions below. Work in small groups. Each group should choose one invention and prepare to argue why this invention has been the most significant and useful of all the inventions. Consider also what life would be like without it.

Speaking

1 Work with a partner and describe the picture opposite by finishing off the following sentences in an appropriate way.

1 I think this is quite an old-fashioned scene because ...

2 In the background I can see ...

3 There is also a group of people who all seem to be ...

4 In the middle of the picture at the front there is a strange-looking machine for ...

5 I think the way this invention works is that firstly there are two men who ...

6 Then they drive to the place where ...

7 A barrel with a tap pours glue onto a big wheel at the front which then ...

8 In front of the big wheel there is some kind of ... which ...

9 This machine consists of a car which is being driven by ...

10 Then attached to the car is a kind of ...

11 At the top of this tower there are ...

12 At the front of the car there is a man who is ...

13 The machine doesn't look very stable. It is held together by ...

14 Other things I can see on the machine are ...

15 Finally, right at the front of the picture there are ...

2 Now listen to an English person doing the same thing and compare what she says with what you said.

W. HEATH ROBINSON.

3

1 Work in small groups. Decide on an invention and then try to draw a rough diagram to show how it works. You may want to choose one of the following inventions:

- a machine for serving breakfast in bed
- a machine for tidying your room
- a way of getting sun-tanned all over without having to keep moving
- a way of eating spaghetti without staining your clothes
- a way of avoiding tears when peeling onions
- a trap for a burglar

2 Now explain your invention to other students. Decide whose invention is the most interesting and useful.

1 Choose the most suitable alternative below to fill in the gaps in the following text.

When the doctor told my mother that I (1) .... have to have a minor operation, she was surprised because I didn't (2) .... a fuss at all. I was actually quite excited about going into hospital. I imagined how interested all my classmates would be when they heard why I was (3) .... from school.

I had a whole day just to get used to (4) .... in hospital before the operation and I spent my time talking to the other (5) .... and watching TV. I was a bit scared when they came to take me from the children's (6) .... to the operating (7) .... . The doctor gave me an (8) .... and told me to count to ten. I didn't get much further than three or four before I fell asleep.

When I woke up back in my bed, my stomach felt very (9) .... . A nurse came to see how I was and told me that it would take a couple of weeks for the wound to (10) .... , but that I would be able to get up and walk around in a couple of days. She took my (11) .... to make sure that I didn't have a fever and I went off to sleep again. When I woke up a few hours later, there was a boy I hadn't seen before in the next bed. He was about the same age (12) .... me with terrible purple bruises all over his face. He'd fallen head first off his bicycle because he had been trying to (13) .... up with his older brother who was riding very fast. He had also (14) .... his left leg. It was going to take him a lot longer to (15) .... than me.

1. **A** will **B** do **C** would **D** am
2. **A** make **B** do **C** get **D** have
3. **A** dismissed **B** allowed **C** permitted
   D absent
4. **A** being **B** be **C** was **D** am
5. **A** customers **B** clients **C** students
   D patients
6. **A** compartment **B** ward **C** section
   D division
7. **A** theatre **B** room **C** place **D** hall
8. **A** puncture **B** injection **C** syringe **D** stab
9. **A** hurt **B** damaged **C** injured **D** sore
10. **A** cure **B** recover **C** heal **D** fix
11. **A** heat **B** climate **C** temperature
    D thermometer
12. **A** like **B** that **C** than **D** as
13. **A** get **B** make **C** put **D** keep
14. **A** ruptured **B** broken **C** smashed
    D crunched
15. **A** recover **B** heal **C** cure **D** better

2 There are mistakes with verb tenses in eight of the following sentences. Find the mistakes and write the sentences out again correctly in your notebook.

1. When I leave school, I am looking for a job in a hotel.
2. I think I go to bed now. I'm very tired.
3. By the year 2000 I will have been studying English for ten years
4. I promise I phone you tonight.
5. I can't come this Tuesday because I'll play volleyball.
6. If I will see her, I will give her your love.
7. Are you making my bed for me this morning? I'm too tired.
8. I'll have done the First Certificate exam by this time next year.
9. When you read this, I'll fly over the Indian Ocean on my way home.
10. Look at those clouds. It will rain.

3 Fill in the gaps in the following text with an appropriate word.

Cooking is fun once you know how to do it. The easiest (1) .... to learn is to borrow (2) .... basic cookery books from the local library or from a friend and (3) .... experimenting. Spend a couple of hours reading through the (4) .... until you find one that you think sounds tasty.

(5) .... a list of the necessary ingredients and check the fridge and cupboards to (6) .... sure you have (7) .... you need. There is nothing worse (8) .... starting to cook a meal and then realising you don't have (9) .... essential like lemons or breadcrumbs. It is really (10) .... to check that you have all the basic equipment like cheese graters and knives as well. The recipes in most cookery books have been tested many (11) .... so the instructions (12) .... be accurate and clear. Read them through carefully and assemble all the things you (13) .... need. Another thing, (14) .... a lot of people forget unfortunately, is that cleaning up as you go along makes cooking easier. My mother, (15) .... was a superb cook, always said, 'The best meals come from a tidy kitchen.'

4 Rewrite the second sentence so that it has a similar meaning to the first sentence using the word in **bold** and other words.

1 I tried as hard as I could, but I still didn't pass.
   best
   I ...., but I still didn't pass.

2 My parents met in 1970.
   since
   My parents .... 1970.

3 I don't share your opinion about military service.
   agree
   I .... you about military service.

4 He has too much free time since he retired.
   hands
   He has too much .... since he retired.

5 Driving on the left will always feel strange to me.
   get
   I don't think I will ever .... on the left.

6 Can you calculate the answers to these sums?
   work
   Can you .... the answers to these sums?

7 She said she wouldn't tell anyone about what happened.
   not
   She promised .... anyone about what happened.

8 The operator had trouble connecting me to the sales department.
   through
   The operator had trouble .... to the sales department.

9 I lived in London as a child, but I don't anymore.
   used
   I .... in London as a child.

10 Could you possibly share your book with me?
   mind
   Would you .... your book with me?

5 There are mistakes of grammar or vocabulary in twelve of the following sentences. Find the mistakes and write the sentences out correctly in your notebook.

1 A: Could I borrow your dictionary?
   B: Yes, of course you might.

2 Her parents gave a party when they heard she had successfully taken all her exams.

3 My family lived in the city since 1963.

4 You lie the table while I finish cooking the dinner.

5 He gained a really big prize in the National Lottery.

6 He failed his driving test for the third time last week.

7 I have finished school two years ago.

8 I'm sorry. I am not agree with you.

9 That dress really suits you. The colour goes with your eyes.

10 You ought take up jogging.

11 Jenny is the nicest person I've ever met.

12 In my point of view, spending a lot of money on expensive clothes is stupid.

13 You really should to go and see that film. It's fantastic.

14 Don't buy her that book. She read all of his novels already.

15 As far that I am concerned, people like that should be sent to prison.

6 Fill in the gaps in the following sentences with an appropriate word. The first two letters of each word have been given to help you..

1 I fell over in the pl.......... at school today and hu.......... my leg

2 The he.......... telephoned my parents when he caught me ch.......... in the final exam.

3 We were lucky enough to get seats in the front ro.......... so we could see all the members of the gr.......... really well.

4 I didn't enjoy that book at all. I thought the pl.......... was too simple and the ch.......... were really artificial.

5 He must have just got up because he was still wearing his py.......... and sl.......... .

6 If you've got such a high te.........., I don't understand why the doctor didn't give you a pr.......... for some antibiotics.

7 Most of the cuts have he.......... since the accident, but she's still got some nasty br.......... on her face.

8 Would you like your eggs sc.........., bo.......... or fr.......... ?

9 Po.......... the sauce over the cauliflower and sp.......... some gr.......... cheese on top.

10 That dress really su.......... you and it was such a ba.......... at only £20.

11 The shop as.......... said they would or.......... a pair of those jeans in my si.......... .

12 Good morning. I'd like to wi.......... some money from my ac.........., but I seem to have left my ch.......... book at home.

7   Read the following text and look carefully at each line. Some of the lines are correct and some have a word that should not be there. If a line is correct, put a (✔) at the end of it. If there is a word that should not be there, circle it. There are two examples at the beginning (**0** and **00**).

0	This summer's fashions should brighten up your wardrobe. ✔
00	Most of the designers have introduced (the) brilliant colours
1	to their collections. There are dresses in bright pinks,
2	yellows and oranges with matching short-sleeved jackets.
3	Many women will have be wearing wide striped trousers in all
4	the colours of the rainbow with matching blouses. You're
5	probably asking what do you will wear on your feet this
6	season. Well, the answer is the very highest of high-heels.
7	And if you are someone who would likes to be comfortable,
8	there are also some very attractive flat sandals for to wear
9	in the evening. The emphasis in this season's men's fashions
10	is on style and comfort. Cool fabrics like cotton and linen
11	are popular with all the designers. There is a wide variety
12	of suits for more formal than occasions, as well as
13	dungarees and T-shirts for casual wear. And hats are back.
14	Men and women will be wearing hats just like the ones our
15	grandparents got used to wear in the forties and fifties.

8   Read the following text and use the word given in capitals at the end of each line to form a word that fits in the gap in the same line.

You don't have to be a (1) .... person to take	**COMPETE**
part in (2) .... , though you do need to be fairly	**ATHLETE**
(3) .... and reasonably fit. You can build up fitness	**ENERGY**
by jogging. It's not the (4) .... that matters, but how	**DISTANT**
long you jog for. You can improve your (5)	**PERFORM**
gradually over a period of weeks. In (6) .... for a	**PREPARE**
long race like a marathon it's (7) .... to run more	**NECESSARY**
than a couple of kilometres most days. (8)	**SUCCESS**
marathon runners work on the (9) .... aspects of	**PSYCHOLOGY**
running long races. Mental (10) .... is just as	**STRONG**
important as being physically fit.	

9   Replace the underlined words and phrases with an appropriate phrasal verb in the correct form.

1   Philip couldn't <u>maintain the same level as</u> the other students in his class.
2   I just won't <u>tolerate</u> his bad behaviour any more.
3   I think we should <u>postpone</u> the party until everyone gets back from their holidays.
4   I'm sure I <u>returned</u> your sweater.
5   Tina, could you help me <u>distribute</u> the books?
6   He <u>revealed</u> his feelings when he blushed at the sound of her name.
7   Could you <u>raise your voice</u> a bit? We can't hear you at the back of the room.
8   You really must <u>stop</u> smoking – it's so bad for your health.
9   They always <u>provide me with accommodation</u> when I'm in Sydney.
10   He said 'no' at first, but in the end he <u>relented</u> and said we could go to the party.
11   Profits are down – I'm afraid we're going to have to <u>increase</u> our prices.
12   She doesn't earn much, but she still manages to <u>save</u> a little money each month.

The planet Earth

Reading

1 Describe what you can see in the pictures.

2 Check that you know the meaning of the following words. Use a dictionary where necessary.

> a meteor   dust   to dye   a sand dune
> a gust   an earthquake   to wrestle
> a tornado   a storm

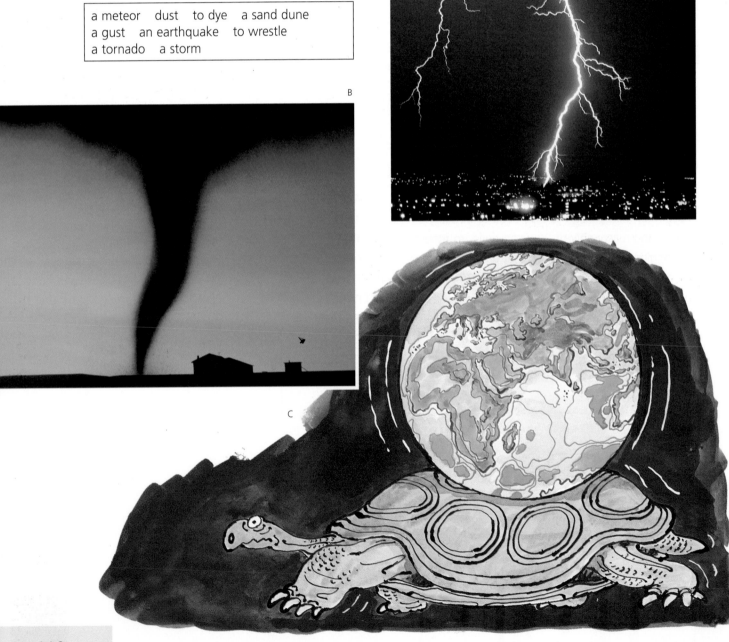

3 Divide into two groups, A and B. Group A should look at the text below, Group B should look at the text on page 187. Each group should read through their text and decide what kind of information is missing in each of the numbered gaps. Is it a name, a date, a thing, a distance or something else?

Group A

Weird Weather Facts

■ The study and forecasting of weather is called (**1**) .... because it was once precisely that – the study of meteors. The idea that meteors were formed in the sky from various combinations of earth, water, air and fire, and that they contributed to weather conditions, goes back to the great philosopher and scientist, Aristotle, in the 4th century BC. It was believed in Europe until late in the 17th century.

■ In AD 582, it rained (**3**) .... on Paris. The terrified local people saw this as a sign from Heaven and responded by repenting for their sins. The true cause of the strange event was the 'sirocco', the wind that sometimes blows from the Sahara across the Mediterranean into Europe. It carries a fine, red dust from the desert interior, and this had (**5**) .... the rain that fell on Paris.

■ On May 29, 1986, twelve schoolchildren in west China were sucked up by a tornado. It put them down again on some sand dunes (**7**) .... km away – completely unharmed.

■ The highest wind speeds ever officially recorded have occurred at the top of Mount Washington in New Hampshire, USA, where gusts have reached 370 km/hour.

■ (**9**) .... believed that the Earth lay on the back of a giant tortoise, and when it shuffled its feet the Earth would quake. One ancient Japanese legend held that the movement of a vast underground (**11**) .... caused earthquakes; a later account said it was a monster catfish. The ancient Greeks blamed huge giants wrestling underground.

■ An average of (**13**) .... tornadoes strike the United States each year. In April 1974, 148 tornadoes hit thirteen states in just twenty-four hours, leaving (**15**) .... people dead.

■ If you are stuck out in a storm, never shelter under a tall isolated tree. Try to get indoors, or into a car. Get away from metal objects and get rid of any (**17**) .... you are carrying. If you're with other people, spread out. Unfortunately, sometimes even being indoors is no protection. In July (**19**) .... a woman was struck by a bolt that came through the window and hit the metal tea-strainer she was holding. The force of the bolt threw her across the kitchen.

from Reader's Digest *Did you know?*

4 Now decide what questions you need to ask to find out what the missing information is.

5 Finally work with a partner from the other group. Ask your partner the questions, listen to the answers and fill in the gaps in the text with the missing information.

Grammar: the article

1 Read the following rules for when we use the definite article (*the*), the indefinite article (*a/an*) and for when we do not use an article at all (the zero article). Then match each of the examples opposite to one of the rules.

THE ARTICLE

The definite article (*the*) is used:

a) with inventions and species of animals e.g. *When was* **the radio** *invented?/I think* **the whale** *may soon be extinct.*

b) with rivers/oceans/seas e.g. **The Amazon** *flows into* **the Atlantic Ocean**.

c) when there is only one of something e.g. **The sky** *is full of stars tonight.*

d) with national groups e.g. **The British** *drink a lot of tea.*

e) with superlatives e.g. *He is* **the kindest person** *I know.*

f) with particular nouns when it is clear what we are referring to e.g. *Could you pass* **the salt**, *please?*

g) with previously mentioned nouns e.g. *There is an apple and an orange. I want* **the orange**.

The indefinite article (*a/an*) is used:

h) with jobs e.g. *She is* **a doctor**.

i) with singular countable nouns (mentioned for the first time or when it doesn't matter which one) e.g. *I live in* **a small house**./*You will need* **a ruler** *in the exam.*

No article (the zero article) is used:

j) with most streets/villages/towns/cities/countries/lakes/mountains e.g. *I'm going to* **Oxford Street** *today./I love living in* **Rome**./*He comes from* **Greece**./*When did the first person climb* **Mount Everest**? (For countries/groups of islands in the plural we use *the* e.g. *He was born in* **the United States**.)

k) with uncountable, plural and abstract nouns used in their general sense e.g. *I like* **orange juice**./*I hate* **cities**./***Travel** broadens the mind.*

Grammar reference p.163 (3)

EXAMPLES:

1 It rained 'blood' on <u>Paris</u>.
2 <u>The highest</u> wind speeds ever officially recorded have reached 370 km/hour.
3 <u>The ancient Greeks</u> blamed huge giants wrestling underground.
4 It blows across <u>the Mediterranean</u> into Europe.
5 When it shuffled its feet <u>the Earth</u> would quake.
6 The idea that <u>meteors</u> were formed in the sky goes back to Aristotle.
7 I'd like to be <u>a meteorologist</u> when I grow up.
8 A later account said it was <u>a monster catfish</u>.
9 <u>The elephant</u> is mainly hunted for its tusks.
10 In July 1982 a woman was struck by a bolt. The force of <u>the bolt</u> threw her across the kitchen.
11 In July 1982 a woman was struck by a bolt. The force of the bolt threw her across <u>the kitchen</u>.

2 Fill in the gaps in the following sentences with *a, an, the* or *(–)* when no article is needed.

1 Could you turn on .... television, please?
2 Watch out! There's .... policeman coming!
3 It's .... best film I have seen in ages.
4 Could I borrow .... piece of paper to make notes on?
5 Is that .... new carpet you were telling me about?
6 I think that .... young people are much more mature these days.
7 We're going to .... Kenya at Christmas.
8 Would you like to see .... photos I took on holiday?
9 They tell me that .... honesty is the best policy.
10 She said that .... carrots were her favourite vegetable.
11 Sometimes I wish .... telephone had never been invented.
12 Look at .... sea. Isn't it beautiful?
13 Why do you think .... Japanese are so hard working?
14 We went sailing on .... Lake Windermere at the weekend.

3 Look back at some of the compositions you have written to check whether you have made any mistakes with the article. If there are mistakes, make sure you understand why.

4 In the following text *the* is missing ten times and *a/an* is missing twice. Insert them in the correct places.

Dead Sea, which lies between Jordan and Israel, is lowest lake in world. It is about 397 metres below sea level and it contains saltiest water in world. This is because several rivers carrying minerals (including salt) flow into lake, but none flow out of it. Surface water evaporates, but all minerals remain behind. Salt makes it easy for swimmers to float – you can even read book while floating on your back. In fact lake contains six times more salt than ordinary sea water so swimmer's body is six times more buoyant than usual.

Vocabulary: weather

1 Put the words in the box into one of the categories below. Some of the words can go in more than one category. Then decide if the words can be used as nouns, verbs or adjectives.

damp	freezing	humid	breeze	drizzle	snow
pour	boiling	hail	gale	shower	warm
chilly	cool	frost	gust	sunny	mild

• **rain** • **wind** • **heat** • **cold** • **wet**

2 Describe what the weather is typically like in your country:

1 at 6.00 a.m.
2 at 1.00 p.m. } this month
3 at 8.00 p.m.

4 in January.
5 in April.
6 in August.
7 in November.

3 Tell a partner what kinds of weather you love and hate.

4 Look at the idioms in *italics* below and try to work out what they mean. Do you have similar idioms in your own language?

1 I'm feeling a bit *under the weather* today.
2 *Make hay while the sun shines.*
3 *It never rains but it pours.*
4 Don't worry. He'll be *as right as rain* in no time.
5 It's just a *storm in a teacup.*
6 He really *put the wind up me* when he said we might lose our jobs.

5

1 Certain adjectives go with or 'collocate' with certain nouns in English. Decide which of the adjectives on the left collocate with the nouns on the right.

● heavy	a) winter
● strong	b) fog
● hard	c) rain
● thick	d) wind
	e) tea
	f) traffic
	g) smoker
	h) opinion
	i) skin
	j) accent
	k) bed

2 Now choose four combinations which are new to you and make sentences which show that you understand the meaning.

EXAMPLE: *It was such **a strong wind** that my hat blew off.*

Pronunciation: homophones

1 Look at the following pairs/groups of words and decide if all the words are pronounced in the same way or if any are pronounced differently.

1 wind/(to) wind (a watch)
2 weather/whether
3 mist/missed
4 pour/paw/poor
5 won/one
6 there/their/they're
7 bear/bare/beer
8 bird/beard
9 so/sew
10 white/wait/weight
11 hat/hate/height
12 flower/floor/flour
13 wear/where/were/we're
14 hurt/heart
15 court/caught
16 whole/hole
17 won't/want
18 sight/site
19 saw/sore
20 (to) row (a boat)
    (a) row (= an argument)
    (a) row (= a line of chairs)

2 Listen and check your answers.

3 Listen to the following sentences and then try to say them with good pronunciation.

1 I saw a bear over there.
2 I wonder whether you could pour me a beer, please.
3 I don't want to wear a flower in my hair.
4 I hurt my shoulder yesterday. It's still sore today.
5 We had a bad row last night. He won't speak to me today.
6 Can you tell me your weight and height, please?
7 We caught a rare bird.

Exam focus

Paper 1 Reading (gapped text)

In this part of the exam you will be asked to read a text from which six or seven sentences (or paragraphs) have been removed and placed in jumbled order after the text. You have to decide from where in the text the sentences (or paragraphs) have been removed. It is important to remember that in the exam one of the sentences (or paragraphs) will not be needed.

1 Discuss what you think the best way is to approach this task type. If necessary, look again at the suggested procedure on page 23 and say if this is what you do, or whether you have a different way of approaching this task.

2 Look at the photos below and discuss the following questions.

1 Where do you think this place is?
2 What are the objects you can see?

3 Now read the following text and find out if you were right.

Easter Island: A terrible warning

The people of Easter Island crossed the ocean to create a peaceful and prosperous 1000-year civilisation. But then their culture collapsed into war and mass starvation. It's a lesson we have to learn from.

The most isolated piece of inhabited land on the planet is in the South Pacific, 3,765 kilometres west of South America and 2,253 kilometres south-east of the nearest island. Easter Island is famous for its astonishing Stone Age culture – hundreds of enormous stone statues, many of them standing on massive stone platforms. **(1 ———)**

The civilisation that produced these amazing constructions has now nearly died out. Today, Easter Island is a 166-square-kilometre museum to that civilisation. Most researchers believe that the first colonists arrived in the first centuries AD and that Easter Island's stone structures were well developed by the 7th century. The archaeological record suggests a single unbroken culture, so there was probably just one major arrival of people by canoe. **(2 ———)**

Over its three million years of existence before humans came along, Easter Island had developed a balanced ecosystem. **(3 ———)** During this early period, the islanders built simple types of ahu (platform), with small statues either on or in front of them.

The second period of the island's history, from about AD 1000 to 1500, was its golden age. As they became more prosperous, the people devoted great energy to building bigger and better ceremonial platforms and hundreds of large statues. As the population grew, probably reaching between 10,000 and 20,000 in about 1500, the need for land increased. **(4 ———)**

The third and final period saw the tragic collapse of the earlier way of life. The causes of the island's change and decline were complex, but mainly due to one thing – the destruction of large numbers of trees. Starting at least 1,200 years ago, this meant that there were almost no large trees left by the time the Europeans came in the 18th century.

Without these trees, statues could no longer be moved and nor could ocean-going canoes be built. **(5 ———)** Deforestation also caused massive soil erosion, which damaged the island's potential for growing crops.

It is impossible to know exactly what happened on Easter Island as there are no records. What is certain is that the civilisation collapsed because of population growth, together with the decline in food and the great expense of effort on wasteful activities (platform building, statue carving and transportation). Starvation led to raiding and violence – perhaps, even to cannibalism.

(6 ———) At that time the population was reduced to about 2000, living in poverty in the ruins of their former culture. The Easter Island story provides a model for disaster. The parallel between the ecological disaster on Easter Island (isolated in the Pacific) and what is happening elsewhere on planet Earth (isolated in space) is far too close for comfort.

4 The following sentences have been removed from the text. Read it again and decide in which numbered gap each sentence should go. There is one extra sentence which you do not need to use.

A This natural balance was disturbed by the arrival of voyagers, probably a few dozen Polynesians.

B So the population was cut off from the important protein supply of deep-sea fish.

C But once settled on the island, the colonists were trapped – it became their whole world.

D By 1722, when the first Europeans arrived, it was all over.

E The foreign visitors also brought with them European diseases which devastated the local population

F However, the story of the island is also a warning to us all.

G There is also evidence of a serious decline of the forest.

5 Discuss the following questions.

1 Are you concerned about the destruction of the environment and the 'wasteful use of resources' on planet Earth?

2 What, if anything, do you think a) governments b) individuals should be doing about it? Consider the following:

– nuclear power stations
– tropical rainforests
– the ozone layer
– recycling of rubbish
– the quantity of traffic
– pollution
– acid rain

from Focus magazine

Grammar: modals of deduction/ criticism (past)

1 Decide which of the underlined words below suggest:

1 certainty   3 criticism
2 impossibility 4 possibility

They <u>must</u>
They <u>might/could</u>   }   have moved the statues on
They <u>can't</u>   wooden rollers.

They <u>shouldn't</u> have destroyed the forest.

2 Complete this dialogue with the correct form of the words in brackets. Then practise saying it with a partner.

A: Do you know why Simon didn't come to my party?
B: He must (1).................... *(be/ill).*
A: Oh no, he can't (2).................... *(be/ill).* I saw him at school this morning and he was fine.
B: Well, he might (3).................... *(forget/about it).*
A: No, he can't (4).................... *(do).* I reminded him about it yesterday morning.
B: Well, he has got an exam tomorrow. He could (5).................... *(stay/at home to work).*
A: Yes, but he should (6).................... *(tell/me)!*

3 Read this short story about Paul. After each part of the story react to each suggested reason for what happened using *must have, might have, could have* or *can't have.*

1 Paul left school early at sixteen although he passed his exams.

   a) not like his teachers
   b) not clever enough

   EXAMPLE: *He **might have left** school early because he didn't like his teachers.*

2 He really didn't want to work in his father's firm, but in the end he did.

   a) no other possibilities
   b) his father promised him a good job

3 He met Sophie, a secretary on a very low salary, at work. They started going out together.

   a) he was after her money
   b) they liked each other
   c) she knew he was the boss's son

4 He suddenly decided to leave his job and go abroad without Sophie.

   a) he loved her very much
   b) she started seeing another man
   c) he wasn't enjoying his job

4 Look at the people in these photos and make deductions about who they are, what their relationship is and what happened just before and in the time leading up to the photo. Use *must have/ might have/can't have.*

5 Write down the names of five people you know. Next to their names write down one thing that they have done wrong in your opinion. Then make a sentence using *should (not) have* and give a reason.

EXAMPLE: *Diana - not set her alarm clock.*
*Diana **should have set** her alarm clock last night because she overslept and was late for school.*

Grammar reference p.169 (10.3/10.4/10.7)

Vocabulary: problems/disasters

1 Fill in the gaps in the following sentences with an appropriate word from the box.

> floods earthquake famine drought disease
> emergency refugees aid charity injuries

1 The crops have failed again and .... is widespread.
2 The latest San Francisco .... measured 4.5 on the Richter scale.
3 In case of .... break the glass and push the button.
4 Half a million .... have now crossed the border in an attempt to find food.
5 I never give to .... I think it should be the government's responsibility.
6 The present government has given more in .... to needy countries than any other in living memory.
7 Many children have suffered terrible .... as a result of the fighting.
8 A new .... has been discovered which causes partial blindness and skin problems.
9 There has been a .... in certain parts of the country due to the lack of rain.
10 There has been so much rain that some rivers have burst their banks and there have been ....

2 Fill in the gaps in the following sentences with the correct form of the words in brackets.

1 The .... of the ozone layer is one of the worst things that has happened. (DESTROY)
2 If we don't send food, there will be .... on a massive scale. (STARVE)
3 We need to find a .... to the problem before things get seriously out of hand. (SOLVE)
4 There was a .... of 100,000 in the centre of London today. (DEMONSTRATE)
5 It is shocking that ten per cent of the population live below the .... line. (POOR)
6 Some of the most beautiful Indian tigers are facing .... (EXTINCT)
7 If the .... gets any worse, I'm going to move to the country. (POLLUTE)
8 I believe the .... of the planet is worth fighting for. (SURVIVE)

Listening: Biosphere 2

1 Look at the photo and discuss where you think it was taken.

2 You are going to hear a radio interview which describes an experiment. Listen and decide if in general it has been a success or a failure.

3 Now listen to the interview again and make a note of the significance of the following.

1 £100 million   5 hairdryers
2 the pigs   6 goats
3 an oxygen tank   7 20 kilos
4 sweet potatoes

Speaking

Imagine you were going to live in the Biosphere for two years. Due to lack of space, you can only take the following possessions with you (all the essentials of life will be provided). Say which ones you would take and why.

- two books
- a video film
- a picture/poster
- a game

- two CDs/cassettes/records
- a musical instrument
- three photos
- one other thing

Writing: transactional letter (2)

Read the following exam task and then the sample answer below. Discuss with a partner what the main problem with the answer is. Then work together and rewrite it in a more appropriate way.

You have seen the following advertisement in a magazine. You have always wanted to take part in an expedition like this one, but would like to have more information. Read the advertisement carefully and the notes which you have made below. Then write your letter.

OPERATION SEA WOLF
Chance Of A Lifetime!

If you want to see the world, visit exotic places, make new friends and work hard as part of a team, this could be just the opportunity you've been looking for.

Operation Sea Wolf sets sail on November 15th and currently needs:
- marine biologists/anthropologists/ geologists
- enthusiastic crew members (no previous sailing experience necessary)

The voyage will last for approximately 6 months and will include research into the animal and plant life of Indonesia.

- any qualifications needed?
- cost?
- what need to take?
- exact date of return?

Dear Sir/Madam,

I was really thrilled to see your super advertisement in Eco Magazine yesterday. I've always wanted to go on a sea voyage ever since I was little and this looks like it could be my big chance.

There are just a few little points that crossed my mind. First of all, I was just a bit worried that I might need some special qualifications or something. Another thing was that you didn't say if we would have to pay anything and I'm actually a bit short of cash at the moment, you know how it is!

If it was alright with you and I did come, my mum wanted me to ask what I would need to bring but I suppose you have some kind of list, don't you? Oh yes, and the other thing was... when exactly do you think we'll be back because I really fancy doing a Spanish course next summer and I can't book it without knowing when we're getting back.

Well, I can't wait to meet everyone. Do write back soon and let me know what's next!
See you soon,

Dieter

1 Six of the following sentences are wrong or unlikely because of a mistake with the article (*a/an* or *the*). Find the mistakes and correct them.

1 Sun rises in the east and sets in the west.
2 That's the car I mentioned before.
3 Put those plates in a washing-up bowl, will you?
4 He's most arrogant man I have ever met.
5 I'd like a glass of wine and a few olives, please.
6 The weather has been marvellous recently.
7 Money has been the cause of a lot of our problems.
8 Australia was everything I imagined it would be.
9 Would you mind if I took car into work today?
10 We're thinking of going to cinema tonight.
11 Are you going to take the dogs for a walk or shall I?
12 Let's go for a drive in country.

2 Match a sentence from Column A with a sentence from Column B.

A

1 It's freezing out there.
2 There were these awful gusts.
3 It's very humid at the moment.
4 There's a gentle breeze coming off the sea.
5 The gales have been terrible.
6 It's very mild for this time of year.
7 Did the storm wake you up last night?
8 Did you know there was a serious earthquake in the capital this morning?

B

a) Yes, the thunder and lightning was really scary.
b) They kept blowing my umbrella inside out.
c) It's great because it stops you getting too hot.
d) Lots of trees have been blown over.
e) You must put your scarf and gloves on.
f) We've normally had some snow by now.
g) I know. The government has declared a state of emergency.
h) I just can't stop sweating all the time.

3 Rewrite the following sentences using the words given so that the meaning stays the same. You will need to use 2–5 words in each case.

1 It wasn't a very good idea for you to sit in the sun for so long.
should
You .... in the sun for so long.

2 I'm sure he hasn't gone far because the car is still here.
can
He .... far because the car is still here.

3 I think it was possibly the cat which scratched the table.
might
The cat .... the table.

4 She was definitely here earlier because she's left her umbrella.
must
She .... here earlier because she's left her umbrella.

5 Buying that car was a real mistake.
should
We .... that car.

6 There's a chance that he phoned, but I haven't been in.
could
He ...., but I haven't been in.

7 There's absolutely no chance that she took the money. I've been with her all the time.
can
She .... the money. I've been with her all the time.

8 I'm sure she's gone to play tennis. She's taken her racket.
must
She .... to play tennis. She's taken her racket.

The great persuaders

Reading

1 Look at the title of the text opposite. How do you imagine this was possible?

2 The following words all appear in the text. Match each one with its correct definition on the right. Then think again about your answer to the question in Exercise 1.

1	a conman	a)	a silly or stupid person
2	a fool	b)	someone who buys and sells material which has been used and finished with but which may still have some value
3	a tender	c)	dishonest behaviour which is intended to deceive people, often in order to gain money
4	a bid	d)	easily tricked or persuaded to believe something
5	a scrap merchant	e)	a gift or favour you give someone in a position of power in order to influence or persuade them to do something
6	a bribe	f)	a statement of the price you would charge for doing a job or providing goods
7	gullible	g)	someone who cheats people by telling them things that are not true
8	fraud	h)	an offer to pay a certain price for something that is being sold

from *The World's Greatest Mistakes,* edited by Nigel Blundell

Conman who sold the Eiffel Tower – twice!

If there is indeed a fool born every minute, for every fool there seems to be a conman ready to make him a little wiser[1].

Two of the most extraordinary conmen of all time were Count Victor Lustig, an Austrian who worked in the French Ministry of Works, and Daniel Collins, a small-time American criminal. Together they managed to sell the Eiffel Tower – not once, but twice.

The count set about arranging the deal by booking a room in a Paris hotel in the spring of 1925 and inviting[2] five businessmen to meet him there. When they arrived, he swore them to secrecy[3], then told them that the Eiffel Tower was in a dangerous[4] condition and would have to be pulled down. He asked for tenders for the scrap metal contained in the famous landmark. The count explained[5] the hotel meeting and the need for secrecy by saying that his ministry wanted to avoid[6] any public anger over the demolition of such a well-loved national monument.

Within the week, all bids were in and the count accepted that of scrap merchant, André Poisson. The deal was made, and a banker's draft was handed over at a final meeting at which the count introduced[7] his 'secretary', Collins. Then the conmen played their best card. They asked Poisson for a bribe to help the deal go smoothly[8] through official channels. The dealer agreed willingly, and gave the money in cash. If he had ever had any suspicions[9], they were now put to rest. After all, a demand for a bribe meant that the two men must be from the ministry.

Lustig and Collins were out of the country within 24 hours. But they only stayed abroad long enough to realise that the outcry they had expected to follow their fraud had not happened. Poisson was so ashamed at being taken in that he never reported them to the police.

The count and his partner returned to Paris and repeated[10] the trick. They sold the Eiffel Tower all over again to another gullible scrap merchant. This time the man did go to the police, and the conmen quickly left the country. They were never brought to justice, and they never revealed just how much money they had got away with.

3   Now read the text and see if you were right.

4   Read the text again and decide if the following statements are True or False.

1   The businessmen promised not to tell anyone that the Eiffel Tower was going to be pulled down.
2   The businessmen all offered money to buy the Eiffel Tower.
3   Poisson finally paid the conmen more than he had originally offered for the Eiffel Tower.
4   Poisson became rather suspicious of the two men before they left France.
5   Poisson didn't tell the police because he didn't realise what had happened.
6   The conmen did finally go to jail.

5   Put the numbered words from the text in the following sentences in the correct form.

EXAMPLE: 1   ...*Wisdom*... is not necessarily something which comes with age.

2   Have you had an .... to Sarah's party?
3   Please don't tell anyone that I'm pregnant. It's still a ....
4   There is no .... of anyone finding out.
5   I'm afraid that .... is just not good enough!
6   I'm really sorry we were late, but it was absolutely ....
7   There is a very good .... to this book.
8   I love the way babies' skin is so ....
9   He is being very nice to me. It's making me rather ....
10   I promise there won't be any .... of this behaviour.

Vocabulary: phrasal verbs (*get*)

● *... they never revealed just how much money they had* **got away with.**

1   Match the phrasal verbs in the following sentences to one of the meanings a)–h).

1   I've been trying to *get through* to you on the telephone all afternoon.
2   If you're unemployed, it's very hard to *get by* on the money the government gives you.
3   Apparently he stole thousands of pounds from the company and *got away with* it for years.

4   It took him a very long time to *get over* the death of his wife.
5   I'm sorry, but I really must *get down to* my English homework.
6   Do you *get on* well *with* your father-in-law?
7   Don't worry. I know how to *get round* my Dad.
8   What are the children *getting up to* now? It's far too quiet?

a)   recover
b)   make contact
c)   start doing seriously
d)   have a good relationship with
e)   persuade someone to let you do something
f)   survive
g)   do something naughty or bad
h)   avoid being caught and punished

2   Now fill in the gaps in the following sentences with the correct particle (*away*, *down*, etc.).

1   You won't get .... with it, you know. Someone will find out!
2   I'm surprised you and Simon don't get .... better. You're so similar in character.
3   Now, don't get .... to anything while I'm out, will you?
4   I've got just enough French to get .... on holiday, but that's about it!
5   If you don't get .... to writing some postcards soon, the holiday will be over!
6   I know she's disappointed about her exam results, but she'll get .... it.
7   If I want an extra day's holiday, I'll have to think of a way of getting .... my boss.
8   It's so frustrating. I just can't get .... to Brian. The line is constantly engaged.

3   Put the words in the following sentences in order.

1   you sister on why get your don't with?
2   in I've Spanish everyday enough got by situations get to.
3   him to will long illness how take it over this get?
4   always can flowers round her get I buying by her.
5   to away what getting while have been you up have I been?
6   business time get to it to down is.
7   it hurt away he me to going get and is with not.
8   hospital Dr Jones easily I to got phoned and through the.

Speaking

1 Discuss what skills and qualities you need to be an effective salesman.

'It's got more special-function keys than you'll find on many of the larger models. It's solar-powered and it even tells you the time in different countries. I'd say that more than makes up for the fact that it doesn't have the number nine!'

2 You are going to be a door-to-door salesman working on a commission-only basis. You are going to try and sell some items to other students, but first you should prepare yourself with some necessary language by doing the following exercises.

A Grammar: modifiers/intensifiers

1 Three of the following sentences are not possible. Decide which ones and why.

a) The film was absolutely incredible.
b) He's a terrific guy. I really like him.
c) The food in that restaurant was very marvellous.
d) John's got a wonderful sense of humour.
e) He's an extremely amazing football player.
f) The number of people at the concert was quite incredible.
g) We had a really great time at Jo's party last night.
h) The special effects in the film were just superb.
i) Her English is really fantastic. She must have lived in an English-speaking country.
j) We saw an absolutely good tennis match on TV this afternoon.

2 Think about the last really good time you had with either your friends or family. Note down some of the key points about it, for example where you went, what you did, why it was so good. Now tell a partner about it. Be very enthusiastic and use some of the modifiers/intensifiers from the sentences in 1.
Grammar reference p.171 (11)

B Writing: linkers (addition)

1 Look at the following ways of linking two positive or negative points about something.

- **Not only** does this machine tell you the time, **but** it **also** makes tea.
- **As well as** tell**ing** you the time, this machine makes tea.
- **In addition to** tell**ing** you the time, this machine makes tea.
- This machine tells you the time. **Moreover/ Furthermore**, it makes tea.

2 Use the words and patterns above to link the information in the following sentences.

a) He is very good-looking. He is also very intelligent.
b) The room in the hotel was dirty. It was also cold.
c) They want us to start working half an hour earlier. They also say they can't pay us any more.
d) The weather in Cairo is fantastic. The people are also incredibly friendly.
Grammar reference p.168 (9.1)

3 You are nearly ready to go to work! Opposite are some of the items you have to sell. Look at the pictures, read the descriptions and decide which item would be suitable for someone who:

a) wants to be seen in the dark.
b) is strongly attracted to metal.
c) wants to look silly at parties.
d) does not mind frightening the birds.
e) never knows where their keys are.

1 Loony Lenses

Just the thing to help you to have fun on those special occasions, these outrageous Loony Lenses have battery powered windscreen wipers and orange headlights. Powered by 2AA batteries (not included). *Price £7.95.*

2 From Drinks Bottle to Rocket

Stand back for the best display of basic rocket engineering you're ever going to see. All you need is an empty plastic drinks bottle and a bicycle pump (not included), and with this amazing kit you can launch your own rocket that will fly up to 30 metres in the air. Adult supervision required for under 14s. *Price £8.95.*

from the *London Science Museum* catalogue

3 Talking Alarm Clock and Keyfinder

A talking pocket alarm on a key ring; at the touch of a button it speaks the time with its 'human' voice. Lost your keys? Just call out or clap your hands and it responds repeatedly from anywhere in the room, helping you to find your keys immediately. Other features include an alarm and LCD visual time display. Button batteries supplied. *Price £13.95.*

4 Giant Horseshoe Magnet

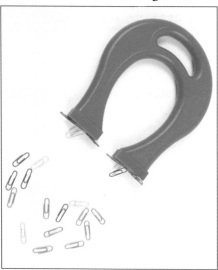

This is a seriously powerful magnet. So strong it lifts up to 2 kilos in weight. It will last for years and is so large (with no small parts) that it is suitable for all children ages 4 and over. The Giant Horseshoe Magnet measures 25 cm high. *Price £6.95.*

5 Glowing Galaxy T-Shirt

As black as night and decorated front and back with inter-galactic action, this exclusive new T-shirt features glow-in-the-dark space craft, astronauts and planets. Printed on 100 percent cotton in a range of sizes for adults and children. *Price £14.95 (Adult), £12.95 (Child).*

4 Now make one or two notes about why someone would benefit from having each item.

5 Work with a partner and roleplay the following situation. You are a door-to-door salesman with these items to sell. You knock on your partner's front door. She/he is in the middle of watching a TV programme. Try and convince your partner to buy as many of the items as possible. Use the language you have just studied where appropriate.

Grammar: *have to/don't have to/ must/need*

- '*The Eiffel Tower* **has to** *be pulled down.*'

1   Can you think of any other ways of saying the sentence above without using *have to* but so that it keeps the same meaning?

2   Answer the following questions.

1   Can you put the following sentence into the past?

- *I must tell John about the party.*

2   In which of these two sentences:

  a) does the speaker probably decide for himself?
  b) is the speaker probably told by someone else?

- *I have to take a holiday before the end of May.*
- *I must take a holiday before the end of May.*

3   Which of these sentences are good English and which aren't? Why?

  a) *I've got to give up smoking.*
  b) *I've to give up smoking.*
  c) *I have to give up smoking.*
  d) *I often have to work until 7 o'clock at night.*
  e) *I often have got to work until 7 o'clock at night.*

4   Is there any difference between these sentences?

  a) *You don't have to wait.*
  b) *You needn't wait.*
  c) *You don't need to wait.*
  d) *You mustn't wait.*

5   Is there any difference between these sentences?

  a) *You are not allowed to smoke in here.*
  b) *You can't smoke in here.*
  c) *You don't have to smoke in here.*

6   Did he do his homework?

  a) *You didn't need to do the homework.*
  b) *You needn't have done the homework.*

Grammar reference p.170 (10.5/10.6)

Watch Out! *supposed to*

1   You *are supposed to* speak English in class.
2   You *are not supposed to* speak Greek in class.

How can we rephrase these sentences using *should*?

---

3   Rewrite the first sentence using the word in **bold** so that the meaning stays the same.

1   It's very important for me to write to my brother.
must
I .... to my brother.

2   It wasn't necessary for them to cook so much food.
need
They .... cooked so much food.

3   They were forced to do their homework before they went out.
had
They .... their homework before they went out.

4   It is not permitted to take photographs in here.
can
You .... in here.

5   There was no need for you to come.
have
You .... come.

6   You shouldn't talk while the teacher is speaking.
supposed
You .... talk while the teacher is speaking.

7   It's necessary for me to work late tonight.
got
I .... work late tonight.

8   No one expected you to wait for them.
need
You .... to wait for them.

4   Complete the first sentence in each of the following short dialogues using an appropriate form of *(don't) have to, must* or *need*.

1   A: .... do photocopying or filing?
  B: No, I don't. That's not part of my job.

2   A: .... take with me?
  B: Just an umbrella, in case it rains.

3   A: .... come to Martin's party if you don't want to.
  B: Are you sure that's OK, I'd really prefer not to.

4   A: .... hit your brother, it's not kind.
  B: But, Mum, why not? He hit me first!

5   A: Oh, no! It's nine o'clock. I've overslept.
  B: .... get up. It's Saturday, stupid!

6   A: .... wear a seatbelt?
  B: Yes, I'm afraid so. It's the law and anyway it will protect you in an accident with another car.

7   A: .... buy any new shoes.
  B: I think you do. Your old shoes are worn out!

5 Work with a partner. Choose one of the following and say what is necessary and not necessary to do to become excellent at it. Use *have to, don't have to, must* or *need* as appropriate.

- play tennis/piano/chess
- speak a new language
- cook
- drive
- paint

Listening: radio advertisements

1 You are going to hear five different radio advertisements. Listen and decide what each one is advertising.

2 Which advertisement did you think was the best? Why?

Speaking

1 Work in groups and choose a product e.g. chocolate, toothpaste, perfume. List the names of a variety of examples of your product e.g. chocolate – Mars, Flake, Bounty, etc. Make a note of the following information where appropriate about each example:

- price
- quantity
- special features
- originality

2 Now compare the products you listed and give each one an overall star rating from ***** (excellent) to * (very poor).

3 Present your findings to the rest of the class and make recommendations about what they should buy.

4 Write a report to summarise your findings. Your report should follow this plan:

- Introduction: explain what your task was and how you did it.
- Summarise your findings about each product.
- Conclusion: recommend which product is best for which type of person.

Vocabulary: media

1 Fill in the gaps in the following sentences with an appropriate word. You have been given the exact number of letters in each case.

1 Are there any interesting head–––––– in today's paper?
2 Mike's a journ–––––– for a local newspaper.
3 The cros–––––– and the cart–––– are the only parts I look at in the paper!
4 Do you know that paper has a circu–––––– of over 3 million a day?
5 Did you read the edit–––––– in the paper today? I agreed with every word it said.
6 I hate the way the papers seem to be so full of gos––– and sca–––– these days.
7 What freq––––– is the BBC World Service on? Can I get it on my radio?
8 I listen to my local radio sta–––– a lot. It has great music and regular news broad––––––.
9 Do you know how many television chan–––– they have in the United States?
10 The picture on our TV isn't very good. Perhaps we should move the aer–––.
11 Give me the rem––– con––––! I hate the way you keep changing what we are watching!
12 Let me phone you back. My favourite so–– is just starting and I never miss it.

2 Discuss the following questions.

1 Do you regularly read a newspaper? If so, which one? Why do you like it?
2 Do you often listen to the radio? What stations do you listen to and what kind of programmes?
3 What are your favourite TV programmes? Are there any TV programmes you can't stand? Why?

Reading

1 Read the following definitions and discuss what you think a 'television ration box' is. How do you think it works? Who might use it?

ration² *v* [T] **1** to limit someone to a fixed amount of something: *On this diet, you are rationed to two eggs a week.* **2** to control supplies of something: *The government had to ration petrol during the war.* **ration** sthg ↔ **out** *phr v* (T) to give out supplies in limited amounts: *He rationed out the water to the sailors.*

2 Now read the article opposite and see if you were right.

3 Read the article again and write appropriate questions for the following answers.

1 It will automatically turn off the TV after a certain period of time.
2 Read or play outside.
3 Randal Levenson.
4 In order to reduce the amount his children watched TV.
5 The screen goes blank.
6 £49.
7 He thinks it has increased his vocabulary.
8 His neighbours.
9 Three thousand five hundred.
10 About two weeks.

4 Discuss the following questions.

1 What do you think about the general quality of TV in your country?
2 What do you think of the idea of a 'television ration box'?

Television Ration Box

1 PARENTS are soon to be offered the ultimate weapon to win the war over how much TV their children watch.

Instead of constantly fighting to ration viewing habits, they will have the job done for them by a coded electronic device.

It will switch off the set once an allotted period runs out, leaving the 10 child to turn to other activities such as reading or even playing in the fresh air.

The gadget, 'TV Allowance', was invented by Miami photographer Randal Levenson, a former engineer, who despaired of ever reducing his three children's screen time.

'There was a lot of anger in the house about the TV and Nintendo 20 usage,' said Mr Levenson, 47.

His response was to build the calculator-sized box which plugs into the TV.

The Levensons now use a code to set the four hours that Moss, 13, Cormac, 11, and Geddes, 6, can watch each week. Each has his own code, and when his time is up, the screen goes blank. He can find out how 30 much time is left by touching a button. The gadget, which will sell in Britain for £49 this summer, also controls video games and the video. It can block out specific periods such as homework time and cannot be disconnected by frustrated youngsters.

'They've got their lives back,' said Mr Levenson's wife, Rusty. 'Not that 40 they were total couch potatoes*, but they certainly spent too much time in front of the TV.

'The problem before was that we were giving up. We could only say "No" so many times. But the unemotional gadget can go on saying "No" for as long as necessary.'

'I thought, "Oh, this is really going to be horrible," said Moss, recalling 50 the first time it was attached to the family set. 'Then you get to live with it and get used to it. I think my vocabulary's ten times bigger now because I'm reading more.'

But, being children and therefore devious, they have found ways of getting round the system, if not beating it.

The set is switched off for 60 advertisements and they barter with each other for TV time. They also decide which programmes more than one child wants to watch. Any time left over at the end of the week can be carried over into the next.

'It teaches kids time management and other business skills,' said Mr Levenson, who decided to market the gadget after neighbours asked him to 70 make units for them. So far, 3,500 have been sold without advertising and he believes that is only the start.

'If I make money, that will be fine. But it was worth it to cut back on the amount of TV my kids were watching. It takes about two weeks but then children accept the situation. They come to find that there are other things in life besides 80 sitting and watching TV.'

* a couch potato = someone who spends a lot of time sitting on the sofa in front of the TV

from The Daily Mail newspaper

Exam focus

Paper 2 Writing (discursive composition)

1 You are going to hear some people giving their opinions about the 'television ration box'. Listen and decide what different arguments you hear:

a) in favour of the idea.   b) against the idea.

2 In Paper 2 you may be asked to write an article of 120–180 words, in which you give your opinion on a certain subject. Here is an example of the type of question you may have.

An English-language magazine is investigating the views of people in different countries on the question:

Should parents limit the amount of television their children watch?

Write a short article for the magazine on this topic, based on your own views and experience.

1 Read the following answer to the sample question. In what areas is it good? In what areas is it weak? Think about:

- length
- grammar
- spelling
- handwriting
- vocabulary
- organisation of ideas and paragraphing
- use of linking expressions
- logical order of argument
- appropriacy of language for context

Should parents limit the amount of television their children watch?

First of all I think it is important to say that the qality of television has improved a great deal in recent years. There is now a wide range of programms suitabel for all ages and intrests. In my opinion, there are many things that children can learn from television. They can, for example, learn about other countrys, other ways of living and so on. As well as this, television can give parents a chance to be free of their children for a short time, which can be very important! On the other hand, sometimes children will just sit and watch rubish for hours at a time and oviously this is not a good thing and needs to be controled. Therefore, I think parents should discuss and aggree just how much TV the children watch. I do think, however, that it is important that children are inwolved in the desision and not just told, otherwise they will want to watch TV even more because it is something they are not alowed to do. To sum up then, parents need to think about how there children use TV and be prepaired to limit the time when it is on if they feel their children are becoming addicted to it in an unhelthy kind of way.

2 Work with a partner. Go through the sample answer above and:

a) correct all the spelling mistakes you can find (there are sixteen).
b) divide it into appropriate paragraphs.

3

1 Which of the underlined linking expressions in the above text are used to:

- give more information (e.g. *and*)?
- introduce a contrasting idea (e.g. *but*)?
- explain the consequence of something (e.g. *so*)?

2 Choose the correct alternative in the following sentences. Then add each new linking expression to the appropriate group above.

a) I like him *although/in spite of* he is rather selfish.
b) *As well as this/In addition to* having a lot of money, he is very good-looking.
c) It was raining *so/therefore* we decided to stay at home.
d) Building a road here will destroy an area of great natural beauty. *Furthermore/And,* all the local people are against it.
e) *Not only/Moreover* was the party awful, but we also had a flat tyre on the way home.
f) They lost the match *despite/however* playing very well.

3 Fill in the gaps in the following sentences with an appropriate linking word/expression from the completed groups in 1.

a) Television kills conversation in families. ...., it has led to an increase in violent crime.
b) We are going to be away for a few days, ... I have asked my mother to come in and water the plants.
c) Tom is a really nice guy .... of seeming quite unfriendly when you first meet him.
d) I really like the job I'm doing at the moment. ...., the salary is awful.
e) The hotel was miles from the sea and .... this, our room was small and badly decorated.
f) .... being very interested in the situation in the Middle East, I still don't understand it very well.
g) I finished reading that book, ... I didn't find it very interesting.
h) We decided not to go to the cinema .... the fact that we all wanted to see the film.
i) The cost of the proposed project is more than we expected and .... we do not feel we can go ahead.

4 Now write your answer to the question in Exercise 2. You should follow this procedure:

- Read the task instructions carefully. Think about what type of text you are writing and what sort of people you are writing for.
- Make a list of points to include in your answer. Turn the question into a statement: *Parents should limit the amount of TV their children watch.* How do you feel about this? Why might this be a good/bad idea? List your ideas under a positive (+) heading, like this:

> **+**
> - *lots of unsuitable programmes*
> - *too much TV reduces time when children should be studying*

- Now imagine someone arguing with your ideas and add their views under a negative (–) heading like this:

> **–**
> - *children can learn a lot from TV*
> - *children should learn to be selective by themselves*

- Write a draft. Organise your article into the following paragraphs:
  1 Introduction: state the general situation/problem referred to in the question.
  2 Give your opinion and specific examples to support your case where possible.
  3 Refer to counter arguments.
  4 Conclusion: summarise your view and possibly give advice or make recommendations to those concerned.
- Read your draft through. Does it answer the question? Is it effective in the various areas listed in Exercise 2 part 1?
- Write a final version.

Speaking

1 Describe in as much detail as possible what you see happening in the pictures. Say which picture best reflects how your family spends its free time.

A

B

C

2 Work with a partner and imagine you have been put in charge of a new TV channel. Decide the following:

1 What kinds of programmes you want to have on your channel e.g. sports, documentaries, quiz shows, films, news, soap operas.
2 How you are going to make it different from existing TV channels.
3 What you are going to call the channel.
4 What a typical evening's viewing will consist of.

1 Choose the correct alternative below to fill the gaps in the following text.

	A		**B**		**C**		**D**
1	can		need		must		got
2	very		really		terrible		absolutely
3	by		through		up		down
4	despite		however		although		though
5	supposed		need		had		got
6	should		necessary		important		supposed
7	wonderful		completely		very		absolutely
8	well		addition		also		moreover
9	over		in		across		through
10	needed		should		must		could
11	from		with		to		off

... and, anyway, I (1).......... just tell you about a (2).......... awful thing that happened to me on Monday. I had just got (3).......... to cleaning the kitchen floor, when I heard this knock on the front door. I went and answered it and there was this man who said he had come to investigate a gas leak. I told him that I didn't have a gas leak, but (4).......... this he insisted on coming in and said he (5).......... to have a look. So, I let him come in. I knew I was (6).......... to check his identification card and he was (7).......... funny when I asked for it. He said he had left it in his van and as (8).......... as this he wasn't wearing the usual overalls. So, I popped upstairs and phoned the gas board to see if they had sent someone round. It took me a long time to get (9).......... to them, but eventually I did and they told me that they hadn't sent anyone and that nothing (10).......... to be done in my area. I went downstairs and the man was putting various things of mine into a large bag. When he saw me, he just dropped the bag and ran out. It gave me quite a shock as you can imagine and to think he nearly got away (11).......... it!

2 Answer the following questions using a word you have learnt in Unit 12.

1 If you gave money to a police officer so he wouldn't give you a fine for speeding, what would you be doing?
2 What is the noun from the verb *to explain?*
3 What is the noun from the adjective *wise?*
4 What phrasal verb means 'to recover from something'?
5 What is the word for the title printed in big letters above a story in a newspaper?
6 What verb means 'to talk or write about other people's private lives'?
7 What do you put on the top of a building so you can receive TV broadcasts?
8 What gadget can you use to change TV channels without actually having to leave your seat?

3 Complete the following sentences in a logical way.

1 Something I really must do this weekend is ...
2 In my secondary school we aren't/weren't allowed to ...
3 If you want to speak English well, you need to ...
4 When I was younger, one of the things I used to get up to was ...
5 The last time I had a really great time out was when ...
6 As well as being really good fun, my best friend is ...
7 I decided not to go to the party in spite of ...
8 It was an incredibly hot day so we ...

It's a mad world

Reading

1 Look at the photos below and opposite and discuss the following questions.

1 Who do you think the people are?
2 What are they doing and why?

2 Read the following text and decide if the things described could happen in your country.

Mad as a hatter OR geniuses at work?

(1 ———)

British eccentrics are famous the world over. We breed eccentrics and we're fascinated[1] by them. Eccentrics are found in all walks of life, whether they are lords or lavatory cleaners, teachers or train drivers. Some wear odd clothes, some collect to the point of obsession, while others inhabit strange environments or hold unorthodox beliefs[2]. Provided they are in no way a threat to society, we usually just avoid them but let them carry on in their own sweet way.

(2 ———)

David Weeks, an American psychologist has conducted the first in-depth psychological study of eccentrics and has concluded that Britain's are still the best in the world. Weeks did detailed personality tests and taped interviews with 130 eccentrics. 'A true eccentric is never acting,' writes Dr David Weeks. 'They are strong[3] individuals with strange inclinations of their own which they are not afraid to express. They refuse[4] to compromise.' He believes one in 10,000 people in the UK is a genuine eccentric, and that for every female candidate there are nine male eccentrics.

(3 ———)

One of his most interesting findings was the good health[5] that eccentrics enjoy. 'Almost all of them visit the doctor only once every eight or nine years; the rest of us go twice a year.' Eccentrics tend to live longer than the rest of us. The theory[6] is that if you have a particular obsession, whether it is eating cardboard or living in a cave, life becomes full of meaning and significance and the resulting happiness strengthens the body's immune system. 'Eccentrics are living proof[7] that one does not necessarily have to go through life

with a fixed set of rules,' says Weeks. 'They are their own b leaders and poor followers, and not feel a need to possess t ordinary things of everyday li They are prepared to stand out fr the crowd.'

(4 ———)

Some, like botanist Al Fairweather, a potato fanatic, ha turned their eccentricity into career – he worked for the Minist of Agriculture, Fisheries and Fo as a potato inspector. He has live for thirty years on a diet of potato boiled in their jacket supplemented by Mars bars, bake beans and Vitamin C. He won't slee in a bed and his idea of a break is visit to the International Potat Centre in Peru. There are othe who are spare time eccentrics, lik Barry Kirk, a computer technicia who likes to paint himself orang and pretend to be a baked bean.

(5 ———)

Some of Weeks's collection – such a the man who climbs down towe blocks dressed as a pink elephant would stick out anywhere, but mos are unremarkable on the surface Weeks believes that inside lie resources of creativity[8] and imagination that are not sufficiently used. 'They are neglected, or no taken seriously, because of the way they express themselves. Often they are convinced that they are ahead of their time and that others have stolen or exploited their good ideas.'

(6 ———)

What counts as eccentricity varies[9] with time and a person's sex as well as location. Adeline Brudenwell, countess of Cardigan, was regarded as extremely eccentric in the 1870s because she would bicycle around London in tight red military trousers and a leopard-skin cape. She would also go for walks in Hyde Park wearing a blond wig, followed by a footman carrying a cushion on which sat a pet dog. Nowadays people would just assume she was an actress or a singer with a new album to promote.

from *Focus* and *Living* magazines

Vocabulary: phrasal verbs (*out*)

1   Match each pair of sentences below to one of the following general meanings of *out* when used in phrasal verbs.

1   to be/go away from home
2   to pay attention (often because of danger)
3   to remove, get rid of
4   to appear clearly (often suddenly)
5   an ending of something (often because there is nothing left)

a)   They are prepared to *stand out* from the crowd.
    Don't *stick* your tongue *out* at me!

b)   *Look out!* There's a policeman coming.
    If you don't *watch out*, you're going to get in serious trouble.

c)   Shall we *eat out* tonight?
    Apparently, he *stayed out* all night. His mother was very worried.

d)   I'm going to *throw out* all my old notebooks.
    You should *rub out* all the mistakes and start again.

e)   I've got to stop playing. I'm *worn out*.
    I'm sorry, we've completely *sold out* of milk today.

2   Look at the phrasal verbs in the following sentences and add each one to the appropriate pair in Exercise 1 according to the general meaning of *out*.

1   *Mind out!* That chair has only just been painted.
2   I can't find any jam. We haven't *run out*, have we?
3   Look at this! I've *come out in* spots all over my face and neck.
4   You should *get out* and enjoy yourself more.
5   I think they should have *cut out* more of the bad language in that film.

3   Decide which of the following headings should go before each of the paragraphs in the text. There is one extra heading which you do not need to use.

A How to stay in good shape.
B Appearances can be deceptive.
C Live and let live.
D Measuring madness.
E Hobby or full-time occupation?
F Some serious research.
G How times change.

4   Put the numbered words from the text in the following sentences in the correct form.

EXAMPLE: 1   That book about the Amazonian Indians is absolutely ....*fascinating*.... .

2   He said it was .... that she had failed all her exams. She normally gets top marks.
3   If that wall isn't .... soon, the whole thing will collapse.
4   His .... to listen to her idea was typical.
5   I think it is very .... the way you eat so much chocolate and drink so much Coca-Cola.
6   It's a .... possibility, but it's not likely to happen in practice.
7   Can you .... you were at home between 6 p.m. and 9 p.m.?
8   His sculpture was a marvellous .... and everyone admired it.
9   These T-shirts are available in a wide .... of colours.

3   Imagine you have just had the most awful week. Make some notes on what has happened to you. Then tell a partner all about it in two minutes, trying to include as many phrasal verbs as possible. Then listen to your partner and see who used the most phrasal verbs from above and from previous units in the book. You can refer to the *Phrasal verbs reference* on pages 181–183.

EXAMPLE: *You'll never believe what an awful week I have had. I'm absolutely **worn out**! It all started on Monday when my Mum told me she had **thrown out** all my old records ...*

Speaking

1 Do the questionnaire opposite to find out how eccentric you are. Tell a partner about your answers, particularly when you answered 'Yes'.

2 Discuss the following questions.

1 What eccentric people do you know/have you heard of? What things do they do/have they done which make them seem eccentric to you?
2 What is the most eccentric thing you have ever done?

Listening: vampire woman

1 Discuss what you know about vampires. What do they typically look like? What things do they like/hate?

2 You are going to hear an interview with a woman who would like to be a vampire. Listen and decide which of the following pictures best matches the woman.

3 Now listen to the interview again and answer the following questions.

1 How long has Carole been interested in vampires?
2 Does she believe she is a vampire?
3 Does she have any brothers/sisters?
4 What colour does she particularly like?
5 Does she believe in reincarnation?
6 Was she born with 'fangs'?
7 Did she enjoy school?
8 Does she often get ill?
9 Where is she planning to visit?

Could you be an eccentric?

TRY OUR TEST!
Only one person in 10,000 is an eccentric. Answer 'Yes' to all these questions, and you could be a member of that most select of social groups.

Creativity
Do you regularly come up with ideas or thoughts that are very different from other people's?

Solitariness
If you do any sports, are they ones you can enjoy alone, such as running or yoga?
Are you more than averagely interested in religion and the paranormal?

Curiosity
Are you constantly asking peculiar questions about everything?
Are you particularly curious about a few special topics, and do you put in a lot of time and effort finding out all there is to know about them?

Non-competitiveness
Is it not important if you come first or last?

Having an unusual childhood
Are you an eldest or only child?
Are/Were your parents very critical?
Do you have eccentrics among your relatives or ancestors?

Feeling different
Do you feel different from those around you, or see yourself as someone who doesn't fit in easily to ordinary society?

Social behaviour
Do you have strong opinions about most subjects which you don't mind expressing however undiplomatic that might be?
Do you dislike small talk?

Ways of thinking
Are you above average IQ, but often make spelling mistakes?
Do you have particularly vivid dreams?

Odd habits
Do you have strong likes or dislikes about food, or do you go to sleep at unusual times or in unusual places?

Temperament
Deep down, are you optimistic, kind-hearted and warm?
Do you pride yourself on your sense of humour?

Finally
Do you believe you're a true eccentric?

from *Focus* magazine

Grammar: conditionals

1 You are going to hear some extracts from the interview with Carole Bohanon. Listen and complete the following sentences with the exact words you hear.

1 If .... in a coffin and drive a hearse.
2 If .... all day and get up at night.
3 If .... were interested, we .... much sooner.
4 I can't bear sunlight; it .... too long.
5 She .... flesh.
6 If .... a trip to Transylvania next year.

2 Read this information on the different types of conditionals. Then look at the sentences from the interview and decide which type of conditional each one is.

CONDITIONALS

Zero Conditional
If + Present Simple + Present Simple: to say what always happens e.g. *If you **mix** blue and yellow, you **get** green.*

First Conditional
If + Present Simple + a future form: to describe what may possibly happen e.g. *If I **see** John, I **will ask** him to ring you.*

Second Conditional
If + Past Simple + *would*: to describe
a) something that is impossible and is just imagined e.g. *If I **were** Prime Minister, I **would reduce** taxes.*
b) which is very unlikely to happen e.g. *If I **had** more time, I **would help** you with your homework.*

Third Conditional
If + Past Perfect + *would have* + past participle: to describe something in the past which could have happened, but didn't e.g. *If I **had gone** to the party, I **would have** seen Michiko.*

Each of the conditionals can be formed using modals e.g.
*If you **see** him, you **should ask** him to come.*
*If you **lost** some weight, you **could wear** my dress.*
*If they **had played** a bit better, they **could have won** the match.*

Grammar reference p.165 (5)

3 There is a mistake in each of the following sentences. Find the mistake and correct the sentence.

1 If I will come to the party, will you give me a lift home?
2 He definitely will pass the exam unless he does a lot more work!
3 I had have a couple of days in bed if I were you. You look awful!
4 You can borrow the car tonight provided that you will take good care of it.
5 I wouldn't have cooked so much food if I had knew they weren't coming.
6 If you pressed that button, you get extra sugar.
7 He might has stayed if you hadn't shouted at him.
8 As long as you have enough money, I'm sure you are having a good time when you go to New York.
9 We won't be able to buy it unless our parents have lent us some money.

4 Make a list of people you might see and things you might do today. Say what will/might happen if you do.

EXAMPLE: *If **I see** André, **I'll tell** him what the homework is.*

5 Imagine you have the opportunity to visit five different places anywhere in the world. Complete the following sentence for each one.

● If I had the chance to visit ..., I would ...

EXAMPLE: *If **I had the chance to visit** the United States, **I would go** to New York because I have always wanted to go up the Empire State building.*

6

1 You are going to hear five people regretting things they did/didn't do in the past. Make a note of what each person is sorry about.

EXAMPLE: a) *He is sorry he didn't go to university.*

2 Now write each person's regret using a Third Conditional form.

3 Tell another student about something you regret that you did/didn't do.

EXAMPLE: *I'm sorry I didn't go to Anna's party last night. I'm sure I would have had a great time.*

7   Look at this cartoon. What do you notice about the grammatical form of the last sentence?

8   Decide which two of the clauses in Column B are most likely to follow the clause in Column A.

A	B
1 If you don't know,	a) you should ask. b) you would have asked. c) ask.
2 When I see him,	a) I might tell him what you said. b) I am going to tell him what you said. c) I will be telling him what you said.
3 If they wanted the house,	a) they will phone. b) they would have phoned by now.· c) they would phone.
4 Do your homework	a) unless you want to be in trouble with your teacher. b) provided that you want to be in trouble with your teacher. c) if you don't want to be in trouble with your teacher.
5 If he hadn't been so stupid,	a) he might not have gone to prison. b) he would not be in prison now. c) he can't be in prison.
6 If I hadn't eaten the fish,	a) I won't be ill. b) I wouldn't have been ill. c) I wouldn't be ill now.

Vocabulary: animals

1   The words in the box are all parts of different animals. Decide which of the animals listed below have which parts. Use a dictionary where necessary.

wings   fur   claws   a trunk   hooves   paws a fin   a tail   a beak   feathers   a mane a hump   a horn

1 bat	5 cow	9 cat	13 snake
2 rhinoceros	6 shark	10 eagle	
3 dog	7 lion	11 fly	
4 elephant	8 horse	12 camel	

2   Work with a partner. Student A should look at the picture on page 188 and describe it for Student B to draw. Student B should look at the picture on page 190 and describe it for Student A to draw. Then look at each other's pictures to find out how like the originals they are.

3   Match some of the animals from Exercise 1 to the following sounds.

a) to purr   c) to moo   e) to hiss
b) to bark   d) to roar   f) to neigh

4   Read the following sentences and try to work out the meaning of the expressions in *italics*. Use a dictionary where necessary.

1 They were trying to keep their wedding a secret, but his father *let the cat out of the bag*.
2 As I was on the way to the shops I thought I would *kill two birds with one stone* so I went in and saw Mary.
3 I've decided to get out of *the rat race* and give up working in advertising. I'm going to move away and grow vegetables in Wales.
4 I am sorry that you and Steve have split up but there are *plenty more fish in the sea*.
5 When I tell my parents that I have failed all my exams, they are going *to have kittens.*
6 I'm afraid you are just going to have *to take the bull by the horns* and tell him you want to leave.
7 If she tells him what she knows, it will really *put the cat among the pigeons*.
8 You know, I heard it *straight from the horse's mouth*, so it must be true.

134

Exam focus

Paper 3 Use of English (open cloze)

In Part 2 of Paper 3 you will read a text with fifteen missing words. The missing words will be mainly 'grammar' words e.g. *has/the/by/might*. Here is a procedure to follow:

- First of all, read the complete text through to get an idea of what it is about.
- Then read the text again and look at the words in the sentences before and after each gap. Think about the meaning and the grammar of the missing word and the words before and after it.

1 Now read the following text quickly. What is it about?

2 Look at gaps 1, 2 and 3 in the text and answer the following questions.

Gap (1) What grammatical structure is involved in the underlined part? What is the one word that must come before *most* with this structure?

Gap (2) What is the main verb here? What tense must be used? Is it in an active or passive form? Is it in the singular or plural? What auxiliary verb must be used here?

Gap (3) What is the main verb here? What period of time is being referred to? What tense must be used? What is the correct auxiliary verb?

3 Now fill in the gaps in the text with an appropriate word.

Victims of reputation

Bats are one of (1)................... <u>most numerous and successful groups</u> of mammals that have ever lived on earth. Over 950 species (2).................... known to exist – that's one quarter of all present-day mammals. Bats (3).................... spread to almost (4).................... part of the world, from the Arctic (5).................... the stormy southern tip of South America.

However, bats all over the world are under pressure (6).................... a fast-growing human population. Loss of suitable places to live, fall (7).................... food supply and environmental pollution are all (8).................... life increasingly difficult for many bat species.

Strangely, there are some wild creatures which are, in fact, little or (9).................... threat to humans, but consistently disturb people by their presence and cause irrational fear. (10).................... them are such animals as cockroaches, spiders, mice and, more often (11).................... not, bats. Exactly (12).................... bats should frighten so many of us is hard to understand, (13).................... they do have many of the characteristics that people seem to find distressing in wild animals.

They are small, fast-moving, capable (14).................... sudden changes in direction and active at night. In (15).................... to this, they have rapidly moving wings, an unpredictable way of flying that can (16).................... them extremely close and a strange, often frightening appearance. Given these characteristics, and the (17).................... that bats often find suitable hiding places around human dwellings, it is perhaps not surprising (18).................... human fears have been transformed into superstition and myth.

Vocabulary: places

1 Look at the photos and discuss the following questions.

1 Which of the places would you like to live in? Why?
2 What do you imagine they are like inside?
3 What kind of people do you imagine live there?

A

B

2 Look at the following pairs/groups of words and decide what the difference in meaning is between each word.

1 a terraced house/a semi-detached house/ a detached house
2 a bungalow/a flat/a bedsit
3 a cottage/a hut
4 a caravan/a tent
5 a town/a city/a village/a suburb/the capital
6 a county/a country/a continent
7 a skyscraper/a penthouse

D

3

1 Match the words in the box to the letters in the picture.

> lawn   porch   flowerbed   fence   shed   patio
> pond   hedge   gate   pavement   cellar   attic
> roof   chimney   drainpipe   TV aerial

2 Describe the place where you live to a partner. What is it like on the outside and inside? Draw a diagram if necessary.

Watch Out! *country*

1 We went to a little hotel in the *country*.
2 It's a very nice *country* for a holiday.

What does *country* mean in each sentence?

4

1 Say why people go to each of the following places.

   a) a theatre   e) a museum
   b) a cathedral   f) a gallery
   c) a market   g) a factory
   d) a stadium

2 Tell a partner about when you last went to these places. Why did you go? Who did you go with? What happened?

Use of English

Read the following description of Romania. There is one extra incorrect word in each line. Try to find the word.

1 Romania's name itself suggests that what makes it different from
2 its neighbours. The connection is with the Imperial Rome and
3 coming from that is a language which sounds as like Italian. The
4 country where is about the size of Great Britain and has a population of
5 23 million, of whom ninety percent there are Romanians.

6 The scenery is varied: mountainous areas with a summer and winter
7 resorts, a very marvellous stretch of the Danube as it descends
8 towards the Iron Gates, not to be mention castles, palaces and
9 monasteries with so impressive frescoes. There are also historic
10 towns from the 13th of century, Black Sea beach resorts and
11 with the astonishing bird-life of the vast Danube delta. And if
12 this is not enough, there are no more fewer than 160 spas
13 offering cures for nearly of every illness known to man.

14 Romania is perhaps the most famous abroad for being the home of
15 Dracula the famous creation of the Irish writer, the Bram
16 Stoker. However, while the story is being fiction, the character
17 is based on a Romanian prince is called Vlad Dracula (son of
18 Dracul) or Tepes (the Impaler) because of such his cruelty
19 towards his enemies. On one occasion he is supposed to have been
20 sat down to a meal to enjoy himself the spectacle of some
21 prisoners having their arms and legs cut them off. He asked for
22 their blood to be collected and brought to him so as a dip for his bread.

23 So, when you visit Romania you may be like to visit Bran Castle
24 which was having built in 1377 and is the castle most closely
25 identified with Dracula. But, if you do, don't forget to how
26 much else there is for to see in Romania.

137

Writing: describing places

1 In Paper 2 you may be asked to write a description of a place such as the one on page 137 about Romania. Read the description again and decide which of the plans below it follows.

A 1 Introduction: where the place is, how to get there and why it became famous.
   2 What you can do there.
   3 Things to do and see nearby.
   4 Conclusion: sum up opinion of place and make a suggestion.

B 1 Introduction: when you visited the place and why.
   2 What happened while you were visiting the place.
   3 Another thing that happened during your visit.
   4 Conclusion: how you felt about the trip when you got home.

C 1 Introduction: factual information about the place.
   2 What there is to see and do there.
   3 Why it is well-known.
   4 Conclusion: some advice.

2 Read the following exam task and decide which of the plans above would not be suitable. Why?

> You work for the local tourist information service. Your boss has asked you to write an article about a place of interest in your area for a tourist information magazine that is distributed free to young travellers. Write a description of a place you know well for the magazine.

3 You are going to write an answer to the question above. You should follow this procedure:

- Look at the instructions carefully and underline the key words.
- Choose a place to describe. Remember, it should interest young travellers and you should know it well.
- Choose one of the two possible plans in Exercise 1. (You may change it if you wish.)
- Make a list of points to include. Answer questions like these and think of others: *Where is it? How do you get there from the airport/centre of town? What is the first thing you notice about the place? When was it discovered/built? When did it become popular/famous? What do people usually do there?* Decide in which paragraph you will include these details.
- As soon as you have decided on the details and where to put them, you can begin to write. Include some conditional sentences with these patterns:
  If you take the road/train/bus from ..., you reach/get to ...
  If you have a little more time, you can also ...
  If you visit ... during/in/at/on ..., you'll be able to ...

1 Name each of the animals in the pictures and the parts of their bodies that are indicated.

2 Name each of the following.

3 Fill in the gaps in the following sentences with an appropriate verb in the correct form.

1 We're always .... out! Can't we have dinner at home tonight?
2 I'm afraid that we've .... out of that particular brand of soap, but we do have other types.
3 That class .... me out. They're such hard work!
4 .... out! You're going to drop those plates if you're not careful.
5 Don't .... out those toys. I might give them to my children one day.
6 You can tell she has had training. She .... out as being by far the best.
7 You should .... the bull by the horns and tell your boss that you've got too much work and you're not being paid enough.
8 I want to know who .... the cat out of the bag. Who said we are going to get married?
9 I thought I would .... two birds with one stone and visit my old school at the same time as we're in Edinburgh on holiday.

4 Fill in the gaps in the following sentences with the correct form of the verbs in brackets.

1 If I .... (know) he was coming to the party, I .... (stay) at home.
2 They .... (might/lend) you their car, if you .... (ask) them nicely.
3 I really don't know what I .... (do) if I .... (win) the lottery.
4 She didn't need to lose the match. She .... (could/win) if she .... (play) a little bit better.
5 We .... (have) a barbecue at the weekend unless it .... (rain).
6 When it .... (be) cold, we .... (put) the central heating on.
7 If Mike .... (not/stolen) that money, he .... (not/be) in prison now.
8 When you .... (speak) English fluently, you .... (be/able) to apply for lots of different jobs.
9 When you .... (press) these two buttons, you .... (get) black coffee with sugar.
10 If I .... (listen) to my father, I .... (not/marry) you in the first place!

14 Guilty or not guilty

Reading

1 Look at the people in the photos and discuss who they are and what they are doing.

A

B

C

2 Read the text and then describe what Batman does.

3 Answer the following questions in your own words.

1 Why had the Joker come to the museum?
2 What mood was the Joker in?
3 What did the water do to the Joker? Did it hurt him?
4 How did Batman get into and out of the museum?
5 What was the Joker impressed by?

1   Vicki could feel the trap close around her. The Joker and a dozen of his men had burst into the museum and set about methodically destroying the paintings. Vicki wondered if there was some way she could run for it, but, within seconds of their arrival, henchmen were covering both main doors and all of the emergency exits as well.

2   Then the Joker saw her. He waved pleasantly as he approached. His face was no longer ghostly white, but his unnatural smile was still there. His good cheer made Vicki feel even more trapped than she had before.

3   She had to keep him away from her. She needed a weapon. She grabbed a water pitcher from the cart and threw it at the Joker.

4   The pitcher missed, but it drenched the Joker with water.

'No!' He cried as his hands covered his face. 'No!'

He bent over double. The tan was coming off on his fingers, revealing the bone-white skin beneath.

'I'm melting!' He fell to his knees.

'I'm melting!' He writhed on the floor. 'Oh, God, I'm melting!'

'Help me!' the Joker croaked, staggering back.

Had she really hurt him? Despite herself, she took a step forward.

He leapt forward abruptly.

'Boo!' he screamed.

5   He was on top of her. She couldn't get away. All she could see was the purple flower, and that big, big grin.

Writing: making your writing more interesting

1 In the Batman text there are various words and expressions that add a dramatic, exciting atmosphere to the story. Find these words and expressions and match them to the following meanings.

1 to enter suddenly and dramatically *(para. 1)*
2 in order and with care *(para. 1)*
3 to take suddenly and roughly *(para. 3)*
4 to make completely wet *(para. 4)*
5 to show *(para. 4)*
6 to move in pain *(para. 4)*
7 to walk unsteadily *(para. 4)*
8 suddenly and unexpectedly *(para. 4)*
9 to cry out loudly in a high voice *(para. 4)*
10 a smile *(para. 5)*
11 to break in many pieces *(para. 6)*
12 to jump *(para. 9)*
13 very surprised *(para. 10)*

2

1 Match the following verbs with a general meaning to a group of verbs in the box.

1 tell	4 hold	7 throw
2 move	5 laugh	8 walk
3 think	6 say	9 eat

a) exclaim/mutter/insist
b) giggle/chuckle/snigger
c) writhe/wriggle/fidget
d) hurl/toss/lob
e) stagger/wander/tiptoe
f) munch/nibble/swallow
g) wonder/consider/reckon
h) order/inform/instruct
i) clutch/grasp/hug

2 Describe in what ways the verbs in each group differ in meaning from each other. Use a dictionary where necessary.

3 You can also make your writing more interesting by using interesting language to modify nouns and adjectives.

EXAMPLES: *His face was no longer **ghostly** white. The tan was coming off on his fingers, revealing the **bone-white** skin.*

Look at the next part of the *Batman* story and discuss more interesting/dramatic ways of expressing the information it contains. Then rewrite it, incorporating your ideas.

Something shattered overhead. Everything was perfect until that noise, the Joker thought. He looked up. Something had come through the skylight, that same dark something that was dropping to the floor.

No, the Joker corrected himself. It wasn't just any old something. It was the Batman. He landed only half a dozen feet away. He pointed his fist at the Joker. There was something attached to the bat guy's wrist. Was Batman going to shoot the Joker? He was too young to die. The Joker considered running, but the bat guy would nail him before he took a step.

The Batman fired. The projectile split in two, each half embedding itself into the walls past the balcony on either side of the Joker. The Joker realized there were wires attached to each of the spikes, and another wire leading from the Batman to his skylight entranceway.

The Batman grabbed Vicki and swung out along the escape wires he had created for himself, plunging off the balcony and straight through an arched doorway marked 'Exit'.

It took the Joker a second to recover.

'Those toys!' he exclaimed at last. 'Where does he get those wonderful toys?' He looked around at his boys. They seemed every bit as flabbergasted as he was.

'Well, don't just stand there!' he yelled. 'Go and ask him!'

They went. The Joker sighed. Did he have to think of everything around here?

It took Vicki a little time to realize she had been rescued from the Joker. Batman held her and before long they were in Gotham Square. He told her to go down a small side street. He followed her and threw a small object behind them. Soon there was smoke in the entrance to the street.

'Get in the car,' he told her. At first she didn't know which one, but then she saw it. It was black and looked strange. 'Ignition,' said Batman and the car started.

4 Now write the next part of the story in an equally exciting style!

from *Batman* (the novel) by Craig Shaw Gardner

141

Vocabulary: crime

1

1 Work in four groups A, B, C and D. Each group should check that they know the meaning and pronunciation of the words in the appropriate box. Use a dictionary where necessary.

Group A

> a thief   a kidnapper   a mugger   a shoplifter
> a pickpocket   a blackmailer   a hijacker
> a forger   a smuggler   an arsonist   a rapist

Group B

> a court   a judge   a jury   a witness
> a defence lawyer   a prosecution lawyer
> the accused   a verdict   a plea

Group C

> a fine   Community Service   capital punishment
> corporal punishment   a suspended sentence
> a jail sentence

Group D

> to arrest   to question   to accuse   to deny
> to admit   to put on probation   to execute
> to release on bail   to acquit

2 Now work in groups of four, one student from Group A, one from Group B, one from Group C and one from Group D. Explain the meaning and pronunciation of your words to the other students in the group.

2 Work with a partner and correct the mistakes in the following sentences, putting the stress on the corrected information.

EXAMPLE: A: A forger sets fire to buildings.

   B: *No, an <u>arsonist</u> sets fire to buildings. A <u>forger</u> makes copies of things in order to deceive people.*

1 A mugger threatens to make secrets known to the public.
2 A shoplifter steals things from people's pockets, especially in a crowd.
3 A hijacker takes goods or people from one country to another illegally.
4 A jury questions the witnesses.
5 The judge pleads guilty or not guilty at the beginning of a trial.
6 You normally get a jail sentence if you are caught driving too fast on the motorway.
7 Some people think capital punishment is a more useful and positive way of punishing people than giving a jail sentence.
8 He denied stealing the car when he saw all the evidence against him.
9 He was put on probation until the case could be heard.
10 They executed him when they found the police had been lying.

> **Watch Out!** *to steal/to rob*
>
> 1 You *steal/rob* things e.g. a watch.
> 2 You *steal/rob* people or places e.g. an old lady, a bank.
>
> What is the correct alternative in each of these sentences?

Use of English:
multiple choice cloze

In Part 1 of Paper 3 you will read a text with fifteen missing words. After the text you will be given a choice of four words for each of the gaps. The missing words will mainly be 'vocabulary' words and not 'grammar' words.

In the following example, all of the alternatives are words connected with crime, but in the exam the words will not be linked to a topic.

Read the text and choose the correct alternative to fill each gap. As you choose, look at each of the four words in the context of the complete sentence and think about:

- its exact meaning.
- its grammar, for example what prepositions or verb patterns it can be followed by.

THE CRIMINAL THEY CAN'T LOCK UP

Burglar, 14, walks free for 33rd time

BY CHRISTIAN GYSIN

1 Britain's most persistent young burglar walked free for the 33rd time yesterday.

Two hours later the politicians promised to take action against tearaways who the law says are too young to be (1)..................... up.

Youngsters aged between twelve and fifteen who repeatedly
10 (2)..................... crimes will be held in ten new 'secure training centres' for up to two years.

The 14-year-old, in (3)..................... yesterday, was responsible for a mini crimewave near his home totalling £58,000. As he was (4)..................... his worried mother said, 'I really thought he would have been
20 locked away.

'I'm worried that he'll be out (5)..................... it again before the week's out.'

Her son had (6)..................... clothes worth £28,000 and (7)..................... into the same branch of one particular shop

three times in one week. He played with the laces of his £100
30 trainers as the court heard he had also (8)..................... his local chemist's at least six times.

Before one (9)..................... a shop assistant was even handed his 'calling card' marked with his initials and advising: 'Ring the police'.

The boy, who cannot be
40 identified for (10)..................... reasons, (11)..................... seven charges of burglary and asked for another 24 to be taken into (12)..................... .

The court heard he was too young to be remanded in custody and that there was no place for him in secure accommodation.

The boy's mother added after
50 the (13).....................: 'I just find it astonishing that nowhere can be found for him. I've (14)..................... him he's living on borrowed time.

'I've tried – but I can't (15)..................... him.'

from *Today* newspaper

1	**A** put	**B** closed	**C** locked	**D** jailed
2	**A** commit	**B** do	**C** make	**D** practise
3	**A** trial	**B** court	**C** dock	**D** cell
4	**A** releasing	**B** freed	**C** innocent	**D** unlocked
5	**A** making	**B** taking	**C** burgling	**D** doing
6	**A** robbed	**B** hijacked	**C** stolen	**D** pickpocketed
7	**A** broken	**B** dropped	**C** popped	**D** smashed
8	**A** taken	**B** stolen	**C** burgled	**D** shoplifted
9	**A** raid	**B** action	**C** rave	**D** steal
10	**A** criminal	**B** illegal	**C** law	**D** legal
11	**A** denied	**B** admitted	**C** confessed	**D** accused
12	**A** consideration	**B** thought	**C** mind	**D** understanding
13	**A** court	**B** custody	**C** crime	**D** trial
14	**A** criticised	**B** explained	**C** warned	**D** pleaded
15	**A** check	**B** control	**C** limit	**D** prevent

Grammar: *make/let/allow*

1   Decide what difference in meaning, if any, there is between the three sentences in Column A.

A	B
1 They allowed him to go home.	a) He was allowed go home. b) He was allowed to go home.
2 They let him go home.	a) He was let go home. b) *No passive form*
3 They made him go home.	a) He was made to go home. b) He was made go home.

2   Choose the correct passive form in Column B of the sentence in Column A.

Grammar reference p.177 (19.2)

3   Fill in the gaps in the following sentences with the correct form of *make, let* or *allow.*

1   They were not .... to open their presents until Christmas morning.
2   Will you .... me go to the party if I promise to be home by 12.00 p.m.?
3   I am never .... to do anything I want. It's not fair.
4   They tried to .... him tell them where his friend was, but he wouldn't.
5   Don't .... him escape! If he gets out onto the road, he'll be run over.
6   He was .... to pay for the damage he had caused to the car.
7   If he hadn't .... me borrow his racket, I wouldn't have been able to play.
8   I am afraid you're never going to be .... to have a party in this house again.
9   If you won't .... him sit down and do his homework, I will!

4   What do you think the boy's parents in the article *The criminal they can't lock up* on page 143 should:

1   make him do?
2   let him do/allow him to do?

Speaking

1   You are going to have a meeting to decide what to do with the young man in the article *The criminal they can't lock up*. His name is Brian North.

Work in groups of five. Each student should take one of the following roles and spend a little time preparing what to say.

- Brian North
- Mrs North
- a representative of the police
- a social worker
- the manager of a local shop

2   Now work with the other students in your group and have the meeting. By the end of the meeting you should have a definite suggestion of what to do with Brian.

3   Finally turn to page 188 and read what actually happened to Brian. Was your decision similar or different?

4   Discuss what, if any, punishment you think would be appropriate for the following people.

1   Three children aged ten, eleven and twelve who deliberately damaged a railway line. As a result, a train came off the line and several people were injured.
2   A single unemployed parent with four children who stole £20 worth of food from a supermarket.
3   A successful businessman who was found to have deliberately not paid £20,000 a year in taxes for the last five years.
4   An animal rights activist who put a bomb in a university laboratory which experiments on animals. The laboratory was destroyed, but no animals or people were hurt.
5   A doctor who had been working for thirty hours without a break and gave the wrong drugs to a patient. As a result the patient died.

Grammar: passives

1   The passive is often used when the agent of the action is either not known or is unimportant.

EXAMPLE: *The boy cannot be identified for legal reasons.*

Look again at the article on Brian North on page 143 and find eight more examples of the passive.

2   Complete this table with the correct passive forms. Use the following words as the base of each sentence:

police/question/suspect

	Active	Passive
Present Simple	The police question the suspect.	The suspect is questioned by the police
Present Continuous	The police are ...	The suspect is ...
Past Simple		
Past Continuous		
Future Simple		
Future Perfect		
Present Perfect Simple		
Past Perfect Simple		
Modals (Present) e.g. *must*		
Modals (Past) e.g. *must have*		

3   Fill in the gaps in this lett with an appropriate active or passive form of the verbs in brackets.

Grammar reference p.171 (12)

Dear Julie,

Well, I arrived safely ... but my luggage didn't! After many enquiries I found that it (1).................. (send) *to Finland instead of England! Apparently, it* (2).................. (label) *wrongly at check-in. Anyway, it finally* (3).................. (arrive) *three days ago and, other than that, I* (4).................. (have) *a great time ever since I arrived.*

The people I am staying with are very nice and I (5).................. (already/show) *all the local tourist sites. I* (6).................. (treat) *exactly like one of the family and I* (7).................. (introduce) *to all their friends. I share a room with Penny, the daughter in the family, who is my age. It's amazing ... every morning we* (8).................. (wake up) *by her mother with a cup of tea! Yesterday (Sunday), we* (9).................. (even/give) *breakfast in bed!*

Today was my first day at my new language school. When I arrived, I (10).................. (take) *to a special room where we* (11).................. (welcome) *by the Director. He* (12).................. (explain) *what was going to happen and who all the staff were. Then we* (13).................. (go) *to a large room where we* (14).................. (give) *a test to do. It was quite difficult, but it was soon over and then we* (15).................. (have) *an interview with a teacher who* (16).................. (check) *our spoken English. As we* (17).................. (leave) *we* (18).................. (hand) *a form to fill in with all our personal details and we* (19).................. (tell) *to arrive early tomorrow to give us time to find our new classes. In the afternoon we* (20).................. (take) *on a guided tour of the city by bus which was very interesting.*

I'm really looking forward to tomorrow when we (21).................. (put) *in our new classes.*

I don't know yet what level I'll be in – apparently we (22).................. (tell) *when we arrive tomorrow. At the same time we* (23).................. (give) *the various books that we need for the course. It's all quite exciting! I just hope I like my teacher!*

Love,
Rosario xxx

Exam focus

Paper 4 Listening (unrelated extracts)

In Part 1 of Paper 4 you will hear a number of short extracts of people talking in different situations (e.g. friends chatting, a stranger asking directions, part of a radio programme). You will have one question about each extract and a choice of three possible answers. You will often be asked about the relationship of the speakers (e.g. *Are they friends/strangers/work colleagues?*), the attitude of the speakers (e.g. *Are they happy/depressed/annoyed?*) or the general subject of the extract (e.g. *Is the person asking for information/making a complaint/booking her holiday?*).

You will hear each extract twice. Here is a good procedure to follow for this task:

- Read the multiple choice questions <u>before</u> you listen the first time. Then select your answers as you listen.
- When you listen the second time, make a note of key words or phrases that justify your answer where possible.

1   Now you are going to listen to people talking in seven different situations. Choose the correct alternative for each question.

1   You overhear this man expressing his opinions in a pub. The original crime he is talking about was

   A shoplifting.
   B mugging.
   C bad driving.

2   Who is the man talking to?

   A his secretary
   B his boss
   C his wife

3   The person speaking is mainly concerned about the listener's

   A diet.
   B general health.
   C physical fitness.

4   You overhear the following exchange on the bus. How does the man react?

   A He is surprised.
   B He doesn't believe the woman.
   C He is angry.

5   You hear someone talking on the phone. She is talking to

   A a theatre.
   B a restaurant.
   C a book shop.

6   You turn on the radio and hear part of a programme about the place of women in society. Does the speaker think that women

   A now have equal opportunities with men?
   B can't get any of the top jobs?
   C have more opportunities than before?

7   You are sitting in a doctor's waiting room when you hear a couple opposite having this conversation. Are they deciding on

   A a birthday present?
   B a present because of academic success?
   C a Christmas present?

2   The following verbs appear in a passive form in the listening extracts you have just heard. Listen again and:

a) decide which extract each verb comes from.
b) write the complete sentence each verb comes in.

1   to give
2   to lock up
3   to confirm
4   to ask
5   to treat
6   to take
7   to offer
8   to allow

Speaking

1 Work with a partner. Student A should look at the pictures below, and Student B should look at the pictures on page 188. The pictures are in jumbled order. Describe to your partner what is happening and together try to work out the complete story in the correct order. Use passive forms where appropriate.

2 Now read the story of what actually happened. Some of the lines are correct and some have one extra word which should not be there. Decide which lines have an extra word and correct them.

1 Jim Crawford had just been left his car in a car
2 park near his office when he was approached by a
3 mugger with a knife who demanded of his wallet. Jim
4 gave to him his wallet and the man ran off. Jim
5 decided to go to the nearest police station and
6 report the crime, but just as he was walking towards
7 it he was being stopped by a second man. This man
8 also wanted Jim's wallet, but Jim tried to explain
9 him that it had already been stolen. The second
10 mugger told him to hand them over his shoes and
11 socks. Jim did it as he was told and then, when the
12 man had gone, walked into the police station. The
13 police were absolutely surprised to see him without
14 any shoes and socks and questioned him about what
15 had happened. After having giving descriptions of
16 the two men, Jim was driven back to his car. But,
17 to his horror, when they got to the place at where
18 he had left it, he discovered that it had been stolen.

A

B

C

D

Listening: Guardian Angels

1   You are going to hear a conversation between a husband and wife. Listen and decide what connection there is between what they say and the picture below.

2   Listen again and decide if the following statements are True or False.

1   Guardian Angels began in America and have since come to Britain.
2   Only a few of them are paid or carry guns.
3   The Guardian Angels do not aim to hurt anyone.
4   There is a 3-month period in which they are taught different skills.
5   They do not like to involve the police if they can avoid it.
6   The official police view about the Guardian Angels is quite negative.
7   The view of the police on the streets is quite positive.
8   The man and woman having the conversation basically have the same view about the Guardian Angels.

3   Discuss the following statements.

- The Guardian Angels are a useful and necessary idea. Citizens should take more responsibility for preventing crime.
- There shouldn't be a need for groups like the Guardian Angels.
- The Guardian Angels are a dangerous idea. Keeping law and order must be left to the police.

Vocabulary: phrasal verbs (*make*)

- *As far as I can* **make out,** *the idea is that ...*

1   Replace the words in *italics* in the following sentences with a phrasal verb with *make* and an appropriate particle from the box. Use a dictionary where necessary.

| up (x 3)   for   of   out (x 2) |

EXAMPLE: Look ... why don't you go and say you're sorry and *become friends again* with Julie?
Look ... why don't you go and say you're sorry and **make it up** with Julie?

1   When it started to rain, we *went to* the nearest shelter.
2   It wasn't true, was it? You just *invented* it, didn't you?
3   He *pretended* that he had been with his best friend, but I knew it was a lie.
4   She tried to *get back* the lost time by getting a taxi.
5   He *couldn't read* what the sign said, because it was so foggy.
6   What do you *think of* that picture? I can't understand it at all!
7   Why don't we *prepare* the spare room for John in case he wants to stay overnight?

2   Work with a partner. You have fifteen minutes to write a short story involving a crime using as many phrasal verbs with *make* as you can. When you have finished, read your story to another group. Who managed to include the most phrasal verbs?

1

1 Write the meaning of the following words.

a) to drench
b) to stagger
c) to grin
d) flabbergasted
e) to yell
f) to fidget
g) to nibble
h) to smuggle
i) a pickpocket
j) a jury
k) a witness
l) to deny
m) to release
n) illegal

2 Fill in the gaps in the following sentences with the correct form of one of the words above. You do not need to use all of the words.

a) He .... towards the telephone, but fell before he could pick it up.
b) The .... was out for several hours before they could all agree on a verdict.
c) He .... being anywhere near the bank on the day the money was stolen.
d) She never eats properly. She just .... at her food.
e) Please stop ....! Sit still.
f) It was pouring with rain and I got absolutely ....
g) I was absolutely .... when she told me I had won first prize.

2

2 The following sentences are all incorrect. Find the mistake and correct the sentences.

1 By the time I got there, John had been gone.
2 Why didn't you let him to borrow the car?
3 I haven't being allowed to stay out late for ages.
4 On one occasion the teacher was made me stand in the corner with my hands above my head.
5 I am be looked after very well by the doctors and nurses.
6 What do you think you will been doing this time next week?
7 He could have delayed by traffic on the way home.
8 You shouldn't be worry. I'm sure everything will be all right.
9 Mike really enjoys be asked to talk about his childhood.
10 You know he made up it all. He wasn't really on holiday at all.
11 We made for to the nearest telephone as quickly as we could.
12 It's very difficult to be make out what it says. The writing is so small.

3

3 Fill in the gaps in the following text with an appropriate word.

A COCK AND BULL STORY

There was never any doubt as to the guilt (1)..................... the accused. In the French county of Valois, in the year 1314, he (2)..................... deliberately killed a man. Several people had witnessed the attack. The accused (3)..................... sentenced to death and hanged soon afterwards. The accused was a bull.

Modern law does not recognise the idea that animals can (4)..................... a crime, but in medieval Europe it was quite common for animals to (5)..................... taken to court on all sorts (6)..................... charges – everything from witchcraft to murder. On one occasion the rats of Atun in central France (7)..................... called before the court on a charge of infesting local houses and barns. When they failed (8)..................... appear, their lawyer explained that their lives would have (9)..................... put in danger by the number of cats in the neighbourhood. He said that (10)..................... court would have to guarantee the safety of each of his clients on their way to and from the trial. The case (11)..................... postponed indefinitely.

In the 15th century, a cock in the Swiss town of Basel was not so lucky. He was accused (12)..................... laying an egg, which the superstitious townsfolk saw as a sure sign that he was a sorcerer. As a result, the cock (13)..................... tied to a stake and burned, along with the egg. And in Lavegny, France in 1457, a sow that had killed and partly eaten a child was hanged (14)..................... murder. Her six piglet accomplices (15)..................... not punished, however, on the grounds that they had been too young (16)..................... know any better.

The power of words

Reading

1 Look at the pictures of different people below and discuss the following questions.

1 What message do you think each person is trying to communicate?

2 Do people use these signs in your country? What other signs do people use?

3 Do you think it is possible for animals to 'talk'? If so, can you give any examples?

2 Read the following text which describes an experiment with animals and answer these questions.

1 What was the aim of the experiment?

2 Did the Gardners believe the experiment was successful?

CHATTING WITH CHIMPS

1 NATURALISTS have long known[1] that the apes, our nearest relatives in the animal kingdom, communicate[2] with one another through gestures, sounds and facial expressions. But it was long believed[3] that only human beings could use words and sentences. In the 1960s, however, determined researchers set 10 themselves the task of teaching chimpanzees and other apes to talk[4] in English.

At first the scientists tried to make the animals speak. But no chimp ever managed to acquire a vocabulary of more than four words, and these were spoken with great difficulty as their vocal tracts are not well adapted for producing the sounds of human speech. 20 The breakthrough came when Trixie and Allen Gardner, a husband-and-wife team of scientists at the University of Nevada, decided[5] to try American Sign Language (ASL), a system of gestures used by the deaf. After four years of dedicated effort they had taught their first chimpanzee, Washoe, to use 132 ASL signs correctly[6] to communicate her wants and needs.

30 Washoe clearly 'understood' words – when she was asked in sign language to fetch an apple, she would bring that fruit rather than, say, a banana. But

her linguistic abilities[7] went muc further. She would not only produ simple combinations like 'give apple' 'please, hurry' to get what she want from her keepers, but also talked herself in sign language when sh 40 thought no one was watching: she w often observed making the sign f 'quiet' for her own benefit alone as sh crept stealthily across the yard towar an area that she had been forbidden enter. Washoe even learned to swea applying[8] the word for 'dirty' anything or anyone she disliked.

The Gardners went on to assemble small community of baby chimps th 50 were constantly in the presence adults who used sign language amon themselves as well as with the anima The researchers reported that th chimps grew accustomed to talking one another in sign language. Th even started inventing[9] their ow words by combining signs they kne for instance, 'water bird' for a swan. Apart from sign language, apes ha 60 been taught by other scientists[10] communicate using plastic tokens on board, having learned that each toke represented[11] an object, action, colo or concept. Some researchers ha noticed that the apes prefer to u symbols in a particular order, and s this as evidence of a primiti grammar. For example, they w request something to drink by signi 70 'more drink' rather than 'drink more' Yet other scientists still doubt wheth the apes are using language in a tru human sense. They point out that th apes rarely put together more than tw words in a sentence, and they spe most of their time exactly copying th series of signs made by their teacher But the Gardners at least are in n doubt[12] that their chimps really can ta 80 with their hands.

from Reader's Digest *Did you kn*

3 Decide which of the following things the chimps were able to do.

1 recognise the meaning of individual words
2 ask for things
3 spell correctly
4 use bad language
5 talk to one another in sign language
6 name new objects by combining words
7 decide on correct word order
8 make grammatically correct sentences

4 Put the numbered words from the text in the following sentences in the correct form.

EXAMPLE: 1 His ....*knowledge*.... of Polish is extremely good.

2 I think there has been a breakdown in .... between the two departments.
3 Did you know that she has had these .... for many years?
4 He's so .... He just goes on and on. It's unbearable!
5 Why are you so .... ? Just make up your mind and tell me what you want to do!
6 I'm afraid number four is .... You'll have to do it again.
7 The facilities for .... people in this building are terrible.
8 Have you filled in your .... form for that job yet?
9 That's a really useful .... I wish I had thought of it.
10 There have been some remarkable .... discoveries this century.
11 I don't think his views are .... of the other people in the class.
12 It is .... whether Xavier is going to be fit to play in tomorrow's match.

5 Discuss whether you think there are fundamental differences between people and animals or whether people are just another type of animal. If you think there are fundamental differences, what are they?

Grammar: expressing hypothetical meanings

1 Complete the sentence in the speech bubble.

I wish I could talk to animals. If I could, I ...

2 Look at these sentences containing the verb *wish*. Then decide which of the rules below are true. If you think there is a mistake in the rules, correct it.

- I wish I had a bit more money.
- I wish I was/were more self-confident.
- I wish I could swim.
- I wish you wouldn't smoke when we are eating.
- I wish you didn't have to go to work today.
- I wish I hadn't argued with my parents last night.

1 When referring to the present or future, *wish* is followed by a present tense.
2 When referring to the past, *wish* is followed by the Past Perfect.
3 When we want to criticise someone else's irritating habit or we want something to change, we can follow *wish* with *would* + verb.

Grammar reference p.167 (8.1)

3 Choose the correct alternative in the following sentences.

1 I wish it *wasn't/wouldn't/isn't* so hot. I hate this kind of weather.
2 The holiday was a disaster. I wish we *didn't go/hadn't gone/weren't going*.
3 I really wish I *can/could/am able to* play the violin like her.
4 Don't you wish that we *didn't/don't/doesn't* have any homework to do.
5 I wish you *weren't/won't/wouldn't* talk with your mouth full. It's very rude.
6 He wishes his parents *are living/have lived/lived* nearer.
7 The party was very boring after you left. We all wish you *had stayed/stayed/would stay*.

4 Imagine your fairy godmother has given you four wishes which must be formed in this way:

1 *I wish* + Past Simple
2 *I wish* + Past Perfect
3 *I wish* + could
4 *I wish* + would

Write your wishes using the correct form.

5 Choose the alternative which correctly interprets the sentence in italics.

1 *It's time they left.* = They have already gone./They haven't gone yet.
2 *If only I hadn't gone to the party.* = I'm sorry I went to the party./I'm sorry I missed the party.
3 *I'd rather you came early.* = I am pleased you came early./ I would like you to come early.
4 *Suppose somebody saw you take it. You'd be in real trouble.* = He is thinking about taking it./He has taken it.

6 Complete the following sentences in a logical way.

1 I wish I … . I'm just so lonely at the moment.
2 If only I …, I wouldn't have failed my exams.
3 I'd rather … tonight because I've got so much work to do.
4 Suppose we … . Do you think anyone would mind?
5 I wish he … . It's so annoying.
6 It's time you … . You've done nothing all day.
7 I think I'd rather …, I haven't had much exercise recently.
8 Suppose you … ? Surely that would put your dad in a good mood?
9 If only we …, then we could come and visit you more often.
10 I'm afraid it's time … . We both have to get up early tomorrow morning.

Watch Out! *'d rather/'d better*

1 I*'d rather* go to an Italian restaurant.
2 You*'d better* finish your homework.

a) Which of the phrases in *italics* means *should* and which means *prefer*?
b) Which *'d* is a short form of *had*? Which *'d* is a short form of *would*?

7

1 You are going to hear a song. Listen and decide what the singer wishes.

2 Match up the two halves of the following lines of the song. Then listen and check your answers.

1 You know I never meant	a) out of sight,
2 But I only passed by	b) right, yeah.
3 All this time I stayed	c) wondering why.
4 I started	d) in your life,
Chorus	e) as a friend, yeah.
5 You said you didn't need me	f) to cause you no pain,
6 Oh, I guess you were	g) I did it again, yeah.
7 Ooh, I never meant	h) to see you again,
8 But it looks like	
Chorus	

3 Look at the appropriate line in the song and imagine possible answers to these questions.

a) *line 1:* why do you think?
b) *line 4:* why what?
c) *line 7:* what pain do you think he caused?

Vocabulary: spoken and written language

1 Look at each of the following verbs and decide when you might do this, in what situation and with whom.

1	to translate	8	to discuss
2	to repeat	9	to row
3	to whisper	10	to beg
4	to mutter	11	to mention
5	to chat	12	to inform
6	to gossip	13	to contradict
7	to shout	14	to speak up

2 Work in a group with two other students. Students A and B should look at page 188 and act out the situations described to Student C. Student C should say what is happening using one of the verbs in Exercise 1. Then Students B and C should look at page 189 and act out the situations for Student A. Finally Students A and C act out the situations on page 190 for Student B.

3 Discuss the following questions.

1 What do you need to do to become 'fluent' in a foreign language?
2 If we say someone is 'bilingual', what do we mean?
3 How much language do you need to 'get by' on holiday in a foreign country where they don't speak your language? What kind of language is most useful?
4 How much use are phrase books when you travel?
5 What skills do you think a) an interpreter b) a translator needs?
6 Which language has the most number of people who speak it as their 'mother tongue'?

4 Work with a partner and decide whether the following are usually written or spoken or both. Try to write a simple definition for each one. Use a dictionary where necessary.

EXAMPLE: ***a telephone directory*** *is a book of all the telephone numbers in one area, usually in alphabetical order.*

1	a telephone directory	8	a diary	15	a prescription
2	a message	9	a shopping list	16	an agenda
3	a novel	10	a love letter	17	a C.V.
4	a play	11	a fax	18	a brochure
5	a lecture	12	a telegram	19	a speech
6	a report	13	a memo	20	a review
7	an instruction manual	14	a will		

Listening: extracts

1 Look at the following written extracts from different types of text. Decide which of the text types listed above each extract comes from. Which one of them is not referred to above?

A
6.20 Blind Date
Cilla Black hosts the popular show which creates new couples and sends them away to surprising locations. This week we hear how Mike and Sandra got on during a cycling holiday in Holland.

B
Department meeting 13/7/96
1. Market share in Europe
2. Recent resignations
3. Projected sales figures for South America (cut off)

C
Wednesday
7.30pm. Squash with Carol

D
Insert the documents FACE DOWN. The unit can accept up to 10 sheets of paper at a time. Enter the phone number of the party to which you wish to send. Confirm in the display whether the phone number is correctly dialled. If you misdial, press the STOP/CLEAR button then enter the correct number. Press the START button. The unit will dial and transmit the documents.

E
I hate being separated from you like this, but just remember it's only another 4 weeks until we can see each other again. Please write soon. Your letters mean so much to me. Fondest love, Geoff.

F
ROWENA, CATCHING MORNING TRAIN TO PLYMOUTH. SHOULD BE WITH YOU FOR LUNCH, LOVE GUY.

G
O Romeo, Romeo wherefore art thou Romeo?
Deny thy father and refuse thy name,
Or if thou wilt not, be but sworn my love, ...

H
Directed by Ridley Scott, this is the story of Thelma (Geena Davis) and Louise (Susan Sarandon) who together decide to get away from their humdrum everyday lives (and men) and take a weekend break. However, a violent incident turns their trip into a nightmare and they end up trying to escape the law instead. The film is built around the relationship between the two women ...

2 Now you are going to hear eight spoken extracts. Listen and decide which of the above texts they are connected to and in what way.

Grammar: *to have something done*

1   Look at the following two sentences and decide what differences there are in meaning and in form.

- I hope all the work you are having done on the house is going OK.
- I hope all the work you are doing on the house is going OK.

Grammar reference p.175 (16)

2   Match a noun in Column A with a verb in Column B and write a sentence with *have* as in the example. Some of the nouns can go with more than one verb.

EXAMPLE: *You can* **have your house painted**.

A	B
a house	to take
a watch	to paint
hair	to test
a sofa	to mend
eyes	to dry-clean
a photo	to cut
trousers	to deliver

3   Look at this extract from Jack's diary. Imagine that today is Thursday. Write complete sentences about:

1 what he had done yesterday.
2 what he is having done today.
3 what he is going to have done tomorrow.

Wednesday

Pick up jacket from dry-cleaners.
Optician 12.15pm (eye-test).
New window in bathroom to be put in
(between 3 and 4 pm).

Thursday

Delivery of new sofa (3-4 pm).
Ken Mills to paint bathroom.
Go to garage: mechanic will change
oil and tyres.

Friday

11.00am TV repairman.
Need special photo taken of me to go
with CV.
Don't forget hair-cut before tonight!!

4   Imagine you have unlimited money to spend. How would you change the place where you live? What would you have done?

EXAMPLE: *I* **would have a tennis court built** *in the garden.*

— **Watch Out!** ◄

I must *have* my hair cut soon.

Which of these verbs can replace *have* in this sentence: *make/get/put/fetch/do*?

Reading

1   Discuss the following questions.

1 What is 'graffiti'?
2 Where do you often find it?
3 What kind of people do it and why?

2 Read the following article and decide if the writer is for or against people who draw graffiti, or whether his opinion is not clear.

Graffiti – a dangerous way of life

Scrawling graffiti is seen as a crime in the UK, yet in the US it has become a recognised art form.

Just a few weeks ago eight graffiti gang members were convicted of causing £5,000 worth of damage on the London Underground. They are among more than 70 hard-core graffiti artists thought to be operating in London today. Most are aged under 20.

Graffiti artists, or 'graffers', operate in many British towns. They often work at night, covering walls, trains and railway stations with brightly painted murals or scrawls in spray paint and marker pen.

Some people regard graffiti as a form of vandalism and a menace. London Underground says that railusers find it ugly and offensive. It spends £2m a year dealing with graffiti, and has even introduced trains with graffiti-resistant paint. 'We don't think it's artistic or creative – it's vandalism. It's a huge nuisance to our customers, and it's ugly and offensive,' says Serena Holley, a spokeswoman for London Underground.

'It creates a sense of anarchy and chaos,' says Richard Mandel, a barrister who prosecuted the graffiti gang. 'Passengers feel as if the whole rail system is out of control.'

British Transport Police has a graffiti unit designed to catch graffers in the act. It spent five months tracking down the recently prosecuted gang.

Graffiti art can also be a dangerous pastime. London Underground says that some teenagers have died in accidents during nocturnal graffiti 'raids'.

However, others say that graffiti at its best is an art form. Art galleries in London and New York have exhibited work by increasingly famous graffiti artists. 'Of course graffiti is art. There's no question about that,' says David Grob, director of the Grob Gallery in London. Even some of those who think graffiti is wrong admit that graffers are talented. 'It's just that their artistic talent is channelled in the wrong direction,' says Barry

Kogan, a barrister who represented Declan Rooney, one of the gang members.

There is a difference between 'good graffiti' and vandalism, says Dean Colman, a 24-year-old graffiti artist. 'I'd never spray private property, like someone's house. Some graffiti are disgusting. There's a big difference between that and graffiti which can brighten up grey walls.'

Dean makes a living as a graffiti artist. His days of illegal spraying are behind him, he says. He has worked on a television programme about graffiti, designed a series of government posters, and decorated nightclubs. He has exhibited his work at Battersea Arts Centre in London, and he has taught graffiti-spraying in youth clubs.

Dean sees himself as an artist, and thinks that graffiti art does not get due recognition. 'There's no graffiti art in the Tate Gallery and there should be,' he says. 'Graffiti is as valid as any other art form.'

from The Guardian newspaper

3 Read the text again and choose the correct alternative to complete the following sentences.

1 The graffiti artists arrested recently in London were

   A put in prison.
   B fined £5,000.
   C wrongly accused.
   D found guilty.

2 The attitude of London Underground is that graffiti

   A is a kind of art, but a problem because some passengers don't like it.
   B is something to be stopped at all costs.
   C is irritating but they have more serious problems to worry about.
   D is causing the price of tickets to go up and therefore needs to be stopped.

3 The British Transport Police

   A have killed some 'graffers' by accident.
   B spent a lot of time trying to catch a group of graffiti artists.

   C have recently criticised the behaviour of the London Underground.
   D don't know what to do about the problem.

4 The lawyer who defended one of the convicted graffiti artists thinks they

   A should show their work in art galleries.
   B should not have been convicted.
   C should use their abilities in different ways.
   D should be more careful when working in the Underground.

5 Dean Colman

   A has never broken the law.
   B is concerned about how little he earns from his work with graffiti.
   C would like to see graffiti taken more seriously by the art world.
   D is worried about young people taking up graffiti-spraying.

Writing: discursive (2)

1 Discuss what you think about graffiti. Is it art or is it crime? What should happen to people who draw graffiti on walls in public places?

2 Look at the following comments about graffiti and decide which are in favour of graffiti and which are against. Which comment is neither for nor against?

1 Graffiti can be colourful, humorous and vibrant. 'The right sort of graffiti can liven up the ugly part of cities,' says Frank Coffield, Professor of Education at Durham University.

2 Graffiti has been a showcase for creative talents. It helped launch the careers of New York artists who used the streets and subways as an unofficial art gallery.

3 Costs of cleaning up graffiti are passed on to rail passengers in higher fares.

4 Some councils have set aside areas which graffiti artists can legally spray. This redirects their energies away from vandalism and, it is said, lets them develop their creative talents in the open.

5 Some people find graffiti offensive, even intimidating. 'I have visited public parks where obscenities and racist slogans have transformed a peaceful and relaxing place into a place of intolerance,' says Professor Frank Coffield.

6 It disrupts travel. London Underground and other rail networks take trains out of service for cleaning when they have been sprayed.

7 Graffiti can be dangerous. At least five graffiti artists have been run over or electrocuted.

8 'Some graffiti art is better than some official public art, because it actually fits into its surrounding – it isn't imposed,' says Zoe Shearman, director of visual arts at London's Riverside Studios.

9 'Graffiti-painting can lead to other crimes,' claims Nicholas Emler, a social psychologist at Dundee University. 'It's often just the starting point for much more serious delinquent behaviour.'

3

1 Look at the following exam task

An international young people's magazine is investigating the question:

Graffiti - the pros and cons.

Write a short article in 120–180 words on the topic, expressing the different sides of the argument.

Note that this time you are being asked to offer arguments for and against, not just your own opinion.

2 Write a rough plan. It should look something like this:

- Introduction: a general statement about the issue.
- Paragraph 2: points against.
- Paragraph 3: points for.
- Conclusion: sum up and state your opinion briefly.

3 Now write your answer. Use some of the arguments for and against graffiti given in Exercise 2 if you wish, and include as many of the following words/phrases as possible.

- To begin with ...
- On the other hand ...
- Another point is that ...
- It is worth remembering that ...
- As far as I'm concerned ...
- However ...
- In addition to this ...
- To sum up ...

Listening: handwriting

1 Discuss whether you think handwriting says anything about a person's character. What do you think your handwriting says about you?

'I'm sorry, but you'll have to ask the doctor to do something about his handwriting.'

2 You are going to hear an expert graphologist (a handwriting expert) analysing some different examples of handwriting. Look at the following samples and say which she refers to first, second and third.

A
We stayed in this great hotel right on the beach. It was fantastic and . . .

B
Why don't you and Chris come for dinner on Friday night?

C
I'm sorry, but I won't be able to make the meeting on Wednesday.

3 Decide if the following statements are True or False from the information given in the radio programme.

1 The way we sign our names alone can tell experts a lot about us.
2 The art of graphology can help people to find a husband or wife.
3 If your handwriting doesn't really slant to the left or right, you are probably quite emotional.
4 The expert thinks the first sample shows the writer is quite a sociable person.
5 People who have small handwriting do not have close friends.
6 The expert thinks the second sample shows the writer is fairly outgoing.
7 The expert suggests that the third sample shows the writer probably likes organising parties.

4 Work with a partner. Look at a piece of written work your partner has recently done. Analyse the handwriting and give an assessment of your partner's personality. Does your partner agree with you? Also, decide if the handwriting is clear and easy to read. If it isn't, what makes it difficult to read?

Exam focus

Paper 5 (a complete interview)

1 You are going to do a complete Paper 5 interview. First consider the following categories:

- grammar
- vocabulary
- pronunciation
- fluency
- ability to communicate

Which of them do you think are your strong points and which are weak areas in speaking?

2 Now listen to a sample interview and give each candidate a grade for each of the categories listed in Exercise 1: poor/satisfactory/good/excellent. The photos they refer to for Part 2 appear below and the pictures for Part 3 appear on page 189.

3 Now work in groups of four and roleplay an interview, similar to the one you have heard, using the same photos and pictures.

Student A

You are the interlocutor. You should keep the conversation going and take the candidates through the different parts of the interview. You will find the questions used on the cassette for Parts 1 and 4 of the interview on page 190.

Student B

You are the assessor. You should refer to the different categories in Exercise 1 for each candidate and give feedback at the end on the strong and weak points of the candidates.

Students C and D

You are both candidates.

After you have finished change roles, so that Students A and B become the candidates.

1

2

3

4

1 Choose the most suitable alternative below to fill in the gaps in the following text.

Good evening. This is Jana Hingis (1) .... from Laguana. The heavy rains that have affected the north of the country have produced serious (2) .... . The Minister for Agriculture said in a statement that the situation is now (3) .... control. (4) .... food supplies have been dropped by helicopter to families who were (5) .... to get to distribution centres. Local charities have also provided clothes and (6) .... shelter for victims of the disaster.

In the south, the (7) .... continues to force thousands of refugees to head north. Many of these people are suffering from (8) .... and are weak from months of famine. International aid organisations are trying to (9) .... them with essential food supplies, but the civil war is (10) .... the job of these organisations extremely difficult.

In neighbouring Kwilulia the cholera epidemic is spreading as a (11) .... of lack of medicines and clean water. The Ministry of Health has issued a (12) .... to all people planning to visit Kwilulia to make sure they are inoculated (13) .... cholera. The extreme temperatures and the high levels of (14) .... are not helping the situation. A United Nations spokesman said this (15) .... turn out to be one of the worst epidemics in the country's history.

1 **A** telling   **B** saying   **C** reporting
   D announcing
2 **A** inundations   **B** flooding   **C** waters
   D overflows
3 **A** under   **B** below   **C** out   **D** away
4 **A** urgency   **B** danger   **C** casualty
   D emergency
5 **A** unable   **B** impossible   **C** unwilling
   D uncertain
6 **A** part-time   **B** partial   **C** half-time
   D temporary
7 **A** dry   **B** draft   **C** drought   **D** draught
8 **A** injuries   **B** damages   **C** diseases   **D** hurts
9 **A** get   **B** reach   **C** arrive   **D** make
10 **A** having   **B** putting   **C** doing   **D** making
11 **A** because   **B** result   **C** reason   **D** cause
12 **A** advice   **B** announcement   **C** warning
   D advertisement
13 **A** for   **B** against   **C** after   **D** by
14 **A** damp   **B** humidity   **C** wet   **D** drizzle
15 **A** should   **B** must   **C** can   **D** could

2 There are mistakes with modals of deduction in eight of the following sentences. Find the mistakes and write the sentences out again correctly in your notebook.

1 That can be you when you were a baby. It looks just like you.
2 Helen must forget that we had a meeting this morning as she still hasn't arrived.
3 Do you think Mum might have bought me those new trainers I wanted for my birthday?
4 You mustn't have been so rude to her. No wonder she won't speak to you any more.
5 That can't be Mike in the photo. He doesn't have a beard.
6 I suppose I could lend you my calculator, but I was sure you'd lose it.
7 You should be freezing. Quickly, come inside by the fire and I'll get you a hot drink.
8 They shouldn't pull down that house. It was one of the oldest buildings in the city.
9 But he can't do it. He was here with me all day.
10 That mustn't be the postman. He doesn't come on Saturdays.

3 Fill in the gaps in the following text with an appropriate word.

Dear Mary,

I'm sorry for not having written for so long, but I've (1) .... busy with exams. They're over now, thank goodness, and I (2) .... relax for a while and write letters to all my friends. I was looking forward to (3) .... to the beach, but unfortunately the weather has turned quite cold all of a (4) .... You (5) .... have finished your exams too. How were they? I hope you (6) .... them all. We are (7) .... to be getting the results next week so I'm keeping my fingers crossed. If I (8) .... studied a bit harder in the first term, I wouldn't have anything to worry about. I did try to (9) .... up for lost time, but you know how it is.

I've been (10) .... to phone Jacqui, but I can't seem to get (11) .... to her. Has her number changed? I wish I (12) .... come and visit you again this summer, but Dad says it's too expensive. Mum is trying to convince (13) .... that it's a good investment because I could improve my English. She can usually get (14) .... my dad, so we might get to see each other after all.

I (15) .... better finish now as it's very late. Write back soon.

Love,
Claudia

4 Rewrite the second sentence so that it has a similar meaning to the first sentence using the word in **bold** and other words.

1 It took her a long time to recover from her illness.
over
It took her a long time .... her illness.

2 I regret saying that to him.
wish
I .... that to him.

3 I'm sure that wasn't Tony we saw. He's in London.
can't
It .... Tony we saw. He's in London.

4 It is important that I post this letter tonight.
need
I .... this letter tonight.

5 I'm sure the children have been doing something terrible while we've been out.
up
I'm sure the children .... something terrible while we've been out.

6 The mechanic checked the tyres on my car.
had
I .... on my car.

7 I think you should go to bed now.
time
It's .... to bed.

8 It was difficult for me to read the number plate in the fog.
make
I couldn't .... the number plate in the fog.

9 Please don't tell Andrew about our conversation.
rather
I'd .... Andrew about our conversation.

10 Unless you start studying now, it's possible that you will fail the exam.
could
You .... you start studying now.

5 Fill in the gaps in the following sentences with a correct form of the verb in brackets.

1 If you .... (mix) yellow and blue, you .... (get) green.

2 If I .... (not/tell) Mary about the party last Saturday, I .... (be able) to go on my own.

3 Unless you .... (start) being a little more responsible, your father and I .... (have) to stop you going out at the weekend.

4 I .... (make) nursery education compulsory for all four-year-olds if I .... (be) Minister for Education.

5 They .... (lose) the championship unless they .... (play) better next week.

6 Provided that you .... (get) home before midnight, you .... (can/go) out tonight.

7 You .... (print) what you've written if you .... (press) this key.

8 As long as you .... (promise) not to say anything, I .... (tell) you what Pat said about Richard.

9 If I .... (realise) we were so late, I .... (go) by taxi.

10 I .... (be) grateful if you .... (can/send) me further information about your courses.

11 .... (buy) a better racket if you .... (want) to improve your tennis.

12 If I .... (not/stay up) so late last night, I .... (not/feel) so tired this morning.

6 Write a word for the following definitions.

1 a very thick mist

2 a light gentle wind

3 a sudden shaking of the earth's surface

4 an organisation that helps people that are poor, sick or in difficulties

5 a long period of dry weather when there is not enough water

6 a person whose profession is writing for a newspaper or magazine.

7 the heading printed in large letters above a story in a newspaper

8 a hollow passage coming out of the roof of a building that lets smoke from the fire out

9 an underground room, usually without windows, often used for storing goods

10 a row of bushes planted close together that divides one garden or field from another

11 to take goods illegally from one country to another

12 a group of people (usually twelve) chosen to hear all the details of a case in a court of law and give their decision on it

13 to speak very quietly so that only a person close by can hear

14 a list of subjects to be discussed in a meeting

15 a small thin book with a paper cover giving instructions or details about a service

7 Read the following text and look carefully at each line. Some of the lines are correct and some have a word that should not be there. If a line is correct, put a (✔) at the end of it. If there is a word that should not be there, circle it. There are two examples at the beginning (**0** and **00**)

0	Apart from listening and speaking, reading for pleasure is a	✔
00	very good way of improving (at) your vocabulary and knowledge	
1	of the grammar in any language. It's fun, too. If you are	
2	studying English, it makes up very good sense to try and	
3	read an English books and newspapers as often as possible.	
4	Magazines like as *Newsweek* are available in many parts of	
5	the world and so they are some newspapers from the United	
6	States, Britain and other English-speaking countries. An	
7	example of an American newspaper that you can often to get	
8	in other parts of the world is the *New York Herald Tribune*.	
9	It has articles on travel, business, sport and all the	
10	latest news from around the world. So if you are visiting in	
11	a city such as Athens or Madrid, have a look at the	
12	news stands to see if there are any English language	
13	newspapers available. You might be get pleasantly surprised.	
14	They may be a bit of expensive, but you'll find that they	
15	are being well worth the money that you spend.	

8 Read the following text and use the word given in capitals at the end of each line to form a word that fits in the gap in the same line.

Unfortunately we have received a lot of (1)	**COMPLAIN**
from customers about late (2) .... of parcels.	**DELIVER**
I have come to the (3) .... that the new system	**CONCLUDE**
we introduced last month is a complete (4) .... . This	**FAIL**
seems to be due to a (5) .... of factors, but one	**COMBINE**
of the most important ones is that some (6)	**EMPLOY**
are not very responsible. The union (7) .... say	**REPRESENT**
it's not the workers but the (8) .... who are at fault.	**MANAGE**
What is clear is that we have to improve (9)	**COMMUNICATE**
within the company. Nowadays there's a lot of (10)	**COMPETE**
in the messenger service industry and we can't afford	
to be less than the best.	

9 Fill in the gaps in the following sentences with an appropriate particle (*in*, *at*, *through*, etc.) or a verb in the correct form.

1 Not only did they sell the Eiffel Tower twice, but they got .... with it.

2 I made .... for lost time by working all night.

3 Those old socks are completely .... out. You should throw them away.

4 If you write in pencil, you can always .... out your mistakes.

5 Let me talk to him. I can always get .... your Dad.

6 I think we should .... out all those old books.

7 He made .... that he was angry, but I knew he wasn't really.

8 I didn't know what to .... of that film. It didn't seem to have a plot at all.

9 The doctor asked me to .... my tongue out so that she could look at my throat.

10 They find it very difficult with four children to support to .... by on the salary he earns.

11 I'm fed up with cooking. Why don't we eat .... for a change?

12 I'm surprised you and Charlie don't .... on better. You're very alike.

161

Grammar reference

Index

1 Adjectives ending in -ed and -ing

1.1 Adjectives ending in -ed

These adjectives end in -ed or have the same form as the past participle of a verb (e.g. *thrilled, relieved, terrified*). We use them to describe people's feelings. The adjectives normally follow *be* or other verbs like *feel, seem, look*, etc.

*She was **excited** about going to the circus.*
*They both looked **astonished** when I told them I was getting married.*
*What's the matter with Iannis? He seems a bit **depressed**.*

1.2 Adjectives ending in -ing

We use these adjectives to describe experiences or events. They can be used before the noun or after *be* and other linking verbs.

*That was an absolutely **terrifying** film. I had my eyes closed for most of the time.*
*Jeff's party was really pretty **boring**.*
*What's that magazine? It looks really **interesting**.*

2 Adverbs of frequency

2.1 Adverbs of definite frequency

The following are common adverbs of definite frequency:

once
twice
five times
several times
} *a day/week/month/year*

every day/week/month/year/morning/afternoon/evening
every three/couple of/few years
on Monday/Wednesday/weekdays, etc.

These adverbs usually come at the end of the sentence.

*My telephone rings **several times a day**.*
*She goes swimming **every morning**.*
*They visit their relatives in Greece **every few years**.*

2.2 Adverbs of indefinite frequency

These adverbs are used to talk about how often we do things. We can put them in order from 'most often' to 'least often' like this:

always   most often
almost always
generally/normally/regularly/usually
frequently/often
sometimes
occasionally
almost never/hardly ever/rarely/seldom
not ... ever/never   least often

In statements and questions these adverbs come towards (but *not* at) the beginning of the sentence depending on the main verb as follows:

- after *be* when it is the only verb in the sentence
  *I **am always** glad to see you.*
- after the first auxiliary verb when there is more than one verb
  *I **have often walked** down this street before.*
- before the main verb when there is only one verb
  *We **sometimes go** to a restaurant for lunch on Sundays.*
- before *used to, have to* and *ought to*
  *She **often used to** come and see me.*
  *We **never had to** wear uniforms when I was at school.*
  *You **sometimes ought to** phone your mother, you know.*
- in questions, after the subject
  ***Don't you usually go** home by bus?*

In negative sentences they come in the middle of the sentence as follows:

- *not* comes before *always* and usually before *generally, normally, often, regularly* and *usually*
  *She's **not always** so friendly. I wonder what she wants.*
  *I **don't usually** go out in the evenings during the week.*

- *not* comes after *sometimes* and *frequently*
  I **sometimes don't** enjoy parties.
  She **frequently doesn't** remember my name.

Always, *often* and *usually* can come at the end of the sentence.

I'll live here **always**.
Do you come here **often**?
I go out with friends on Saturdays **usually**.

Always and *never* come at the beginning with imperatives.

Always have a clean handkerchief with you.
Never say that to me again!

3 The article

3.1 The definite article: the

Use the definite article *the* to talk about the following:

- inventions
  When was **the telescope** invented?
- species of animal
  The domestic cat has lived alongside humans since the time of the Pharaohs.
- oceans and seas
  My sister says **the Pacific** is not as blue as **the Aegean**.
- mountain ranges
  Are **the Andes** as high as **the Dolomites**?
- island groups
  The Galapagos Islands are off the coast of Ecuador.
- areas
  There's flooding in **the northwest** and a terrible drought in **the south**.
- rivers
  You can take a cruise along **the Rhine**.
- deserts
  The sand on this beach was imported from **the Sahara**.
- hotels
  They spent the first night of their honeymoon at **the Ritz**.
- cinemas
  That film Robert Redford directed is on at **the Odeon**.
- theatres
  They're putting on a production of Miss Saigon at **the Palais.**
- newspapers
  You can get **The Times, The Guardian, The Independent** and several other British newspapers here.
- national groups
  The Welsh are famous for their singing.

Also use the definite article:

- with superlatives
  He's **the tallest, the most handsome** and **the nicest boy** in our class.
- when there is only one thing
  The sun was shining brightly, but it was still very cold.
  I sometimes think **the world** is not a very nice place.

- to talk about particular nouns when it is clear what we are referring to
  Where's **the dog**? I want to take him for a walk.
  Close **the window**, will you? It's freezing in here.
- to talk about previously mentioned things
  Take one egg, a small onion and a bunch of parsley.
  Break **the egg** into a bowl.

3.2 The indefinite article: a/an

Use the indefinite article *a/an*

- with (singular) jobs, etc.
  She's **an engineer**.
  Is your father **a football fan**, too?
- with singular countable nouns (mentioned for the first time or when it doesn't matter which one)
  I'd like **a small salad** and **a glass of mineral water**.
  What you need is **a decent holiday**.
- With these numbers: 100, 1,000, 1,000,000
  There were over **a hundred people** at the party.
  He wants **a thousand pounds** for that old car of his.
  He had made **a million dollars** by the time he was sixteen.
- in exclamations about singular countable nouns
  What **a fantastic view**!

3.3 The zero article

Use no article (the zero article) to talk about:

- continents
  They're travelling through **Asia**.
- countries
  Have you been to **Peru**?
- mountains
  They have reached the summit of **Mount Everest**.
- lakes
  Are **Lake Constance** and **Lake Como** both in Switzerland?
- villages
  San Andres is a village just along the coast from here.
- towns
  Horsham is a pleasant town near the Sussex coast.
- cities
  And now it's over to Jack Russell for the latest news from **Washington**.
- streets, roads, etc.
  Oxford Street and **Tottenham Court Road** are very busy shopping streets in London.
- magazines
  Do you read **Time** magazine?
- illnesses
  The twins have got **measles** and I've got **flu**.
  (But: I think I'll go and lie down – I've got **a headache**.)
- uncountable, plural and abstract nouns used in their general sense
  We buy **fruit and vegetables** at the market, but we get **bread** from a bakery near our house.
  I don't like **people** who try to impress you with how much **money** they've got.
  Love makes the world go round.

Also use no article in the following expressions:

to/at/from school/university/college
in/to class
to/in/into/from church
to/in/into/out of prison/hospital/bed
to/at/from work
for/at/to breakfast/lunch/dinner
by car/bus/bicycle/plane/train/tube/boat
on foot

4 Comparison

4.1 Types of comparison

There are three types of comparison:

1 **to a higher degree** (comparative form + *than*)
*People are **more concerned** about environmental issues **than** they used to be.*
*This dessert is **sweeter than** the one you made last night.*
2 **to the same degree** (*as ... as*)
*Those trainers cost just **as much as** mine.*
*Nicholas isn't **as/so friendly** to me **as** he used to be.*
3 **to a lower degree** (with *less* + *than* and *the least*)
*My younger sister is **less self-confident than** I am.*
*That was **the least difficult** question in the exam.*

4.2 Comparative and superlative form of adjectives

One-syllable adjectives
Add *-er* and *-est* to form the comparative and superlative of one-syllable adjectives.
*Unemployment is at the **lowest** level for five years.*

Two-syllable adjectives ending in -y, -ow and -le
1 for two-syllable adjectives ending in *-y*, drop the *-y* and add *-ier* and *-iest*
*That was the **easiest** test I've ever done.*
2 for two-syllable adjectives ending in *-ow*, add *-er* and *-est*
*As they crawled through the cave it became **narrower** and narrower.*
3 for two-syllable adjectives ending in *-le*, add *-r* and *-st*
*Use Marvel washing up liquid. It's **gentler** on your hands.*

Note: for other two-syllable adjectives see 4.4 below.

4.3 Spelling

1 With one-syllable adjectives:
- that end in a vowel + a consonant, double the consonant e.g. *fat fatter fattest, big bigger biggest*
- that end in *-e*, add *-r* and *-st* e.g. *fine finer finest*
2 With two-syllable adjectives that end in *-y* after a consonant, replace *-y* with *-i* e.g. *tidy tidier tidiest*

4.4 more and most + adjective

Use *more* and *most* with:
- two-syllable adjectives (except for those listed in 4.2)
*Riding a mountain bike is **more tiring** than jogging.*
*It was **the most boring** film I had ever seen.*

- adjectives with three or more syllables
*I think this exercise is **more difficult** than the last one.*
*Bungee jumping is **the most exciting** sport I've done.*

4.5 Irregular comparative and superlative adjectives

These are the most common irregular forms:

good better best
bad worse worst
little less least
much more most
far further/farther furthest/farthest
old elder eldest (people only; the regular forms, *old older oldest* are used for buildings, towns, animals, trees, etc.)

*Jim is a **better** player than I am, but John is **the best**.*
*That must have been **the worst** movie I've ever seen. It was even **worse** than the one we saw last week and that was really **bad**.*
*You live even **further** from the centre than I do, but Pedro lives **the furthest** away.*

4.6 Adverbs

1 Most adverbs of manner have two or more syllables. Therefore they form their comparatives and superlatives with *more* and *most*.
*If you correct your mistakes **more clearly**, you won't have to write your composition out again.*
*She works **the most carefully** in the class.*

2 Adverbs with the same form as adjectives form their comparatives with *-er* and *-est*.
*I know you like driving fast, but if you drive any **faster**, I'll get out at the next set of traffic lights.*
*The people who arrived **the earliest** got the best seats.*
*You'll just have to try a bit **harder**.*
*Suzanne took **longer** to finish than Michelle.*
*My sister eats **the quickest** in our family.*

4.7 Irregular comparative adverbs

1 *badly* and *well* use the same comparative and superlative forms as *bad* and *good*.
*She did **worse** in the tests than she expected, but **better** in the final examination.*

2 Other irregular forms include: *late later last, much more most, little less least.*
*Michael arrived **later** than Paul, but Tim arrived **last**.*
*I still don't see my family **much**, but I see them **more** than I used to.*
*I like Justin **less** than Mike, but I like Terry **least** of all.*

4.8 Modifying comparison

You cannot use *very* with comparatives, but you can use the following:

much bigger   *a lot* cheaper
far less expensive   *a bit* faster
very much better   *I don't think it will be **any** quicker*
a little happier   *to go by car.*

5 Conditionals

5.1 Conditional linking words and punctuation

Some common conditional linking words are:

if, when, as/so long as, until, unless , even if, no matter how/who/what/where/when, provided (that)

When the clause with the conditional linking word (*if, unless,* etc.) is at the beginning of the sentence, there is a comma. When the main clause begins the sentence, there is no comma.

If you lend me your basketball, I'll help you with your homework.
Can we go out and play basketball when we finish our homework?
You can't go out and play basketball until you finish your homework.
As long as you finish your homework, you can go out and play basketball.
I won't lend you my basketball unless you help me with my homework
I won't lend you my basketball even if you help me with my homework
No matter how much you help me with my homework, I won't lend you my basketball.

5.2 Zero conditional

FORM: *If,* etc. + Present Simple + Present Simple in the main clause

USE: to say what always happens.

If you stroke our cat, she purrs.
Unless you are on top of a mountain, water boils at 100° C.

5.3 First conditional

FORM: *If,* etc. + Present Simple/Present Continuous/Present Perfect + Present Continuous, Future or imperative in the main clause

USE: to describe what may possibly happen.

Tell Mary to phone me no matter how late she gets back.
If you're passing through London, you are always welcome to come and stay with us.
Unless you've finished before 5.00, I won't be able to pick you up.

5.4 Second conditional

FORM: *If,* etc. + Past Simple/Continuous + conditional in the main clause

USE: to talk about something:

- that is impossible and just imagined
  If I had a younger brother, I'd teach him to play football.
  If I were/was a millionaire, I'd invite all my friends to spend their holidays on my private island.

- which is very unlikely to happen in the future
  No matter how safe it was, I wouldn't try bungee jumping.
  Unless I won a really big prize in the lottery, I wouldn't give up my job.

Also, the second conditional is often used to give advice.

I'd buy a decent dictionary if I were you.

5.5 Third conditional

FORM: If + Past Perfect + *would have* + past participle in the main clause

USE: to describe something in the past that could have happened, but didn't or shouldn't have happened, but did.

I wouldn't have cooked a vegetarian meal unless I had thought they were vegetarians.
She would have passed the exam if she had answered all the questions.

5.6 'Mixed' conditionals

It is possible to have sentences that mix:

- an *if* clause referring to the past with a main clause referring to the present or future
  I would be happily married now if I hadn't told Mary I didn't love her.
  She wouldn't let us go to the match unless we had finished our homework.

- an *if* clause referring to the present or future with a main clause referring to the past
  He would have invited you if he wasn't already coming to the dance with his girlfriend.
  She would have ordered something else if she didn't like spaghetti.

5.7 Modal verbs in conditional sentences

Modal verbs *can, could, might,* etc. can be used in first, second and third conditionals.

I might go to the match if there are any seats left.
If she had private classes, she could pass the exam.
If they had taught us how to use the machine safely, the accident might never have happened.

5.8 Polite expressions

- *would* can be used after *if* in polite expressions.
  If you wouldn't mind waiting for a moment, the porter will take your cases up to your room.
- *should* is used in the *if* clause to make it even less likely. This is common in formal letters.
  If you should require any further information, please do not hesitate to contact us.
- *should* can replace *if* in formal letters.
  Should you wish to contact me, I can be reached at the above address.

6 Countable and uncountable nouns

6.1 Uncountable nouns

These have no plural. The following are common nouns that are *usually* uncountable:

accommodation, advice, behaviour, bread, copper, (and all other metals), *English,* (and all other languages), *furniture, health, information, knowledge, luggage, news, progress, research, rice,* (and all other grains and cereals), *salt,* (and all other condiments e.g. pepper), *scenery, spaghetti, traffic, travel, trouble, water* (and all other liquids), *weather, work.*

6.2 Nouns which can be countable or uncountable

The following nouns can be both countable and uncountable:

1 Nouns we think of as single things or substances:
- egg
  *Would you like **a boiled egg** for breakfast?*
  *You've spilt **egg** on your tie.*
- chicken
  *I bought **a chicken** to have for Sunday lunch.*
  *There was a choice between **chicken** or fish on the plane.*
- iron
  *We'll have to buy **a new iron**. This one just doesn't get the creases out.*
  *People learned to make implements from **iron**.*
- glass
  *Pass me **a glass** and I'll pour you a drink.*
  *What did people use for windows before they invented **glass**?*
- hair
  *Waiter! There's **a hair** in my soup.*
  *She's got long blonde **hair**.*

2 Normally uncountable nouns which are used to refer to particular varieties.
*Would you like **wine** with your meal?*
*They produce **a very good white wine** on that island.*

3 Words for drinks e.g. *coffee, tea, beer.* The countable noun means a *glass of, a cup of, a bottle of,* etc.
Coffee is very expensive at the moment.
*Why don't we stop for **a coffee**?*
*People in Belgium drink **beer** more than wine.*
*There's **a beer** in the fridge if you want one.*

4 *time, space, room*
*I'm sorry I haven't got **time** to talk to you now. Can you call me later?*
*We had **a really good time** at José's party.*
*All this old wardrobe does is take up **space**.*
*Fill in **the spaces** with a suitable word.*
*There's **room** for one more in this compartment.*
*Have you got **a single room** with a shower?*

6.3 Determiners used with countable and uncountable nouns

1 *few*
Use *few* with plural countable nouns. It means 'some but not many'. Before *few* you can use:
- the indefinite article *a*
  A few of my friends and I are going out to dinner together this Saturday.
  *There were only **a few people** on the bus.*
- the last, the first, the next, every
  *Over the next **few days** I want you to make sure you get plenty of rest.*
  *For the first **few months**, I felt a bit shy and insecure.*
  *We see them **every few weeks**.*

2 *fewer*
Fewer is the comparative of *few.* It can be followed by *than.*
*There were **fewer people** at the party **than** we had expected.*
*There will be **fewer jobs** in industry in the future.*

3 *a little; a bit of*
- Use *a little* and *a bit of* before uncountable nouns. It means 'at least some'.
  *I'll have **a little time** this afternoon if you would like to come and see me.*
  *Could I have **a bit of cheese**? It looks delicious.*
- *little* without the indefinite article means 'almost none'.
  Little money was spent on the building and it began to fall down almost as soon as we moved in.
  *She made **little effort** and didn't do well in the exam.*
  Note: use *a slice, a lump* and *a piece* with uncountable nouns for food.
  *How much sugar do you want? **One lump** or two?*
  *I'll just have **a small slice of cake**, thanks.*
  *Would you like **another piece of toast**?*

4 *many*
- Use *many* with plural countable nouns.
  How many twins do you know?
  *There are **many countries** in the world where you can enjoy excellent skiing.*

5 *much*
- Use *much* with uncountable nouns.
  *I don't have **much money**.*
  How much salt does it say to put in the sauce?

6 *lots/a lot of*
- Use *lots/a lot of* with plural countable and uncountable nouns.
  *I've had **lots/a lot of spaghetti**. I don't think I could eat another thing.*
  *They've got **lots/ a lot of friends and relatives** in Australia.*

7 Gerunds and infinitives

7.1 Verbs followed by the gerund form -ing

I **considered buying** a flat in Monte Carlo, but they were too expensive.

Here are some common verbs which are followed by the gerund:

admit, deny, appreciate, can't help, can't stand, consider, delay, deny, detest, dislike, enjoy, escape, excuse, face, feel like, finish, forgive, give up, imagine, involve, mention, mind, miss, postpone, practise, put off, resent, risk, suggest, understand

7.2 Verbs and phrases followed by the infinitive without 'to'

You **must answer** all the questions.

Here are some common verbs/phrases which are followed by the infinitive without to:

can, could, may, might, must, need, had better, would rather

7.3 Verbs followed by an object + the infinitive without 'to'

She **made me do** it.

Here are some common verbs which are followed by an object and the infinitive without to:

let, make, know, hear, feel, help.

Mum **won't let me go** to the beach today.
I'**ve never known him** be so rude.
I **heard her sing** in New York.
Can you **feel his heart beat**?
Would you **help me put** my bag in the overhead locker?

In passive sentences these verbs are followed by an infinitive with to.

He **was made to return** the money.
They **are known to be** very valuable.

7.4 Common verbs followed by an infinitive with 'to'

I can't **afford to buy** a new overcoat.

Here are some common verbs which are followed by an infinitive with to:

afford, agree, appear, arrange, ask, attempt, bear, begin, care, choose, consent, decide, determine, expect, fail, forget, happen, hate, help, hesitate, hope, intend, learn, like, love, manage, mean, offer, prefer, prepare, pretend, promise, propose, refuse, regret, remember, seem, start, swear, trouble, try, want, wish

7.5 Common verbs followed by object + infinitive with 'to'

He **encouraged me to try** again.

Here are some common verbs which are followed by an object and the infinitive with to:

advise, allow, ask, cause, command, encourage, expect, forbid, force, get, hate, help, instruct, intend, invite, leave, like, mean, need, oblige, order, permit, persuade, prefer, press, recommend, request, remind, teach, tell, tempt, trouble, want, warn, wish

7.6 Verbs followed by a gerund or an infinitive with a difference in meaning

1 **remember, forget, stop, try**

remember: the gerund is used when the action happens before the remembering; the infinitive refers to an action that happens after.
I **remember walking** along the beach holding hands.
Did you remember to tell Maria about the party?

forget: when used with the gerund this means 'forget what you have done'; when used with the infinitive with to this means 'forget what you have to do'.
I **had** completely **forgotten seeing** him in Paris that year.
I **forgot to post** the letter you gave me.

stop: when used with the gerund, this means 'stop something you do'; when used with the infinitive with to, this means 'stop in order to do something'.
I **stopped drinking** coffee because I couldn't sleep.
We **stopped to have** a coffee on our way into town.

try: when used with the gerund this means 'make an experiment' – doing the action may not be successful; when used with the infinitive this means 'make an effort' – the action may be difficult or impossible to do.
Try drinking a glass of water to stop your hiccoughs.
Try to study for two hours a day even if you are busy.

2 **can't bear/stand, hate, like, love, prefer**
When these verbs are used with the infinitive they refer to more specific situations. When they are used with the gerund they refer to more general situations. The difference in meaning is very slight.

I **prefer to go** to school by bus.
I **can't bear getting up** so early, but I have to.

8 Hypothetical meaning

8.1 wish

● We use wish + Past Simple to express a wish that has not come true in the present. We also use wish + Past Simple to talk about wishes that might come true in the future.
I **wish** Jackie still **lived** here.
Don't you wish you **played** tennis as well as she does?

- If the verb is *to be,* we can use the Past Simple (*I/she/it was; you/we/they were*) or *were* with all persons (*I/you/she/it/we/they were*).
  We all wish the exam **wasn't/weren't** tomorrow.
  I wish she **was/were studying** here, too.
- We use *wish + would* and *could* to refer to general wishes for the future.
  I wish I could come to your party, but I'm afraid I'll be away that weekend.
  I wish it would rain.
- *wish + would* is often used to talk about other people's irritating habits. This form is not often used with *I* or *we.* To talk about our own irritating habits we use *could.*
  I wish you would stop tapping your foot like that. It's driving me crazy.
  Don't you wish he wouldn't wear that terrible old sweater?
  I wish I could stop eating so much chocolate.
- We use *wish* + Past Perfect to refer to things we are sorry about in the past.
  I wish I had studied harder.
  She wishes she hadn't sold her apartment.

8.2 If only

- *if only* is used with the same verb forms as *wish,* and is used when your feelings are stronger. It is often used with an exclamation mark (*!*). It is used very commonly with *would/wouldn't* to criticise someone else's behaviour.
  If only I could see her now!
  If only grandfather were here today.
  If only I didn't have to work so hard.
  If only she hadn't stolen the money.

8.3 It's time

- *it's time* is used with the Past Simple to talk about the present or future. We mean that the action should have been done before. We can also say *It's **about** time* and *It's **high** time.*
  It's time you went to bed, young man. It's already ten o'clock.
  It's about time you started doing some more work on phrasal verbs.
  It's high time they were here. Their plane landed hours ago.

8.4 I'd rather (would rather)

- We use *I'd rather* + Past Simple when we want to say what we want someone or something else to do in the present or future.
  I'd rather you didn't stay out too late tomorrow night.
  Would you rather I came back later? You look very busy.
  I'd rather the meeting started a little earlier.
- We use *I'd rather* + Past Perfect when we want to say what we wanted to happen in the past.
  I'd rather you hadn't said that.
  I'd rather she had gone out more warmly dressed.

- *I'd rather* + infinitive without *to* is used to talk about our preferences or other people's preferences in the present or future.
  I'd rather go to the beach than to the mountains.
  They'd rather go by bus.

8.5 Suppose

suppose means 'What if ...?'. It is used with:
- the Present Simple to describe something that may possibly happen or may have happened.
  Suppose someone **knows** she was with us.
  Suppose someone **sees** you going into the building tomorrow morning.
- the Past Simple to talk about something that is just imagination or which is unlikely to happen in the future.
  Suppose she knew you loved her. What would you do?
  Suppose you won the lottery. How would you spend the money?
- the Past Perfect to talk about something that could have happened but didn't in the past.
  Suppose we hadn't studied so hard. Do you still think we would have passed?
  Suppose you had married Ted. Would you have been happy together?

9 Linking words and phrases

9.1 Addition

Use *as well as, in addition (to), moreover, furthermore, not only ..., but also ..., what is more* to add more information or reinforce (make stronger) what you have already said.

As well as offering an excellent way of improving your English, the automatic translator is fun to use.
In addition to finding you a place to stay in London, our friendly staff will meet you at the airport.

After *not only* use inversion (the word order you use in questions).

Not only was she extremely rude to the customers, she also stole money from the till.

9.2 Listing ideas, giving emphasis, describing a process

Use *firstly, first of all, in the first place, to begin with, secondly, thirdly, finally* to list ideas and emphasise them.

Firstly, I would like to say that we have raised over £200 pounds. **Secondly,** I want you to know that we have raised that money by knocking on doors in the neighbourhood. **Finally,** I should tell you that all of that money will be spent on a day trip for disabled children in the area.

9.3 Showing the relationship between causes and results

Use *as a result, because, because of (this), so* and *therefore* to show the relationship between causes and results.

She went out without an umbrella or a raincoat even though they had forecast rain. **As a result** she caught a terrible cold and had to spend a week in bed.

There are not many good basketball players in our country. **Because of this** teams try to recruit foreign players.

Because there are not many good basketball players in our country, teams try to recruit foreign players.

I told him I thought he had behaved very badly, **so** he's not speaking to me.

People whose diet is deficient in certain vitamins and minerals often become tired and depressed. **Therefore** it is important to make sure your patients eat a balanced diet.

9.4 however, although, in spite of, etc.

Use *however, although, even though, though, despite* and *in spite of* to show that what you are saying is surprising or unexpected in relation to something else you know to be true.

1 *however*

When you use *however*, you talk about the surprising thing in a sentence.

*I was sure I was going to miss the plane. **However**, there was no traffic, so we got to the airport in plenty of time.*

2 *although, even though* and *though*

When you use *although, even though* and *though* you can express the two ideas (the thing you know to be true and the surprising thing) in one sentence.

***Although** he trained every day, he couldn't improve his speed.*
***Even though** it's summer, you still need a pullover.*
***Though** there are a number of advantages, there are also serious disadvantages.*

Though can be used at the end of a separate sentence that expresses the surprising thing.

*We didn't have enough money to go out very much. We still had a nice time, **though**.*

3 *in spite of* and *despite*

in spite of and *despite* are prepositions. They must, therefore, be followed by a noun (often *the fact*) or a gerund. *Despite* is slightly more formal.

***In spite of the fact** that it's known to be harmful, many people continue to smoke.*
***Despite the terrible weather**, they reached the top of the mountain.*
***Despite arriving** early we still could not get tickets.*

9.5 but

But is used to link two contrasting ideas in one sentence. It is not normally used at the beginning of the sentence.

*I eat chicken and fish **but** I don't eat eggs.*
*She is staying at home **but** we are going out.*

9.6 On the one hand ... On the other hand ...

We use *On the one hand ... On the other hand ...* when we want to introduce an opposite point in a discussion. We don't always use *On the one hand ...* .

(On the one hand) if I do the exam in June, I'll be able to spend the summer with my family. **On the other hand** if I leave it until December, I'll have more time to prepare.

10 Modal verbs

FORM: modal verbs do not change in the third person. They are followed by the infinitive without *to*.

10.1 Ability

1 *can*

We use *can* to talk about present and future ability.

*I **can pick you up** on Saturday morning.*
***Can't you ride** a bicycle?*

2 *could*

We use *could* to talk about general past ability.

*I **could read** before I started school.*
***Could Einstein speak** English when he went to live in the USA?*

10.2 Asking for and giving permission

1 *can*

We use *can* to ask for and give permission.

***Can I borrow** your calculator for a few minutes?*
*You **can stay up** and watch the late night film, but then you have to go to bed.*

2 *could*

We use *could* to ask for permission when you are not sure what the answer will be.
(**Note**: *could* is **not** used for giving permission)

*A: **Could I ask** you a few questions?*
*B: Yes, of course **you can**.*

3 *may*

We use *may* to ask for or give permission in formal situations.

***May I leave** early today? I've got a dentist's appointment.*
***You may leave** the exam room after the examiner has collected your paper.*

10.3 Possibility

1 **Theoretical possibility**

a) **can** We use *can* to:
   ● say that things are possible without saying what chance there is that they will happen.
      *Anyone **can learn** to use a word processor.*
   ● talk about typical behaviour of people or things.
      *Dogs **can be** jealous of small babies.*

- speculate or guess about past events
  (**Note**: this is only in questions and negative sentences.)
  FORM:
  can't + *have* + past participle
  can + subject + *have* + past participle
  Wh- word + *can* + subject + *have* + past participle
  She **can't have understood** *what you meant.*
  Can he have thought *we'd left already?*
  Where can they have gone?

  b) *could*
  We use *could* to talk about theoretical possibility in the past.
  Uncle Tony **could be** *very funny sometimes.*

2 **Factual possibility: *could, may* and *might***
  We use *could, may* and *might* to:
  - say there is a chance that something might happen in the future
    We **may go** *to Australia* **next Christmas**.
    It **could snow tonight**.
    She **might stay for a few days**.
  - say that something is possibly true at the moment of speaking
    She **might be angry** *about something you said.*
    He **may be away** *for the weekend.*
    We **could be wrong**.
  - talk about the possibility that past events happened
    FORM: *could/may/might* + *have* + past participle
    They **may have decided** *to stay the night there.*
    He **might have met** *her at Joe's party.*
    She **could have seen** *him leaving the building.*

10.4 Obligation: should and ought to

We use *should* and *ought to* to talk about obligations and duties in the future, present and past.

You **ought to/should** *treat your mother better.*
Oughtn't we to/Shouldn't we tell *someone about the accident?*
Shouldn't we have/Oughtn't we to have invited *Susan if we invited Charlie?*

Should + *have* + past participle is often used to criticise your own or other people's behaviour.

I **should have got** *some more soap when I was at the supermarket.*
You **shouldn't have said** *that.*

10.5 Strong obligation and necessity

1 ***must***
  We use *must* to:
  - talk about present and future strong obligations and necessities that come from the speaker.
    You **must check in** *at least two hours before your flight departs.*
    I **must remember** *to tell Ted about the meeting.*

- ask about what the listener wants you to do
  Must I eat *all the vegetables?*
- tell people **not** to do things
  You **mustn't speak** *Greek in class.*

2 ***have to/have got to***
  We use *have to/have got to* to:
  - talk about present and future strong obligations that do not come from the speaker. *Have got to* is used more in British English than it is in American English.
    We **have to wear** *uniforms at our school.*
    Do we have to write *in pen or in pencil?* (more common in American English)
    I **haven't got to go** *to school tomorrow.* (more common in British English).
  - talk about past and reported obligations of all kinds
    They **told us we had to check in** *two hours before departure.*
    We **had to wear** *uniforms when I was at school.*
    I **knew I had to do** *something. I meant to tell Ted about the meeting.*

10.6 Lack of obligation

1 ***needn't, don't need to*** and ***don't have to***
  We use *needn't, don't need to, don't have to* to talk about a lack of obligation in the present or future.
  You **don't need to/needn't come** *to the airport. I'll get a taxi.*
  We **don't have to go** *to school tomorrow. It's a holiday.*

2 ***needn't*** + ***have*** + past participle
  We use *needn't* + *have* + past participle to say that somebody did something, but that it was unnecessary.
  You **needn't have written** *it out again.*

3 ***didn't need to*** + infinitive
  We use *didn't need to* + infinitive to say that something wasn't necessary without saying whether the person did it or not.
  You **didn't need to bring** *an umbrella.*

10.7 Deduction

1 ***must***
  We use *must* to say that we are sure about something in the present or past.
  That **must be** *Elena when she was a baby*
  You **must have enjoyed** *your trip to Mexico.*

2 ***can't***
  We use *can't* in negative sentences **not** *mustn't.*
  That **can't be** *Jack. He drives a Fiat.*
  Alex **can't have been** *away. The lights were on in his flat.*

11 Modifiers and intensifiers

a) We use the adverb *very* before gradable adjectives (that is adjectives that can be used in the comparative) and gradable adjectives followed by nouns. *Very* makes the meaning of the adjective more intense. *Very* can also be used before adverbs.

The film was **very interesting**.
She's a **very thoughtful girl**.
That restaurant is **very expensive**.
He drives **very slowly**.

b) Other intensifiers that can be used instead of *very* are: *so*, *rather* and *pretty* (weaker than *very*), *extremely*, *particularly*, *really*, and *terribly* (for extra emphasis).

I felt **terribly embarrassed** when he gave me the flowers.
She's a **rather shy** girl.
I was **pretty pleased** when I heard I got a 'B' in the exam.

c) The following groups of non-gradable adjectives cannot normally be used with *very*.

- nationality adjectives e.g. *Peruvian, German, Japanese*
- colour adjectives e.g. *scarlet, navy, blue, purple*
- adjectives describing permanent attributes of activities e.g. **atomic** *physics*, **plastic** *surgery*
- extreme or absolute adjectives e.g. *terrible, disastrous, marvellous, wonderful*

Note: with the extreme or absolute adjectives, we can use *really* and *absolutely*.

The party was **absolutely disastrous**. No one came!
You look **really marvellous**. Have you been on holiday somewhere?

12 Passives

FORM: appropriate tense of *be* + past participle

Present Simple:	Audio and video tapes **are kept** in the resource centre.
Present Continuous:	Our car **is being repaired** at the moment.
Past Simple:	The parcel **was delivered** right on time.
Past Continuous:	I dreamt I **was being chased** by a tall blond man with a moustache.
Present Perfect:	**Have you been invited** to Simon's party?
Past Perfect:	We **had been told** to get there no later than ten o'clock.
Future *will*:	She**'ll be looked** after very well there.
Future Perfect:	The house **will have been** completely **repainted** by the time you get back.

going to:	The procession is **going to be led** by the Lord Mayor.
Modals:	The door **must have been left** open.
	Sale items **may not be returned**.
Passive Gerund:	Our cat doesn't like **being patted**.

Note:

1 Verbs that do not take an object (e.g. *ache, arrive, sit down*) do *not* have passive forms. It is not possible to say: *I was ached*.

2 Stative verbs like *have, fit, suit* are not used in the passive with the same meanings.
Do you **have** a car? (have = own)
They've only given us £5.00 change. We**'ve been had**. (have = deceived)
Those jeans don't **fit** you any more. (fit = be the right size)
The laboratory **is being fitted** with all the latest equipment. (fit = provided with)
That dress **suits** you. (suit = look nice)
Mary and Tom **are not really suited** to each other. (suit = are not compatible).

USE: the passive is used for the following reasons:

- to talk about actions, events and processes when the action, event or process is seen as more important than the agent. This is often the case in scientific writing.
Santa Cruz **was founded** in 1495.
The pigeons **were fed** a diet of seeds and lettuce.
- to put new information later in the sentence.
The film **was directed** by Quentin Tarantino.
- to put longer expressions at the end of the sentence.
I was offended by the way she pushed past me.

12.1 by + agent

When we are interested in the agent, we use the preposition *by*.

The games **were designed by a new Japanese company**.
They **were rescued by some climbers** who found them wandering along the track.

13 Questions

There are three main types of questions:

1 *Yes/No* questions (the expected answer is 'yes' or 'no')
A: Are you from Greece?
B: **Yes, I am**.

2 *Wh-* questions (*who? whose? where? why? what? which? when?* and also *how?*)
Whose books are these?
Where does he live?
Why did they do that?

3 Alternative questions (which expect the answer to be one of two options)
Do you want to **go out to eat** or **stay at home**?
Which would you rather have, **coffee** or **tea**?

13.1 Yes/No questions

a) FORM:

- with *be*, *have (got)* and modal verbs like *may*, *can*, *could*, *would* and *should* the question is formed by inverting the subject and the verb: She has got a car. =
  Has she got a car?
  Is she having lunch?
  Should I buy a dictionary?
  Was she pretty when she was younger?
  Did anyone call while I was out?
- with other verbs use *Do/Does/Did* + subject + infinitive
  Do you like fish and chips?
  Does she know Antonio?
  Did they enjoy the picnic?

b) Negative *Yes/No* questions

These are questions which expect a particular answer.

Don't you spend the summer on Andros? (expected answer 'yes')
Aren't you Carmen's sister? (expected answer 'yes')
Hasn't he told you yet? (expected answer 'no')
Haven't you got any money? (expected answer 'no')

c) Question tags

These questions also expect a particular answer.

FORM: the tags are formed with the auxiliary of the main verb. The most common question tags are formed like this:

- positive statement + negative question tag
  He **likes** swimming, **doesn't he?**
  You**'re doing** the exam in December, **aren't you?**
  You**'d met** Max before, **hadn't you?**
- negative statement + positive question tag
  You **don't know** which bus goes to the market, **do you?**
  You **haven't seen** my keys anywhere, **have you?**
  You **wouldn't like** it if I stayed out all night, **would you?**

Notes:
1 It is also possible to have positive statement + positive question tag.
  You **like** Jacky, **do you?**
2 Question tags can also be added to imperatives (form the tag with *will* or *can*).
  Open the door, **will you?**
  Turn on the light, **can you?**
3 Where *let's* is used, the tag is formed with *shall*.
  Let's go to the beach, **shall we?**

13.2 Wh- questions

a) FORM: *Wh*- word + auxiliary + subject + main verb

Where do they live?
Why are they laughing?
Why did she say that?

b) *Wh*- questions with prepositions

The preposition comes at the end of the sentence or the clause except in very formal writing and speech where *whom* is used after the preposition.

Who did you buy those flowers **for?**
For whom did you buy those flowers? (very formal)
Who did you speak **to** when you phoned before?
To whom did you speak when you phoned before? (very formal)

c) Questions with *how*

How means 'in what way'. It is used for asking about temporary states.

How are you?
How was the exam?

Note: *How do you do?* is not a question but a very formal greeting. The answer is *How do you do?*

d) Questions about the subject

You do not use the auxiliary or inversion. The word order is the same as it is for statements.

CONTRAST
Who wants an ice cream? (question about the subject)
What is black and yellow and dangerous to eat? (question about the subject)
Who knows the answer to number five? (question about the subject)
WITH
Who did you see at the party? (question about the object)
What did Lucy buy her mother for her birthday? (question about the object)

Note: contractions of auxiliaries are often used in speech and informal writing.

Who**'s already passed** the exam? (has)
Who**'s going to drive** you to the airport? (is)
What**'ll he do** without you? (will)

13.3 Alternative questions

There are two types of alternative questions. One type is like a *Yes/No* question the other is like a *wh*- question.

Shall we go to the cinema tonight or on Friday?
What do you want to do this weekend, stay at home or go to the country?

13.4 Indirect questions

All indirect questions use statement word order. Indirect *Yes/No* questions use *if* or *whether*.

I'd like to know how much all this is going to cost.
Could you tell me if/whether there's a train to Luton?
I don't know if/whether I'll go to the party.
Would you mind telling me where I can get a ticket for the show tonight.
I wonder if/whether she still works here.

14 Relative clauses and pronouns

14.1 Relative pronouns

The most common relative pronouns are:

who, whom: to refer to people
which: to refer to things
that: to refer to either people or things
whose: the possessive of *who* and *which*
when: used after nouns referring to time
where: used after nouns referring to place
why: used to refer to reasons

1 **Defining relative clauses**
   In defining relative clauses:

   ● the relative clause defines or identifies the person, thing, time, place or reason
   *Jane is the woman **whose daughter I met in Los Angeles**.*
   *That's the house **whose roof was blown off in the storm**.*
   *August is the month **when Tom is coming to visit**.*
   *I can't remember the name of the street **where they live**.*
   *The reason **why I left you is** that I don't love you any more.*

   ● *that* can be used instead of *who* or *which*
   *The girl **that (who) shares an office with me** talks all day long.*
   *The library **that (which) is being opened next month** will offer much better facilities than this one.*

   ● the relative pronoun can be left out if it is the object of the verb in the relative clause
   *The man **(who/that) I spoke to yesterday** told me it would be open.*
   *Sue bought **the blouse (which/that) we saw** when we were in town the other day.*

   ● no commas are used before and after the relative clause.

2 **Non-defining relative clauses**
   The relative clause gives extra information which **can** be left out. Commas are used before and after the relative clause.

   *Mary Wilcox, **who is about to start work on a new book**, will speak to us about her travels in India.*
   *Susan, **whose brother you met at the party**, is going to work in Brazil.*
   *My new car, **which I love very dearly**, is being repaired.*
   *Paris, **where I lived for three years**, has become very expensive.*

3 **Prepositions in relative clauses**
   Prepositions can come before the relative pronoun or at the end of the relative clause depending on whether the sentence is formal or informal.

   *The person **to whom I spoke** told me the hotel was fully booked.* (Formal)
   *Jane, **who I bought my car from**, has gone to the States.* (Informal)

15 Reported speech/direct speech

15.1 Direct speech

This is when we report the exact words that someone says or writes.

'Do you want to come to my place for tea?' she asked.
In your postcard you said, 'Come and stay whenever you like.'

15.2 Reported speech

This is when we report something that has been said or written. If the report is after the time the thing was said or written, the verb form generally changes as follows:

Direct speech	Reported speech
1 Present Simple/ Continuous	Past Simple/Continuous

*'I **am working** in my father's office,' she said.*
*She **said she was working** in her father's office.*

2 Past Simple/Continuous	Past Simple/Continuous or Past Perfect Simple/Continuous

*'Classes **started** last week,' the director explained.*
*The director **explained that classes started/had started** the week before.*

3 Present Perfect Simple/ Continuous	Past Perfect Simple/ Continuous

*'I **have lived** in the country all my life,' the old man told me.*
*The old man **told me (that) he had lived** in the country all his life.*

4 will	would

*'I**'ll** cook supper,' she said.*
*She **said she would** cook supper.*

5 must (obligation)	had to

*'You **must** change the verb form,' the teacher explained.*
*The teacher **explained that we had to** change the verb form.*

6 can	could

*'I **can** count up to one hundred,' said Jenny.*
*Jenny **said she could** count up to one hundred.*

The verb form does not need to change when:

● the thing being reported is still true
*'Caterpillars **turn into** butterflies,' the teacher explained.*
*The teacher **told us that caterpillars turn into** butterflies.*
*'Paper 3 **starts** at 3.30,' said the examiner.*
*The examiner **told us that Paper 3 starts** at 3.30.*

● the thing reported contains the modals *would, could, might, ought to* and *should* as well as *must* for logical deduction
*'You **ought to** tell him what you think of him,' she said.*
*She **said I ought to** tell him what I think of him.*

*'I **might not be able** to stay for long,'* she said.
She **said she might not be able** to stay for long.
*'I think he **must be** ill',* she said.
She **said she thought he must be ill**.

- the thing being reported contains the Past Perfect
*'He **had been missing** for several months,'* she said.
She **said he had been missing** for several months.

Other changes that occur in reported speech are:

Direct speech	Reported speech
tomorrow	the next day, the day after, the following day
yesterday	the day before, the previous day
last week	the week before
here	there
this/that	the
this morning	that morning
today	that day
next Friday	the following Friday
ago	before

15.3 Reported statements

FORM: verb (+ *that*) + clause

'I took the money,' she admitted
She **admitted (that) she had taken** the money.
'He studies during the week and plays volleyball at the weekend,' she said.
She **said (that) he studied** during the week and played volleyball at the weekends.

15.4 Reported questions

1 **Reported Yes/No questions**

FORM: when there is no question word in the direct speech question, we use *if/whether*. Word order is the same as in the statement. The verb tense and other changes are the same as for other types of reported speech.

*'**Are you going** to Pete's party?'* she asked.
She **asked if/whether we were going** to Pete's party.

*'**Do you like** Greek food?'* he asked.
He **asked us if/whether we liked** Greek food.

2 **Reported *wh-* questions**

FORM: when *wh-* question words are used, the *wh-* word is followed by statement word order, that is the subject followed by the verb. All the tense and other changes are the same as for other types of reported speech.

*'**What's** your favourite colour?' **she asked** him.*
She **asked** him **what** his favourite colour **was**.

*'**Where do** Andy and Lucy live?' he **asked** her.*
He **asked** her **where** Andy and Lucy **lived**.

15.5 Reported orders

FORM: verb + (*that*) + clause *or* verb + object + infinitive with *to*

*'**Take up** sport,'* the doctor **said**.
The doctor **recommended (that) I take up** sport.

*'**Go** to the shops and get me some tea, will you?'* she **said**.
She **told me to go** to the shops and get her some tea.

15.6 Reported suggestions

FORM: suggest + *-ing*
        suggest + *that* + *should* + infinitive without *to*
        suggest + Past Simple

*'**Let's have a surprise party** for Eddie,'* she **said**.

She **suggested having a surprise party** for Eddie.
She **suggested that we should have** a surprise party for Eddie.
She **suggested we had** a party for Eddie.

Note: we cannot say: *She **suggested to have** a party for Eddie.*

15.7 Reporting verbs

1 Verb + object + infinitive
She asked me to come.

Other verbs with the same pattern are:
advise, beg, encourage, invite, order, persuade, remind, warn

2 Verb (+ *that*) + clause
She says (that) she doesn't want to speak to you.

Other verbs with the same pattern are:
say, claim, admit, explain, promise

3 Verb + object (+ *that*) + clause
He told us (that) he worked for a big international company.

Other verbs with the same pattern are: *remind, warn*

4 Verb + gerund
He admitted lying to the teacher.

Other verbs with the same pattern are:
admit, deny, recommend, suggest

Note: verbs in groups 2, 3 and 4 can also be used with *that* + clause.
He admitted that he had lied.

5 Verb + preposition + gerund
She apologised for being so rude.
She discouraged me from taking up smoking.

Other verbs with the same pattern are:
accuse (of), apologise (for), blame (for), congratulate (on), discourage (from), insist (on)

6 Verb + infinitive
We agreed to meet again in September.

Other verbs with the same pattern are:
agree, decide, offer, promise, refuse, threaten

16 *to have something done*

FORM: *have* + object + past participle (the most common form)

get + object + past participle (also possible when people are speaking informally)

USE: we use *to have something done* to say that someone else did something for you because you wanted them to or to you even though you didn't want them to.

*Go and **get your hair cut**. It looks terrible.*
*We're **having the front of our building painted**.*
*How **will you have your suit cleaned**? The dry cleaner's is closed on Saturday afternoon.*
***Did those windows get broken** in the storm?*
*Charles I **had his head cut off**.*

17 Verb tenses

17.1 Present Simple

FORM: a) Positive statements
    *I/you/we/they **eat** chocolate.*
    *He/she/it **eats** chocolate.*

    b) Negative statements
    *I/you/we/they **don't eat** chocolate.*
    *He/she/it **doesn't eat** chocolate.*

    c) Questions
    ***Do** I/you/we/they **eat** chocolate?*
    ***Does** he/she/it **eat** chocolate?*

    d) Short answers
    ***Yes**, I/you/we/they **do**.*
    ***No**, I/you/we/they **don't**.*
    ***Yes**, he/she/it **does**.*
    ***No**, he/she/it **doesn't**.*

USE: we use the Present Simple:

a) with routine or regular repeated actions (often with adverbs of frequency like *always, often, sometimes, never, every Saturday morning, once a week*)
*We **go** to Greece for our holidays **every summer**.*
*She **doesn't drink** coffee **after midday**.*
*My father **goes** to the market **every Saturday morning**.*
*I **never get up** before nine o'clock on Sunday.*

b) in time clauses with a future meaning after *when, as soon as, if, until*
*I'll phone her **when/as soon as I get** home.*
*Say 'hello' to Tim **if you see** him.*
*I'm not going to speak to him **until he apologises**.*

c) when we are talking about permanent situations
*I **come** from Melbourne.*
***Does she still live** in a flat?*

d) when we are talking about the future as expressed in timetables, regulations and programmes.
*The train **leaves** at 5.33.*
***Do classes begin** at the same time as last year?*

e) with scientific facts
*Bees **make** honey.*
*The planets **revolve** around the sun.*

f) with 'state' verbs which are not normally used in continuous forms: *be, have, depend, know, think, understand, disagree, like, want, hear, love, see, smell, taste*
*I **don't have** much money.*
***Does she understand**?*
*I'm sorry, but **I disagree** completely.*
*That perfume **smells** too strong.*

g) in spoken instructions, sports commentaries, jokes and formal letters
*First you **put** the cassette in the machine.*
*Romero **runs** towards goal and he **kicks** the ball.*
*A man **goes** into a restaurant and orders some soup.*
*I **enclose** a copy of my curriculum vitae.*

17.2 Present Continuous

FORM: the present form of *be* + the *-ing* form of the verb.

Contracted forms: *I'm (I am), you're (you are), s/he's (s/he is), it's (it is), we're (we are), they're (they are)* + *-ing* form.

USE: we use the Present Continuous when we are talking about:

1 actions happening now
*I think she**'s having** lunch.*
2 changing/developing situations
*My toothache **is getting** worse.*
3 temporary situations
*I **am working** in my father's restaurant this month.*
4 plans and arrangements in the future
***Are you doing** anything special this weekend?*
5 annoying or surprising habits with *always*
*She**'s always losing** her belongings.*
*They**'re always holding** hands even after fifty years of marriage.*

17.3 Present Perfect Simple

FORM: *have/has* + past participle

USE: we use the Present Perfect Simple:

1 when we are describing situations that have continued from some time in the past until now
*Mike **has lived** in Japan for three years.*
*I**'ve been** in love with Bill since 1984.*
2 when we are describing recent events
*I**'ve eaten** two packets of crisps, a bar of chocolate a plate of spaghetti and four bananas so far today.*
3 when we are describing repeated actions that have continued from some time in the past until now
*We**'ve seen** three movies this week.*
*I**'ve been** to every one of their concerts since they started playing together.*
4 with 'state' verbs e.g. *be, believe, have, know, think, like*
*I**'ve disliked** bananas since I was a child.*

5 to talk about experience, that is things that have happened at some time in our lives
*We**'ve been** to Athens before.*
*She**'s read** all of Graham Greene's novels.*
***Have you ever been** rock climbing?*

6 when we can see a present result of past actions
*Oh no! Someone**'s let** the dog into the living room and there are paw prints all over the sofa!*

7 when we talk about our first, second, etc. experience of something
*That's the first time I**'ve tried** rock climbing.*

8 when we use the superlative
*Maria is the most beautiful girl I**'ve ever seen**.*

17.4 Present Perfect Continuous

FORM: *have/has + been + -ing*

USE: we use the Present Perfect Continuous:

1 to talk about a recent activity when you can still see the effects of that activity
A: *What's that green stuff on your hands?*
B: *Paint. I**'ve been painting** the bathroom.*

2 to emphasise how long an action has been going on for
*I**'ve been painting** the bathroom all morning.*

3 to suggest that an activity is temporary
*I**'ve been learning** to drive, but I'm going to give up.*

4 to suggest that an action is not complete
*I**'ve been reading** that new Stephen King novel, but I haven't finished it yet.*

17.5 Past Simple

FORM: verb + *-ed* (remember there are many irregular verb forms)

USE: we use the Past Simple:

1 to talk about events in the past that are now finished
*I **went** to a really fantastic concert last night.*
*She **took out** her key, **opened** the door and **got** into the car.*

2 to talk about habits in the past
***Did you go** to the beach often when you were younger?*

3 to talk about situations in the past
*When I **was** a child, I didn't enjoy playing sports at all.*

4 in reported speech
*She **said she didn't feel** like coming.*

17.6 Past Continuous

FORM: *was/were + -ing*

USE: We use the Past Continuous:

1 to talk about actions in progress in the past
*I **was reading** that grammar book you lent me.*

2 to talk about temporary situations in the past
*This time last year she **was preparing** for her FCE exam.*

3 to talk about anticipated events that did not happen
*They **were going** to Wales on holiday that summer, but there was a train strike and they had to cancel their trip.*

4 to talk about an event that was in progress when another event happened
*I **was having** a shower when the doorbell rang.*

5 to talk about actions in progress at the same time in the past
*While I **was doing** the washing up, Joanna **was having** a shower.*

17.7 Past Perfect

FORM: *had* + past participle

USE: we use the Past Perfect:

1 to refer to a time earlier than another past time
*By the time I saw her again, she **had already married** Tom.*

2 in reported speech
*She said she **had told** him.*

17.8 The future

FORMS:
- *shall/will* + infinitive
- *going to* + infinitive
- Present Continuous (see 17.2)
- Present Simple (see 17.1)
- Future Continuous (*will + be + -ing* form)
- Future Perfect (*will + have* + past participle)

USE:

1 We use *going to* or *shall/will* + infinitive for predicting something when there is no present evidence.
*I think it **will be** cooler tomorrow.*
*You**'ll meet** someone and fall in love eventually.*
*It**'s going to be** a really good summer.*
Note: we cannot use the Present Continuous in this case.

2 We use *shall/will* + infinitive for promises, threats, offers and requests.
*If you play that CD one more time, I**'ll throw** it out the window.*
*I promise I **won't tell** anyone.*
***Will you turn** that stereo down?*
*I**'ll pick you up** at the airport if you like.*
Note: we cannot use *going to* in this case.

3 We use *going to* and the Present Continuous to talk about things that have already been decided.
*We**'re having** a few friends over for dinner this Friday.*
*When **are you going** to take a holiday?*
Note: we cannot use *will/shall* + infinitive in this case.

4 Use *going to* to talk about things that are certain to happen. We know this because there is present evidence.
*Look at those clouds. It**'s going** to rain.*
*I**'m going** to be sick.*
Note: we cannot use *will/shall* + infinitive or the Present Continuous in this case.

5 We use *will/shall* + infinitive to talk about future actions decided at the time of speaking.
*I think I**'ll lie down** for a moment.*
*I**'ll do** the dishes.*

6 We use the Future Continuous (*will/shall* + *be* + *-ing*) to say that an action will be in progress at a definite time in the future.
I'll be lying on a beach soaking up the sun by the time you receive this.

7 We use the Future Perfect (*will/shall* + *have* + past participle) to describe something that will be completed before a definite time in the future.
I'll have flown over a thousand hours by this time next year.

18 *used to/would*

18.1 *used to*

FORM: Positive statements
    used to + infinitive
    Negative statements
    did/didn't + *use to* + infinitive
    Questions
    Did you/she/they, etc. *use to* + infinitive

USE: we use *used to* to talk about past habits and states that do not occur now or no longer exist.

We ***used to walk*** to school, but now we get the bus.
What ***did they use to do*** at night before TV was invented?
He ***used to be*** really shy, but he's much more·confident since he started his new job.

Notes:
1 *used to* is not used to say how often things happened or how long they took.
2 Be careful not to confuse *used to* with *be/get used to* + noun/gerund which means 'be/become accustomed to something' because you have been doing it for a while.
I'm ***used to working*** nights.
I can't ***get used to living*** alone.
Do you think we'll ever ***get used to*** the noise?

18.2 *would*

Would is also used to talk about past habits and repeated actions but **not** about past states.

When I was little, I ***would dress up*** in our mother's old clothes.

19 Words that cause confusion

19.1 *like*

1 *like* as a verb
    FORM:
    a) *like* + object
      I ***like*** *Tony, but I don't love him.*
    b) *like* + *-ing* (= enjoy doing)
      Do you ***like studying*** *English or do you just do it because you have to?*

    c) *like* + *to* + infinitive (= choose to do)
      She ***likes to finish*** *her homework on Friday evening.*
    Note: short answers to *Yes/No* questions with *like* are always formed with *do, does* or *did.*
    A: *Do you like living here?*
    B: *Yes,* ***I do.***
    d) *would like* + (object) + infinitive with *to* is used as a polite way of saying 'want'. It refers to one occasion in the future.
      I'd ***like her to phone*** *me later today.*

2 *like* as a preposition, which means 'similar to' or 'in the same way as'
Do you ***look more like*** *your dad or your mum?*
That ***sounds like*** *rain.*

3 *like* which means 'such as/for example'
Let's buy him something nice, ***like*** *a book or a CD.*

4 *feel like* + object/*-ing*, used to talk about something that we want or want to do
I ***feel like (eating)*** *a big plate of spaghetti.*

19.2 *make/let/allow*

FORM:
1 *make*
  ● *make* + object + infinitive without *to*
    He ***made her do*** *the exercise again.*
    Note: in the passive, *make* is followed by an infinitive with *to.*
    She ***was made to do the exercise*** *again.*

2 *let*
  ● *let* + object + infinitive without *to*
    Why won't you ***let us go*** *and see that movie?*
    Note: *let* has no passive form. *Allow* or *permit* are used instead.
    We ***were allowed to go*** *and see the movie.*

3 *allow*
  ● *allow* + object + infinitive with *to*
    I won't ***allow you to go out with*** *that boy again.*

19.3 *so/such*

1 *so*
so + adjective/adverb/determiner/verb (+ *that* clause)
I was ***so embarrassed (that)*** *I wanted to die!*
She was behaving ***so strangely (that)*** *we phoned a doctor.*
They earned ***so little money (that)*** *they could never save.*

2 *such*
such + (adjective) + noun (+ *that* clause)
She's ***such a terrible liar (that)*** *no one ever believes her.*
We had ***such fun*** *at the picnic.*

Paper 2 Writing reference

This writing reference section contains:

1 a **checklist** of key points you should be thinking about when writing for Paper 2.
2 a variety of **key expressions** you may wish to use as you attempt the different tasks in Paper 2.

Checklist

When writing any composition you will need to check that you have paid attention to the following points:

- Have you answered all the parts of the question?
- Have you answered the question directly?
- Have you communicated your meaning clearly?
- Have you written the appropriate number of words?
- Is your writing clear and easy to read?
- Have you punctuated your work appropriately?
- Have you organised your work appropriately, in paragraphs where necessary?
- Are there any mistakes of basic grammar, vocabulary, spelling, etc. that you can correct?
- Have you used a variety of grammatical structures and not only, for example, used the Past Simple in telling a story?
- Have you used a range of vocabulary and not only, for example, simple adjectives like *bad, happy, fast,* etc.?
- Have you used linking words/phrases like *however, so, in addition, as soon as,* etc. where appropriate?
- Have you used language of an appropriate style? Is it too formal/informal? (Remember *who* exactly the audience is that you are writing for.)
- Have you made your composition interesting/amusing where appropriate, so that reading it is an enjoyable experience?

Key expressions

Informal letter

(For work on informal letters see p.12.)

There is more than one way to organise an informal letter, but here is one standard way:

> 14 Clivedon Road,
> Finstock,
> Oxford OX7 3BY
> 23/6/96 [1]
>
> Dear Stuart,
> Thank you very much for your ....
>
>
> Best wishes, [2]
> Robert

[1] The date can be written in various ways e.g. *23rd June 1996, June 23rd 1996, 23 June 1996.*

[2] There are various ways of closing letters to friends depending on your relationship to them. Some of them are:

(With) best wishes,
All the best,
(With) love,
With all my love,
Lots of love,

Here are some useful phrases/expressions to use when writing informal letters.

TO BEGIN THE LETTER:
- ***Thank you for your letter. It was great to hear from you.***
- ***Sorry, I haven't written for so long. I've been really busy just recently.***
- ***I thought I'd better write and let you know that*** ...
- ***This is just a short note to tell you that*** ...

TO END THE LETTER:
- ***That's about all my news. Do write soon and let me know what you've been doing.***
- ***Once again, thanks very much for all your help*** ...
- ***I'm (really) looking forward to seeing you on*** ...
- ***Give my love to*** ...

TO APOLOGISE:
- ***I'm really sorry that*** we couldn't come to your party on Saturday, ***but unfortunately*** both of us had really bad flu.

TO INVITE SOMEONE:
- **Why don't you come** and stay with us next weekend?
- We're having a few friends for dinner on Friday night and **we were wondering if** you and Paula would like to come.

TO RESPOND TO AN INVITATION:
- **Thanks for the dinner invitation.** Paula and I **would love to come.**
- **It was really kind of you to invite us for the** weekend**, but I'm afraid** we've already arranged to go and see Jill's parents in Scotland.

TO MAKE A REQUEST:
- As you know, our car is at the local garage at the moment, and **I was wondering if there was any chance that** we could borrow yours while you are away next week?
- **One of the reasons why I am writing is to ask a favour. Do you think you could** find out how much a reasonable hotel would cost for bed and breakfast for two people for one night?

TO CONGRATULATE SOMEONE:
- **Congratulations on** gett**ing** the job! Does this mean you will be moving up north?
- **Well done on** pass**ing** your driving test first time! All you need now is a car!
- Jim and I **just wanted you to know how pleased** we were that you did so well in your university exams.

Formal letter

(For work on formal letters see pp.20–21, p.96 and p.118.)

There is more than one way to organise a formal letter, but here is one standard way:

```
                                    14 Clivedon Road,
                                    Finstock,
                                    Oxford OX7 3BY
                                    23/6/96

The Manager,¹
Leisure and Business Travel,
73 Chorleywood Road,
Rickmansworth,
Herts WD3 0QL

Dear Sir/Madam²,
As you are probably aware, my family and I ....



Yours faithfully,

Robert Smith
```

1 With more formal letters the address of the person or company you are writing to should be on the left-hand side of the page, positioned below the address of the sender.

2 If you begin the letter *Dear Sir/Madam,* you should end it with *Yours faithfully.* If you begin the letter *Dear Mr (or Mrs/Ms/Miss) Jenkins,* you should end it with *Yours sincerely.*

Here are some useful phrases/expressions to use when writing formal letters:

TO REQUEST INFORMATION:
- **I am writing in response to** your advertisement in Friday's edition of The Times. **I would be grateful if you** could send me a copy of your summer brochure.
- **I am writing to enquire whether** you could let me have some information about your pension scheme.
- **I would like to know more about** the type of accommodation that you can provide.

TO MAKE A COMPLAINT:
- **I am writing to you about an unfortunate incident that** took place in your shop on Tuesday.
- **I have now been waiting** a month for a replacement.
- **To make matters worse,** we were told that there was no record of our reservation.
- **I would be grateful if you could** refund the cost of the holiday as soon as possible.

Discursive composition

(For work on giving opinions, etc. see p.63 and pp.126–127.)

Here are some useful words/phrases/expressions to use when writing a discursive composition:
- **It is often said that** children watch too much television. **However, in my opinion,** television can have an important educational role.
- **Firstly,** it has been clearly shown that passive smoking can seriously affect your health.
- **Although a number of people think that** capital punishment is an effective deterrent**, it is also the case that** a number of people have been sentenced for crimes they did not commit.
- **From my point of view,** we all need to take responsibility for the environment.
- **While it is true that** learning a foreign language can be hard work**, on the other hand** it might mean you can get a better job in the future.
- **Finally, it is important to remember that** you can often be delayed for several hours at the airport.
- **On balance then I feel that** boxing should be banned.

Narrative

(For work on narrative compositions see p.44 and p.141.)

Here are some useful structures/phrases/expressions to use when writing a narrative composition:
- **I was** eat**ing** an ice-cream and Sarah **was** sunbath**ing when** we first saw the shark.
- **I was just about to** open the door, **when** I heard a shout from the kitchen.
- **By the time** I got to the house, Peter had left.
- **As soon as** John arrived, we got in the car.
- **We had been** play**ing** cards **just before** it happened.

- *It wasn't until* I got home *that* I realised how much I wanted to see him.
- *After* wait*ing* for some time, I decided to leave.
- *A few seconds later* there was panic.
- *Eventually* everyone went home.

Descriptive (people)

(For work on writing descriptions of people see p.81.)

Here are some useful structures/phrases/expressions to use when writing a description of a person:

- *She is in* her twenties.
- *She looks like* her mother, but in many ways *she takes after* her father.
- *She's got* short blonde hair and blue eyes.
- *He (generally) wears* casual clothes, like jeans and sweat shirts.
- *He's (quite)* well-built and *he's got* a beard and a moustache.
- *She is very* easy-going and rarely gets angry.
- *She is (much) more* flexible *than* I am.
- *He is not (nearly) as* interesting *as* his brother.
- *She used to* smoke, but she doesn't anymore.
- *The first thing you notice about her is* her smile.
- *You can tell* he has suffered a lot *by* the expression on his face.

Descriptive (places)

(For work on writing descriptions of places see p.138.)

Here are some useful structures/phrases/expressions to use when writing a description of a place:

While Chicago is perhaps most famous for its gangsters of the twenties and thirties*, it must also be remembered that it is* the centre of American commerce and transportation. O'Hare airport is the busiest airport in the world. Forty-four million passengers pass through it every year. *Chicago is also a* great inland port. *It makes* steel and refines oil, but it also stands on the edge of the Great Plains. So the cereals and beef from the prairies pass through the city.

Chicago has a population of over three million including a wide variety of different ethnic groups, who celebrate their own festivities at different times of the year.

The city has a powerful personality of its own which is very American. It has the two tallest skyscrapers in the world and much of its architecture is magnificent and very original. *There are many interesting things to see and do in Chicago, including* visiting some of its beautiful parks and impressive museums.

Reports

(For work on writing reports see pp.72–73.)

You may, for example, be asked to write a report for school or for your employer. Here are some useful words/phrases/expressions to use when writing a report:

- *As I was asked, I* spoke to a number of tourists about their opinions of the island.
- *I found that* there were a variety of opinions on the subject. Most people I talked to thought that smoking should be banned in all public places. *However,* a small number felt that this was quite unreasonable.
- *Having talked to* a number of young people about what they do in their free time*, I discovered that* there were three main areas of interest.
- *I contacted* over fifty different organisations *and had replies from* forty-three of them.
- *As a result of my inquiries, I would like to make a number of points. Firstly* ...
- *One of the most positive aspects of* the resort is the wide variety of restaurants which cater for a range of tastes.
- *There are a number of ways in which* the facilities for disabled people in this town could be improved. Firstly ...
- *In conclusion, then, I strongly recommend that* video cameras are installed throughout the Kingsway Shopping Centre to help reduce the level of crime.

Applications

(For work on writing applications see p.103.)

You may be asked to write an application, which could be for a job, scholarship, etc. It might be a letter or it might be part of an official form. Here are some useful expressions to use when writing an application:

- *I am writing in reply to your advertisement for a* sales assistant in the Evening Standard on 13th November.
- *I have always been interested in* work*ing* with tourists and *this is one of the main reasons why I am applying for this job.*
- *I have done a lot of work with* children over the past few years.
- *I have a lot of experience of* sell*ing*, particularly in the field of computers.
- *I recently completed a course in* marketing, which I believe will be very relevant for this job.
- *I can speak* French and German fluently and am due to take the Cambridge First Certificate of English examination in June.
- *I am available to start work from* the 15th May.
- *I would like to apply for the FPT scholarship which I* read about in the Education Today magazine.
- *Having this scholarship would mean that I could* spend a further year studying in Britain.
- *I would be very grateful if you would consider my application for this scholarship.*
- *Please don't hesitate to contact me at the above address if you need any further information.*

Phrasal verbs reference

The grammar of phrasal verbs

There are four main types of phrasal verbs:

(1) **Verb + adverb (no object)** e.g. *get on* = have a good relationship with someone
*Mike and Sally aren't **getting on** very well at the moment.*

The verb and adverb <u>cannot</u> be separated by other words.

(2) **Verb + adverb + object/Verb + object + adverb** e.g. *give away* = distribute for free
*He **gave away** all his money. OR He **gave** all his money **away**.*

The verb and adverb <u>can</u> be separated, but if the object is a pronoun (e.g. *it*, *me*, *them*), the adverb must come <u>after</u> the object e.g. *He **gave it away**. NOT He gave away it.*

(3) **Verb + preposition + object** e.g. *look after* = take care of
*He **looked after** his parents for many years.*

The verb and preposition <u>cannot</u> be separated.

(4) **Verb + adverb + preposition + object** e.g. *put up with* = tolerate
*I don't know how she **puts up with** his terrible behaviour.*

The verb, adverb and preposition <u>cannot</u> be separated.

The grammatical type of each phrasal verb below is indicated by the number in brackets.

break down (1) p.47: stop working, usually a machine or vehicle e.g. *If my car **breaks down** again, I am going to sell it.*

break (something) down (2) p.47: destroy something such as a door or wall e.g. *The firemen **broke** the door **down** and ran inside to look for the children.*

bring (someone) up (2) p.27: look after and educate a child e.g. *Do you think it is difficult to **bring** children **up** as a single parent?*

carry on (3) p.17: continue doing something e.g. *He **carried on** watching TV even though his mother had told him to go to bed.*

catch on (to something) (1) p.61: understand e.g. *The teacher explained it at least three times, but Helen still didn't **catch on**.*

close (something) down (2) p.47: end an activity e.g. *I read in the paper last night that they are **closing** my old school **down**.*

come down (1) p.47: fall to the ground e.g. *Did you see that the apple tree next door **came down** in the night?*

come out in (something) (4) p.131: often when your body develops spots or rashes e.g. *He **came out in** red marks all over his face and neck.*

cut (something) down (2) p.47: bring to the ground e.g. *If we don't **cut** that tree **down** soon, it will fall down.*

cut down on (something) (4) p.47: reduce the amount e.g. *You must **cut down on** all the chocolates and cakes you eat. It's not good for you.*

cut (something) out (2) p.131: remove e.g. *If you **cut** some of these late nights **out**, you won't feel so tired in the mornings.*

die down (1) p.47: come to an end e.g. *She waited until the laughter **died down** before she continued her speech.*

eat out (1) p.131: eat in a restaurant instead of at home e.g. *I'd like to **eat out** tonight. How about going to that little Italian restaurant on the high street?*

get (something) across (2) p.61: communicate an idea e.g. *He had an interesting plan for reducing the level of pollution in the city, but it took him a long time to **get** his ideas **across**.*

get away with (something) (4) p.121: avoid being caught and punished e.g. *He is always late for work. How does he **get away with** it?*

get by (1) p.121: survive e.g. *It was hard to **get by** on one salary when Tom lost his job, but things are OK now.*

get (something) down (2) p.47: make a written record e.g. *Simon, could you make sure you **get** his telephone number **down**?*

get down to (something) (4) p.121: start doing seriously e.g. *I really must **get down to** writing my Christmas cards otherwise it will soon be too late.*

get on (with someone) (1) p.27 = have a good relationship e.g. *My brother and I are different kinds of people. I've never really **got on** with him.*

get out (1) p.131: have time outside the home e.g. *You should **get out** more. It's not good always being inside with the children like this.*

get over (something) (3) p.121: recover from e.g. *Her grandmother died a couple of months ago and it's taking her a long time to **get over** it.*

get round (someone) (3) p.121: persuade someone to let you do something e.g. *My father doesn't want to lend me his car, but I know how to **get round** him.*

get through (to someone) (1) p.121: make contact, often by telephone e.g. *I've been trying to **get through** to you all day, but your phone has been constantly engaged.*

get up to (something) (4) p.27: do something, often naughty or bad e.g. *OK, kids, what did you **get up to** while we were away?*

give (something) away (2) p.81: 1 donate for free e.g. *I think we should **give away** all these old toys to the local children's hospital.*
2 show, reveal e.g. *His bored expression **gave away** how he really felt.*

give (something) back (2) p.81: return e.g. *Lend me £10, will you? I promise I'll **give** it **back** tomorrow.*

give in (to someone) (1) p.81: surrender, agree to what someone else wants e.g. *You shouldn't **give in** to him if you think he is wrong.*

give off (something) (3) p.81: produce e.g. *Plastic **gives off** a horrible smell when it is burnt.*
(Note that in this case the verb and the adverb cannot be separated.)

give (something) out (2) p.81: distribute e.g. *The teacher **gave** files and books **out** to all the students.*

give (something) up (2) p.81: stop e.g. *All my friends have **given** smoking **up** this year. It's incredible.*

go down (1) p.47: fall e.g. *The price of houses has **gone down** by five per cent in the last year.*

go on (1) p.17: continue doing something e.g. *She **went on** talking while he made lunch.*

grow up (1) p.27: become an adult e.g. *I **grew up** in the north of England, but I moved down to London for my first job.*

hold on (1) p.17: wait e.g. *Could you **hold on** for a moment while I get a pen and paper?*

keep on (1) p.17: continue doing something e.g. *It **kept on** raining for the rest of the day.*

keep up (with someone) (1) p.61: maintain the same level e.g. *It's very difficult to **keep up** with her because she walks so fast.*

let (someone) off (2) p.61: give someone a light punishment or no punishment at all for something they have done wrong e.g. *As it was his first offence the judge **let** him **off** with a small fine.*

look after (someone/something) (1) p.27: take care of e.g. *Would you mind **looking after** our cats while we are away on holiday?*

look out (1) p.131: pay attention, be careful e.g. ***Look out**! There's a car coming.*

look (something) up (2) p.61: find information, often in a reference book e.g. *He **looked up** all of the new words in his bilingual dictionary.*

look up to (someone) (4) p.27: admire, respect e.g. *I have always **looked up to** my mother. She's so patient and kind.*

make for (someone/something) (3) p.148: go towards e.g. *They **made for** the nearest café when it started to rain.*

make of (something) (3) p.148: think of e.g. *What do you **make of** that new book by Jason Bryant? I couldn't understand a word of it!*

make out (1) p.148: pretend e.g. *She **made out** that she had been at home all evening when in fact she had gone out to see Martin.*

make (something) out (2) p.148: see clearly e.g. *I can see someone coming towards us, but I can't **make out** who it is.*

make (something) up (2) p.148: invent e.g. *I don't believe what she told us about meeting Elton John. I think she is **making** it **up**.*

make (a room, bed, etc.) up (2) p.148: prepare e.g. *We need to **make** the spare room **up** if Jim is going to stay here tonight.*

make (time) up (2) p.148: get back e.g. *We left late, but if I drive fast, I think we can **make up** the lost time .*

make up (with someone) (1) p.148: become friends again e.g. *You shouldn't get angry with your sister. Please go and find her and **make up**.*

mind out (1) p.61: pay attention e.g. ***Mind out**! You nearly walked in that puddle.*

pick on (someone) (3) p.61: treat someone badly or unfairly e.g. *The other boys are really horrible to Michael. They're always **picking on** him.*

pick (something) up (2) p.61: learn e.g. *He's very quick. You just tell him how to do something once and he's **picked** it **up**.*

put (money) by (2) p.90: save e.g. *I try and **put** a little **by** each month. We'd like to go on a holiday to the Greek islands next year.*

put (an animal) down (2) p.90: destroy e.g. *It was very sad. Our horse broke its leg and was in terrible pain. We had to have it **put down**.*

put (someone) down (2) p.90: criticise someone or try and make them look stupid or insignificant e.g. *I think he **puts** me **down** in meetings because he never has any ideas of his own.*

put (something) down (2) p.47: write, make a record of e.g. *A lot of people seem interested. Why don't you **put** all their names **down** and then we'll send them a copy.*

put (something) off (2) p.90: postpone, make later e.g. *Can we **put** the football match **off** for a week because some of our team are ill with flu?*

put (something) out (2) p.90: extinguish e.g. *Could you **put** your cigarette **out**, please? This is a no-smoking area.*

put (someone) through (2) p.90: connect (especially by telephone) e.g. *Could you **put** me **through** to Mr Jenkins' secretary, please? I need to change the time of my appointment.*

put (someone) up (2) p.90: give accommodation e.g. *Of course we can **put** you **up** for a few days while you're looking for a flat. There's no problem – we've got a spare room.*

put (the price) up (2) p.90: increase e.g. *If we **put up** our prices again, we're going to lose some of our best customers.*

put up with (someone/something) (4) p.90: tolerate e.g. *I can't **put up with** the noise from next door's party anymore. I am going to ask them to turn the music down.*

rub (something) out (2) p.131: remove something (usually with a rubber or a cloth) e.g. *I think you should **rub** the first part of your essay **out** and try again.*

run out (of something) (1) p.131: finish, have no more left e.g. *Could you buy some more milk when you go to the shops. We have nearly **run out**.*

sell out (of something) (1) p.131: finish because everything has been bought e.g. *I'm sorry, we've **sold out** of bread. Why don't you try the supermarket?*

slow down (1) p.47: reduce speed e.g. *Please **slow down**. You're driving so fast, it's making me frightened.*

speak up (1) p.61: say things more loudly e.g. *You need to **speak up** a little, I'm afraid I can't hear very well.*

stand out (1) p.131: appear clearly e.g. *He usually **stands out** in a crowd. He's well over two metres tall!*

stay out (1) p.131: remain away from home e.g. *Your mother doesn't like you **staying out** all night. Please be home by midnight.*

stick out (1) p.131: appear clearly e.g. *I'm going to really **stick out** at school. I'm the only person who hasn't got a pair of the right kind of trainers.*

take after (someone) (3) p.27: be similar to in character e.g. *He **takes after** his father, he's very friendly and outgoing.*

take (something) down (2) p.47: write, make a note of e.g. *Sharon, could you **take down** the following letter for Brian Stevens at CBC?*

take (someone) in (2) p.40: make someone believe something which isn't true e.g. *When he told her he had come to check the gas meter, she was completely **taken in**.*

take off (1) p.40: suddenly increase, do well e.g. *Interest in the environment **has taken off** in the last couple of years and I don't really understand why.*

take (someone) off (2) p.40: imitate someone to make other people laugh e.g. *You should hear Simon **taking off** the Prime Minister – he's very funny.*

take (time) off (2) p.40: have a holiday/change e.g. *You should **take** a few days **off** work, you're not looking at all well.*

take (someone) on (2) p.40: employ e.g. *I'm thinking of **taking** another secretary **on**. Do you know anybody suitable?*

take (something) over (2) p.40: take control e.g. *He's very dominating. When he joins a discussion, he usually **takes over** and no one else has a chance to say anything.*

take (something) up (2) p.40: start a new hobby e.g. *I've **taken up** yoga recently. It's changed my life.*

take up (space/time) (2) p.40: occupy e.g. *This sofa **takes up** far too much room in here. We should move it downstairs.*

tell (someone) off (2) p.27: speak to someone angrily because they have done something wrong e.g. *My Maths teacher **told** me **off** for not paying attention in class.*

throw (something) out (2) p.131: get rid of e.g. *Don't **throw** those boxes **out**. They might come in useful one day.*

watch out (1) p.131: pay attention e.g. ***Watch out**! There's a car coming.*

wear (someone) out (2) p.131: to make very tired, no energy left e.g. *I've spent the day shopping, cleaning and cooking and now I'm **worn out**.*

work (something) out (2) p.61: calculate e.g. *You've been trying to do that puzzle for ages. Haven't you **worked** it **out** yet?*

Communication activities

Unit 1, Speaking Exercise 2, p.6

Scoring

Add up your total and see if the person described below sounds like you:

	a)	b)	c)
1	1	0	2
2	1	2	0
3	1	2	0
4	2	0	1
5	2	0	1
6	2	1	0
7	0	2	1

1–3 Very low on thrill-seeking. You like your comfort above all else. You'll do everything possible to avoid dangerous or unpredictable situations. Why not try taking an occasional risk now and then? You might surprise yourself!

4–6 You are cautious and sensible at all times. You occasionally think about breaking out of your normal routine, but you don't generally go through with it. Why not do something different and more exciting with a friend?

7–10 You seem to have found a very good balance between healthy excitement and unnecessary risk. You give yourself challenges which keep you alert and make you an interesting person to know.

11–14 The ultimate thrill-seeker. You're a bit of a wild one! Watch out though that you don't start taking stupid or dangerous risks just for the buzz. Remember it can be addictive!

Unit 3, Pronunciation Exercise 2, p.30

1 Shut the door, will you love?
2 Your uncle's got a bad cough.
3 Apparently they're having some trouble at the bank.
4 Give this cap to your mother.
5 There's blood on my ankle.
6 Your cousin came home. He won the match.
7 I drank too much on Monday.

Unit 3, Vocabulary Exercise 5, p.34

Student A

Unit 4, Grammar Exercise 4, p.39

The photo is of Nigel Kennedy, one of the world's most accomplished violinists. He was born in Brighton, England in 1958. Both his parents were musicians. His father left his mother before he was born. He is famous for wearing unorthodox clothes and behaving more like a pop star than a famous classical musician. He has a very friendly manner and gives the impression that he really wants people to like him. He is a keen supporter of the English football club 'Aston Villa'.

Unit 4, Grammar Exercise 6, p.43

Joke B

have	seem	be	go	sit	reserve
enjoy	remark	like	read	reply	

A wealthy man (1) .... in the theatre with his pet elephant. He (2) .... the best seats so they could (3) .... a good view. Everyone (4) .... very surprised at how interested the elephant (5) .... to be in the play and at the end of the play the manager of the theatre (6) .... up to the wealthy man and (7) .... on this.

'Your elephant certainly seemed (8) .... himself. I must say I was surprised he (9) .... the play so much.'

'So was I,' (10) .... the wealthy man. 'When he (11) .... the book the play was based on, he didn't like it at all.'

Unit 6, Reading Exercise 6, p.58

IQ puzzles

1 Four girls, Helen, Sharon, Claire and Donna, have an average age of twenty. Sharon is eight years older than Helen and fifteen years older than Claire. The sum total of Helen's and Sharon's ages is forty-six, whilst the sum total of Sharon's and Claire's ages is thirty-six. How old is Donna?

2 Ten of these shapes can be fitted together to form a circle. Which are the three pieces that are **not** needed?

3 If you were given a 7-litre container and an 11-litre container and were asked to measure out exactly 8 litres of water using just these two containers, how would you do it?

4 Divide this square up into five segments so that each contains two dots, two squares and one circle. Four of the five segments must be of identical size and shape.

●	●	●	○	□
□	□	□	●	□
●	□	○	●	●
□	□	○	○	●
○	●	●	□	□

Turn to page 189 for the answers. How well did you do?

Unit 7, Grammar Exercise 4, p.71

Student A

In the small circle in the top left-hand corner, write the name of a hobby/free-time activity you have done for a long time and really enjoy.

In the rectangle in the top right-hand corner, write the name of the place where you live now.

In the square in the bottom left-hand corner, write down the number of times you have been abroad.

In the circle in the middle at the bottom, write down the most exciting thing you have ever done.

On the horizontal line in the middle, write the name of the most disgusting thing you have ever eaten.

Unit 8, Vocabulary Exercise 4, p.79 (student B)

Unit 8, Reading Exercise 3, p.80

Group B

Part B

1 According to photographer Terry O'Neill: 'The public just don't realise how hard these supermodels work. They'll jump on a plane, go to Milan, go to bed, get up really early, do four fittings, do six shows a day for a week, no spare time whatsoever, jump on a plane, go back to New York, get up really 10 early, do a modelling assignment. **It**'s non-stop. I'm amazed the top girls have any private life at all. They work harder than Olympic athletes. Naomi is the best at it – she's there on the phone with her diary on her lap while she's having her make-up done, making appointments, running her life and her business affairs at the same time 20 as getting ready to be photographed. She's always doing twenty things at once. You've got to admire her.'

Whatever doubts there may be about her book, the album is definitely her own work. Has a music career been a long-held ambition?

'It was something like that. I studied singing at school. Dance 30 used to be my main subject and performing arts is what I've studied since I was five. So **it** was something I wanted to get back to. I love music ... listening to it, dancing to it. I know there are people out there saying, "She's just a model, can she sing, what's she doing?" But I wouldn't have got my contract and got other people to work with 40 me if I hadn't got some voice. I've given it one hundred per cent and you can't feel bad about yourself for that.'

And how does a supermodel enjoy herself in time off from her busy schedule?

'Cooking, having friends over, going to clubs sometimes, if I know the DJs and if there's going to be 50 good music.'

And how about men?

'Oh,' Naomi puts her head to one side and smiles sweetly. 'My ideal man is creative, intense, intelligent, humorous, very loving and affectionate.' She has had a number of celebrity boyfriends (including Mike Tyson, Sylvester Stallone, Robert De Niro, Sean Penn and U2's 60 Adam Clayton), but now she talks about wanting a steady boyfriend and wanting babies,' ... but not for a while yet. I'll never give up travelling altogether – I like **it** too much – but at the moment I've got too much I want to achieve to be starting a family. Don't feel sorry for me, though. I live out of a suitcase, but I love my life – I really love it!'

Unit 9, Vocabulary Exercise 5, p.91

Student A mime the following actions for Student B:

1 Fry an egg.
2 Squeeze some lemon on an oyster, then eat it.
3 Ladle some soup into a bowl.
4 Boil some water and then make some tea.
5 Eat some peas with chop sticks.

Unit 10, Vocabulary Exercise 5, p.103

Student A ask Student B the following questions:

1 What's your home telephone number?
2 How much do you weigh?
3 How tall are you?
4 When were you born?
5 What percentage of the people in this room have black hair?
6 What is ¾ minus ¼?
7 What is the speed limit on motorways in your country?
8 What temperature does water boil at?

Unit 11, Reading Exercise 3, p.111

Group B

Weird Weather Facts

■ The study and forecasting of weather is called meteorology because it was once precisely that – the study of meteors. The idea that meteors were formed in the sky from various combinations of earth, water, air and fire, and that they contributed to weather conditions, goes back to the great philosopher and scientist, (2) ...., in the 4th century BC. It was believed in Europe until late in the 17th century.

■ In AD 582, it rained 'blood' on Paris. The terrified local people saw this as a sign from Heaven and responded by repenting for their sins. The true cause of the strange event was the (4) .... the wind that sometimes blows from the Sahara across the Mediterranean into Europe. It carries a fine, red dust from the desert interior, and this had dyed the rain that fell on Paris.

■ On May 29, 1986, (6) .... in west China were sucked up by a tornado. It put them down again on some sand dunes 20 km away – completely unharmed.

■ The highest wind speeds ever officially recorded have occurred at (8) ...., where gusts have reached 370 km/hour.

■ The Algonquin Indians of North America believed that the earth lay on the back of a (10) ...., and when it shuffled its feet the Earth would quake. One ancient Japanese legend held that the movement of a vast underground spider caused earthquakes; a later account said it was a monster catfish. The ancient Greeks blamed huge (12) .... wrestling underground.

■ An average of 708 tornadoes strike the United States each year. In April (14) ...., 148 tornadoes hit thirteen states in just twenty-four hours, leaving 315 people dead.

■ If you are stuck out in a storm, never shelter under a (16) .... Try to get indoors, or into a car. Get away from metal objects and get rid of any metal you are carrying. If you're with other people, (18) .... Unfortunately, sometimes even being indoors is no protection. In July 1982 a woman was struck by a bolt that came through the window and hit the (20) .... she was holding. The force of the bolt threw her across the kitchen.

Unit 13, Vocabulary Exercise 2, p.134

Student A

Unit 14, Speaking Exercise 3, p.144

The boy was 'reluctantly' bailed to appear before the juvenile court again next month.

Magistrates ordered him to observe a 5 p.m. to 7 p.m. curfew because most of the offences have been committed at night.

They also ruled that he should live with his grandparents and report daily to his local police station.

Unit 14, Speaking, p.147

E

F

G

H

Unit 15, Vocabulary Exercise 2, p.153

Students A and B

1 A *shout* at B because she/he borrowed your Walkman and then lost it.
2 *Chat* together about what you're both thinking of doing at the weekend.
3 B tell A what she/he thinks the English homework is. A *contradict* B and tell her/him that it is something completely different.

Unit 15, Exercise 2, p.158

Pictures for Part 3

Unit 3, Vocabulary Exercise 5, p.34

Student B

Unit 6, Reading Exercise 6, p.58

Answers to the IQ puzzles on page 185.

1 Donna is twenty-two years old.

2 Shapes 3, 6 and 9 are not needed.

3 Fill the 11-litre container and from this fill the 7-litre container, which leaves 4 litres in the 11-litre container. Empty out the 7 litres and pour in the 4 remaining litres from the 11-litre container. Then fill the 11-litre container again and from this fill the 7-litre container. This will leave you with 8 litres in the 11-litre container.

4

●	●	●	○	□
□	□	□	●	□
●	□	○	●	●
□	□	○	○	●
○	●	●	□	□

Unit 15, Vocabulary Exercise 2, p.153

Students B and C

1 *Gossip* together about someone you both know.
2 B *whisper* something to C.
3 C *inform* B that she/he has to retake all her/his exams because she/he did so badly.

Unit 7, Grammar Exercise 4, p.71

Student B

In the small circle in the top left-hand corner, write the name of the friend you have had for the longest time.

In the rectangle in the top right-hand corner, write the name of the most awful place you have ever been to.

In the square in the bottom left-hand corner, write down the number of pets you/your family has had.

In the circle in the middle at the bottom, write down the name of the most interesting person you have ever met.

On the horizontal line in the middle, write down the most embarrassing thing you have ever done.

Unit 9, Vocabulary Exercise 5, p.91

Student B mime the following actions for Student A:

1 Eat a bowl of spaghetti.
2 Chop an onion.
3 Eat some prawns, taking all the shells off first.
4 Grate some cheese.
5 Whisk some egg whites together until they become light and fluffy.

Unit 10, Vocabulary Exercise 5, p.103

Student B ask Student A the following questions:

1 How old are you? (in years and a fraction)
2 What do you think is the average height of men in your country?
3 What's the home telephone number of a good friend of yours?
4 What is ½ times ½?
5 When is your mother's birthday?
6 What is the normal temperature of people?
7 How much did the last piece of clothing you bought cost?
8 What is ⅛ in decimals?

Unit 13, Vocabulary Exercise 2, p.134

Student B

Unit 15, Vocabulary Exercise 2, p.153

Students A and C

1 A ask C what something in English means and C *translate* it into your language.
2 C *beg* A to lend you her/his bicycle/motorbike/car for the evening.
3 Have a *row* about whose turn it is to do the washing-up.

Unit 15, Speaking Exercise 3, p.158

Student A

Questions for Part 1
- Where are you from?
- How long have you lived here/there?
- What's it like living here/there?
- Why are you studying English? What might you do with your English in the future?
- What do you like doing in your free time?

Questions for Part 4
- How important is it that schools prepare pupils for life as well as teach academic subjects? Should school education be more practical?
- Should pupils go straight from school to university or should they have time off in between?
- What do you think is a good size for a class at school?
- Why do some teachers have problems keeping control of their classes at school?
- At what age do you think pupils should be free to leave school?

Language index

(GR refers to the Grammar reference)

Watch Out!

Watch Out! boxes
The following are items that appear in Watch Out! boxes:

Addison Wesley Longman Limited,
Edinburgh Gate,
Harlow,
Essex
CM20 2JE
England
and Associated Companies throughout the world.

First published 1996

Fourth impression 1996

Set in 10/12.5pt Frutiger 45 Light

Printed in Spain by Mateu Cromo

ISBN 0 582 25300 4

Author acknowledgments

I would especially like to thank the following people:

• Sue and Emma for their continuing support and encouragement

• all the Longman team and, in particular, Judith King (Senior Publisher), Frances Woodward (Senior Editor), and Emer Wall

• Matthew Barnard, Charlie Crawford and Kristina Teasdale for their comments and advice at an early stage of the project.

We are grateful to the following for permission to reproduce copyright material:

The Editor, *Best* Magazine for an adapted extract from the article 'Are you Hooked?' by Caroline Sweet in *Best* Magazine 14.6.94; the author, Tony Buzan for an extract based on his 'Mind Maps' (r) in *Use Your Head* published by BBC Books; Carlin Music Corporation – UK Administrator for adapted lyrics to the songs '9 to 5' by Dolly Parton and 'Blue Suede Shoes' by Carl Perkins; the author, J. Collard for an extract based on his article 'Supermodel Sensation' in *Attitude* Magazine, published by Northern & Shell PLC; EMAP Publications Ltd for an adapted extract from the article 'Would you set yourself on fire ...' from *Just Seventeen* Magazine; Futura Publishing Co Inc. for an adapted extract from *Batman* by Craig Shaw Gardner; Granada Television and the Chiappi family for an extract based on the article 'Open House' in *TV Times*, 29 Aug – 4 Sep 1992. p7; Gruner & Jahr Ltd for extracts based on the articles 'Could you be a 'Type T' Personality?' & 'Why do we risk it?' in *Focus* Magazine, March 1993; 'Why laughter is the best medicine' by Janet Fricker in *Focus* Magazine, May 1993; ' Invent your way to riches' by Matt Bacon in *Focus* Magazine, May 1994; Guardian Syndications for an adapted extract from the article 'Virtual Reality' by Bob Swain in *The Guardian*, 15.6.93; Robert Harding Syndication for an adapted extract from the article 'Great Adventures' by David Wickers & Jenny Barnett in *Marie-Claire*, November, 1992; Hit & Run Music for adapted lyrics to the song 'I Wish It Would Rain Down' by Phil Collins. (c) 1989 Philip Collins Ltd/Hit & Run Music Ltd; IPC Magazines Ltd for an adapted extract from the article 'Why are Brits so strange?' by M. Jaffe-Pearce in *Living* Magazine, February 1989; The London Science Museum, Innovations Group for extracts from the text in *The London Science Museum Catalogue Collection,* Spring 1995; the author, Harold Gale for extracts from *Mensa Mind Teasers.*; NMC Enterprises Division for an extract from the article 'The Brain: A User's Guide' by Edward Fox in

Esquire Magazine, December 1993. (c) National Magazine Company; Newsgroup Ltd for adapted extracts form the articles 'Father fires son for 10 years of laziness' in *Today* Newspaper, 26.4.91, 'Twin Sisters' by Pam Francis in *Today* Newspaper 22.5.91, 'One love affair that lasted' by Alison James in *Today* Newspaper, 5.12.92; 'The criminal they can't lock up' by Christian Gysin in *Today* Newspaper, 3.3.93; Penguin Books Ltd for an extract from the Longman Structural Reader edition of *The Go-Between* by L. P. Hartley (Hamish Hamilton 1953). copyright (c) L. P. Hartley, 1953. Reproduced by permission of Hamish Hamilton Ltd; Polygram International Music Publishing Ltd for adapted lyrics to the song 'Your Song' by Elton John and B. Taupin, 1970. This Record Co Ltd; Random House UK Ltd on behalf of the Roald Dahl Foundation for the poem 'My Sister' by Lisa Tilbury from *Wondercrump Poetry* edited by Jennifer Curry, published by Red Fox; The Reader's Digest Association Ltd for adapted extracts from 'Mountain Men' p345, pp65, 86, 69, 77, 'Cock & Bull Story' p60, 'Chatting with Chimps' p120 all in *The Reader's Digest: Did You Know?* (c) 1990; Reed Consumer Books Ltd for extracts from *The World's Greatest Mistakes* by Nigel Blundell, published by Octopus Books; Solo Syndication Ltd for an adapted extract from the article 'Television ration box' by Tony Burton in *The Daily Mail*, 12.1.93.

We have unfortunately, been unable to trace the copyright holders of the article 'From Cradle to Gravy' by Anita Chaudhuri from *Time Out* Magazine, December 9–16 1992 and would appreciate any information that would enable us to do so.

We are grateful to the following for permission to reproduce copyright photographs:

All Action/Dave Hogan for 46, The Advertising Archives for 26, Colorific for 46,114t,154t, Elizabeth Whiting Associates for 136mr, Frank Spooner Pictures for 37r,131/Bolcina/Nelss for 78tl/Eric Brissauo for 104bl/Evrard-Liaisd for 148/Francois Lochon for 114b, Michael Freeman for 58, Granada TV/Chiappi family for 32t, Gamma sport/Hotcher for 6, Hulton Deutsch for 13bm,46,78ml, 78mr,78tr, Hutchison Library for 16bl, Idols/Ben Watts for 46, Image Bank/Patti McConville for 104/Juan Alvarez for 102/Gordon for 102, J Allan Cash for 102, Katz/John Reardon for 84l, Kobal Collection for 42,48,85tl,85br,85r,140r, 140bl, Longmans/Gareth Boden for 12mt,12tl,12mb,158bl /Maggy Milner for 32b,86,91, Madame Tussauds for 79, The Mansell Collection for 14, Moviestore Collection for 13b,68t, Museum of the Moving Image for 74, Network for 104tl,116t/Mike Goldwater for 104tr/Jenny Matthews for 98/Mike Abrahams for 116b, Pictor for 102, Punch for 25,36l,90,101,122,125b,155, Rapho/Robert Doisneau for 52, Redferns/Mick Huston for 16br/Steve Gillett for 39, Rex Features for 13,16tr,22l,36r,46,78b,80,102,130b,136cl, 154b,16l, Ronald Grant Archive for 140tr, Science Museum for 37l,123tl, 123bl, S.O.A for 137m,137t/Stern for 137b, Solo Syndication/Mail Newspapers plc for 117, The Spectator for 125, Sygma/D Hudson for 103t, Telegraph Colour Library for 11,13t,13m,16tl,16c,16cr,60b,61,110l,135,136b,136t, 138,16l, Tony Stone Images for 54l,60t,102,110r,158r, United Feature Syndicate for 134, W Heath Robinson for 106.

We have been unsuccessful with our trace for the copyright holders of the images that appear on the following pages; any help with this would be appreciated:
41 and 150.

Illustrated by Gary Andrews, Kathy Baxendale, Jonathan Bentley, Rachel Busch, Peter Byatt, John Chamberlain, Kim Harley, Maggie Ling, Ed McLachlan, Gary Swift, Lis Watkins